I0827692

IMAGES
of America

DETROIT LAKES

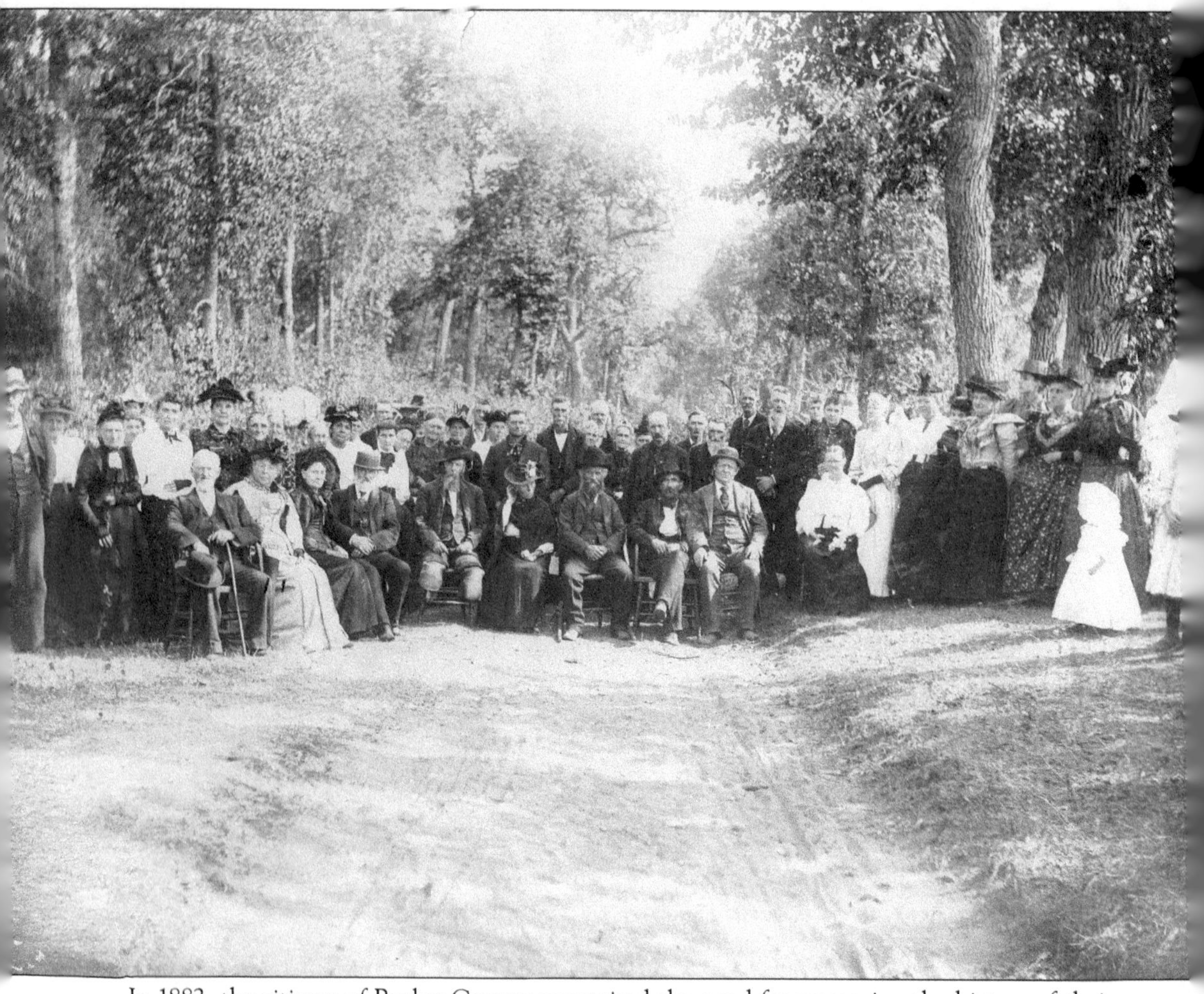

In 1882, the citizens of Becker County recognized the need for preserving the history of their community. The result was the Pioneer Settlers Union. The group, comprised of many founding residents, worked actively to preserve the history of their burgeoning community as it was happening. In 1924, this organization was renamed the Becker County Historical Society. (Courtesy Becker County Historical Society.)

ON E COVER: Taken by Johnson Photography in 1909 at the peak of Detroit Lakes' building and onomic boom, the image on the cover shows a busy day on Washington Avenue. This stree the central corridor of the Detroit Lakes business district, remains the heart of downtown. There re companies still operating today that were established well before this photograph was taken 0 years ago. (Courtesy Becker County Historical Society.)

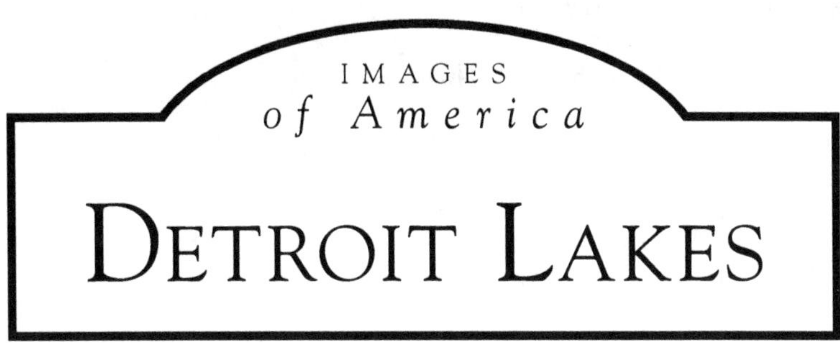

Becker County Historical Society
with help from Amy Degerstrom and Kelsey Opsahl

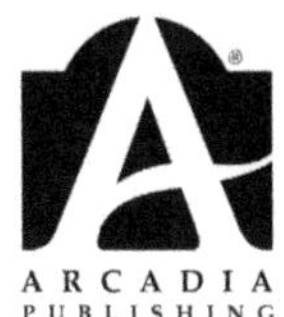

ISBN 978-0-7385-8404-1

Published by Arcadia Publishing
Charleston, South Carolina

Printed in the United States of America

Library of Congress Control Number: 2011940518

For all general information, please contact Arcadia Publishing:
Telephone 843-853-2070
Fax 843-853-0044
E-mail sales@arcadiapublishing.com
For customer service and orders:
Toll-Free 1-888-313-2665

Visit us on the Internet at www.arcadiapublishing.com

For Kelsey, without whom this project could not have happened. Thank you!

Contents

ACKNOWLEDGMENTS

The staff and volunteers of the Becker County Historical Society and Museum have come together to create what we hope will be an interesting and vibrant look at the visual history of our home, Detroit Lakes, Minnesota. As the executive director of this organization, I was privileged to work with so many wonderful people on this project and would like to take this opportunity to thank them. First, I would like to thank Kim Bettcher, who had the idea and was gracious to hand us the opportunity. I would also like to thank Virginia Weston and Peggy Stellmach for their many Mondays of research and finding answers to tough questions. I would like to thank the staff of the Becker County Historical Society, namely Jeannie Johnson, Margie Rousu, and Fran Kennedy, who took lists and helped make them captions, and took photographs and found them a date. Particularly, I would like to thank Kelsey Opsahl, whose interest and dedication to this project helped our ideas organize into a book. Your work has been phenomenal, and your help has been invaluable. A special thanks to Winnie Rodgers, who has been a great support and contact at Arcadia Publishing. I would also like to thank the business owners and managers who have continued to make our community thrive, and who help to keep our history alive and strong. We appreciate you! Mostly, we would like to thank those folks who have thought about preserving their history, and the history of the region, by donating their precious photographs and stories to the Becker County Museum collections. Without you, our book could not exist! Unless otherwise noted, all images appear courtesy of the Becker County Historical Society. A particular thanks to my husband, Sean, and to Bev Olander and Fred Floan, who took the time to read the text and who helped make this project a reality. Thank you.

—Amy Degerstrom
Executive Director
Becker County Historical Society and Museum

I would like to thank my wonderful family and friends for their support during this process. I also want to thank the staff at the Becker County Museum for all their help with the research. Without Jeannie, Margie, and Fran, none of this would have gotten done! A big thank-you to my husband, Troy, for his support and patience during the hours I worked on typing captions in the evening and on weekends. And to Amy, it was a great time working with you on this project, and I feel that we now know more than we ever wanted to about Detroit Lakes (but the coffee meetings in the morning at La Barista were definitely worth it!).

—Kelsey Opsahl
Museum Assistant

Introduction

The city of Detroit Lakes, Minnesota, has a rich and vivid history. The Ojibwe and Dakota people were the area's first residents, but the fur trade and timber industry brought early white settlers, primarily the French Canadians. European settlement began after the establishment of Becker County in 1858 and the drawing of boundary lines for the White Earth Reservation in 1868. The first community on the site of Detroit Lakes was known as Tylertown, developed along the joining of the Pelican River and Detroit Lake. This settlement was later annexed into the city of Detroit Lakes, but many of Tylertown's early street names, such as Frazee and Pioneer, remain.

The city's cultural diversity as a result of this early settlement is echoed by a unique eco-diversity. Becker County straddles the forest and prairie, and inhabits three biomes. Coniferous forest fills the eastern and north-central portions, deciduous forest the central, and prairie the western. Detroit Lakes, falling at the southern center of these environments, sits at the crossroads of all three of these biomes, making it a city with vast water, rich vegetation, and high, flat overlooks. The city, incorporated in 1871 as Detroit, fast became the financial and cultural headquarters of the county. Its location and vast water supply encouraged settlers to flock to the area, just as it continues to draw vacationers today.

Over the years, Detroit Lakes has grown and flourished, thanks to a variety of forward-thinking individuals and groups. The arrival of the railroad in the early 1870s provided access to the rest of the country. Men like John K. West, considered the father of tourism in Detroit Lakes, created pamphlets that were sent east. They espoused the glorious and curative mineral springs, the beautiful waterways on which to take a leisurely steamboat ride (on boats provided by him, naturally), and the lush landscape and rich commerce that rivaled any place in America. These same ideas were echoed by investors like E.G. Holmes, who purchased huge tracts of land, developed them, and then sold them bit by bit, thereby growing the city. As time moved on, retail giants, such as Blanding's, Norby's, and Nunn's, were established and brought much-needed services and supplies to the area. John Teague opened a pharmacy and worked with early physicians, such as Dr. Leonard C. Weeks, to establish health care. The needs of the early settlers often outweighed the influence of cultural norms, allowing women like Emma Ogden, the first female physician in Minnesota, to settle here in the 1880s and have a thriving business. A newspaper, the *Detroit Record*, was established and began publication in 1872. Churches were built, opera houses were established, schools and government offices opened, and the outline for what the city is today was firmly planted.

In the 20th century, Detroit changed its name to Detroit Lakes because of postal mix-ups with Detroit, Michigan. The city sent its men and women to war—twice—and established a National Guard armory. House calls became a thing of the past when a new, modern hospital was constructed. The automobile industry caused a shift from saddle and harness shops to garages and sales lots, and at one time, more than 40 existed in the city limits. These new cars gave rise to the drive-in, both as restaurants, such as the Red Hen and Sandwich Hut, and as a drive-in movie theater. Neighborhood grocery stores, once numbering more than 50, gave way to centralized superstores. The city shifted focus from the railroad to the lakes, with a sand swimming beach being added and Clem's Big Dock offering boat rentals. Housing developments grew up on the outskirts of the original city footprint, with traffic moving from the central corridor of Washington Avenue to the lakeshore and edges of town. The 1980s were a time of economic struggles in the region, bringing about an entrepreneurial spirit for small businesses to develop and a need for well-established business to re-brand and market their goods.

Today, Detroit Lakes is a thriving resort community, more than doubling in population each summer. Events like WE Fest, the Northwest Water Carnival, Fourth of July by the Lake, the Becker County Fair, the Detroit Lakes Street Faire, and Art in the Park bring out the community as well as thousands of visitors between May and September. The Historic Holmes Theater at the Detroit Lakes Cultural and Community Center and Shakespeare in the Park bring performers to the region. The bypass of Detroit Lakes by the new State Highway 10 in 2008 changed the layout of the city, moving portions of the business district west. Old streets and buildings have disappeared to make way for new development along the highway. Pioneer and mid-century landmarks, such as the original town hall, courthouse, and the steam whistle, have given way to malls and chain stores. New development, focused along the new highway corridor, creates opportunity for the city. However, ties to the past remain, with firms like Norby's still operating after more than 100 years. The Becker County Historical Society keeps this history alive, telling the story of the region and preserving history as it happens.

All in all, a marshy tract of land along a series of lakes has become what the pioneers had envisioned—a strong, stable, diverse, and culturally rich city that remains the heart of the lakes region in Northwest Minnesota.

One

The Early Years 1871–1889

The legend of Detroit's naming is said to have happened in the years before its settlement, when a Catholic priest was traveling through the area. He camped for the night on the north shore of what is now Detroit Lake, in plain sight of where a long sandbar stretched across the surface. The water was low, and the dim outline of the bar as it stretched across the lake was glimmering in the light of the setting sun. The priest exclaimed to some of the attendants, "See what a beautiful *detroit*!" *Detroit* is the French word for a narrow place in a body of water, but in this instance, it referred to the bar reaching across the lake.

The settlement that eventually became Detroit Lakes started with Merwin M. Tyler, who constructed a 12-by-14-foot cabin next to the Northern Pacific Railroad line where the Pelican River meets Detroit Lake. Tylertown, as it was originally known, served as a hotel and post office for early visitors to the area. Mail delivered by the railroad was emptied onto a bed for the locals to sort through. This village was eventually annexed into the city of Detroit.

Col. George Johnson selected the area for a formal settlement in 1871. He built a flour mill on the Pelican River, and as the Northern Pacific Railroad was constructed through Becker County, the settlement quickly grew. Civil War veterans, having been paid in land rather than cash, quickly came to take up soldier's homesteads, and 364 of them eventually settled in the area. Detroit was named the county seat in 1877. By 1884, several businesses had been established, such as the Hotel Minnesota, the *Detroit Record*, and the Holmes Opera House. The foundation for the first courthouse was laid that same year. The first major industry, the Fargo-Detroit Ice Company, was established and began to supply ice for not only the region, but also for the Northern Pacific Railroad. In 1885, the village hall was constructed and housed the county fire department. Detroit grew quickly during this period, with 307 people listed in the 1870 census and 1,510 by 1890.

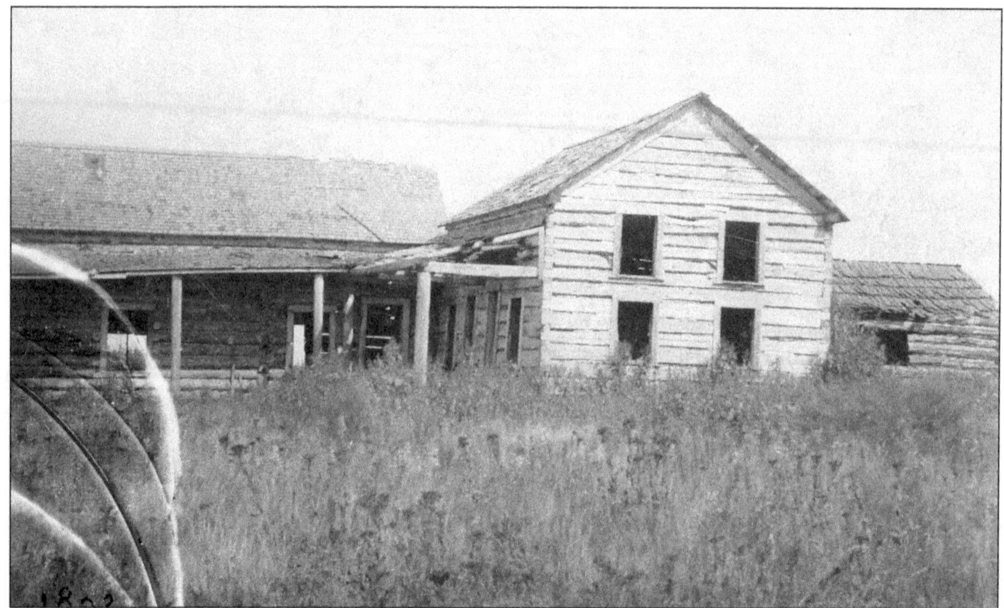

On July 28, 1870, Melvin M. Tyler settled on the northwest quarter of Section 34, Detroit Township, where he built a small, 12-by-14-foot log cabin. It was later enlarged and became the Tyler Hotel, standing for many years on the north side of the railroad near the Pelican River. It became a meeting place for officials and also served as a post office.

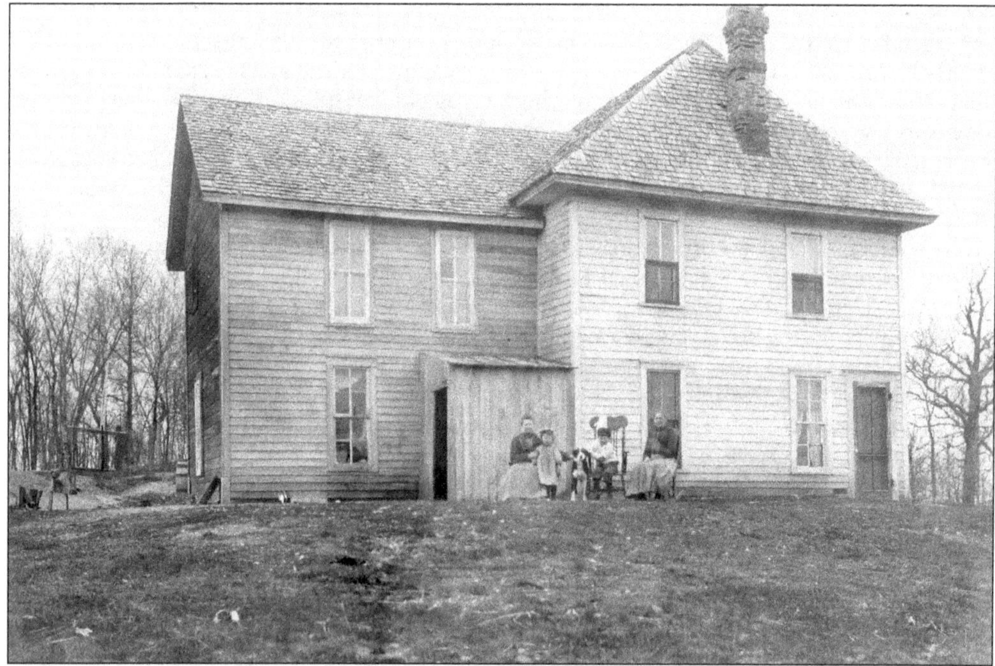

Pictured above is an example of one of the first frame-built, two-story homes that existed in Detroit Township. The owner of the home, Capt. I.M. Thomas, came to Becker County in the spring of 1871 and his family followed in June of the same year. He is remembered as the man who ran the water tank and pumped the water for the Northern Pacific Railroad Company for more than 20 years.

When the people of Detroit began to build up their village, they discovered that they were nearly surrounded by lakes and impassable swamps. The old Red River trail passed around the east side of the village, and through tortuous winding, afforded a tedious outlet to the northwest and the southwest. The people of Detroit, however, went about the road problem with commendable energy. At a heavy expense, they built the entire road from Detroit to White Earth via the village of Richwood. These roads, while expensive, were the making of the town. Their construction provided Detroit with a momentum that has persisted to the present day. The photograph on the right shows Washington Avenue looking south, and below is Main Street looking west.

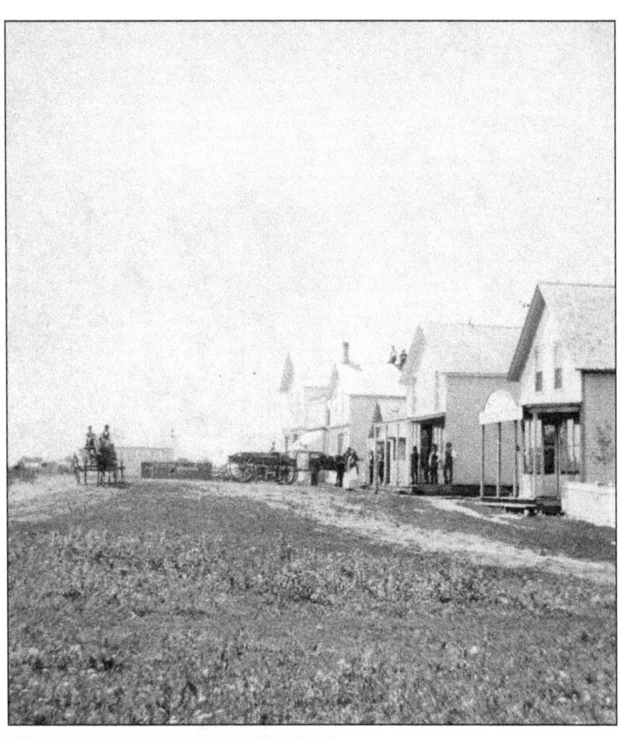

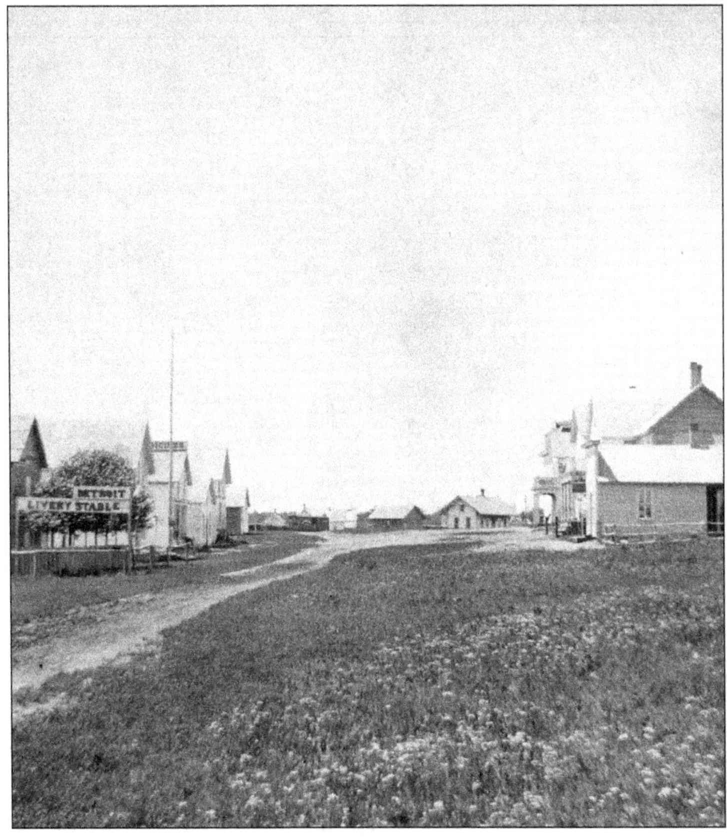

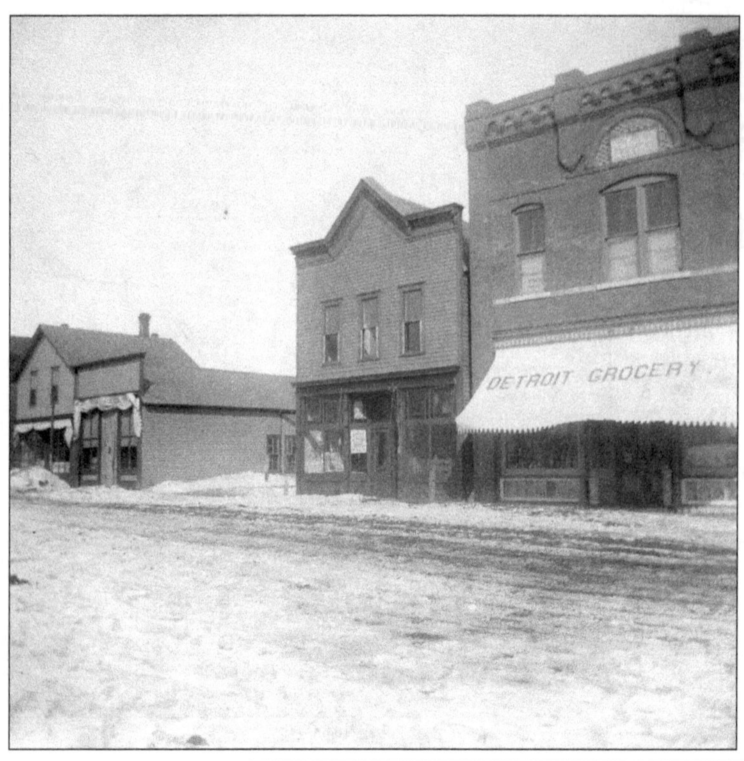

The Detroit Wholesale Grocery Company was the largest, best-equipped, and best-stocked wholesale grocery establishment east of the Twin Cities. Designed by Frank L. Bolen, the Holmes Artificial Stone and Brick Company had the contract for the stone and masonry work. Since it was located on the trunk lines of the Northern Pacific and Soo Line Railroads, it had the advantage of loading the goods right on the cars without the expense and inconvenience of cartage.

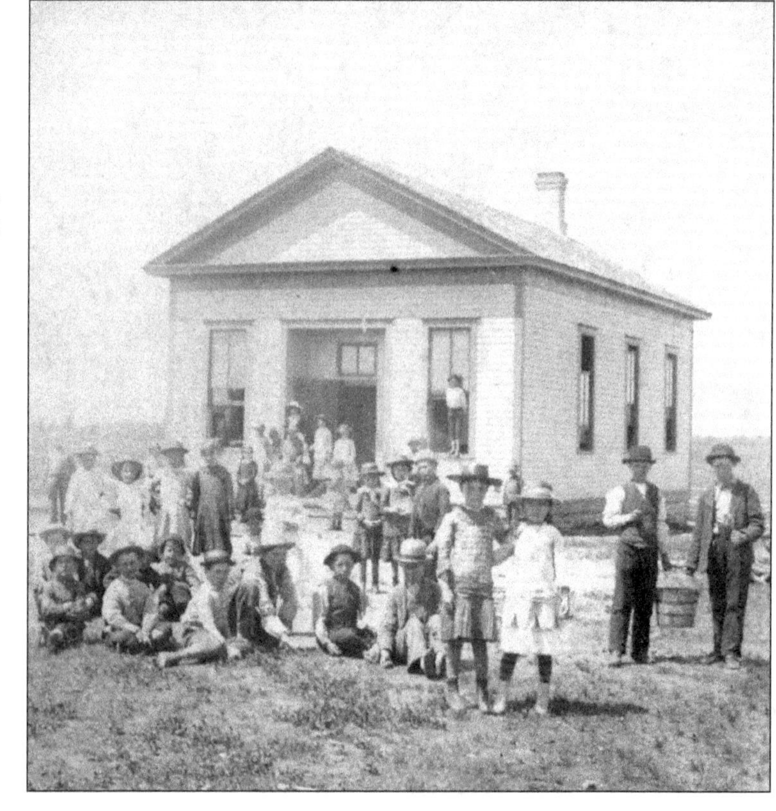

On March 12, 1872, the board of county commissioners granted a petition to create school district no. 1. Detroit's first common school was opened on July 2, 1872. In February 1873, the Baptist church was rented and the school moved there under the management of Miss Amelia Brigham for five months. On August 30, 1873, the first schoolhouse was completed where the Washington School was located (now a senior living complex).

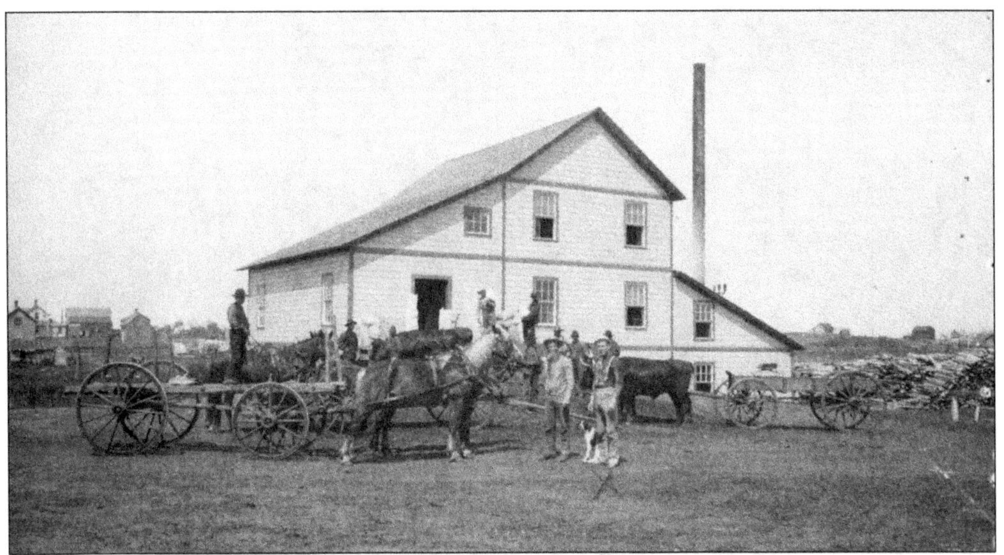

Turnbull Mill, which was located at the intersection of State Street and Curry Avenue, was purchased from Mrs. James Turnbull by Charles Knuth and J.F. Taylor. They enlarged and improved the mill, renaming it the Detroit Roller Mills. They put in the best and most improved machinery and had a first-class flour mill with a daily capacity of 75 barrels. The mill was doing really well, but a fire destroyed it in 1900.

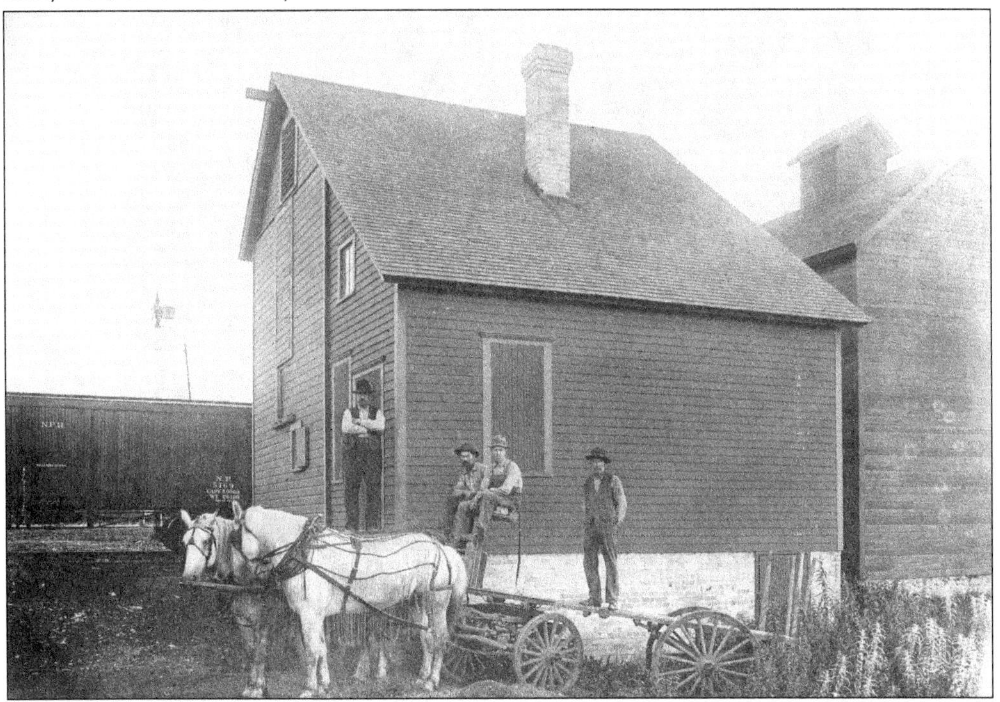

Ground was broken for the Detroit Brewery in June 1885. It was located just east of Detroit on the north side of the Northern Pacific tracks, down in Tylertown and on the east side of the Pelican River. The owners were A. Werner and J.J. Hass of Perham, and Charles Schmarback of Detroit. That fall, the saloons in the village were handling large schooners of the homemade product. Detroit Brewery burned down in 1892.

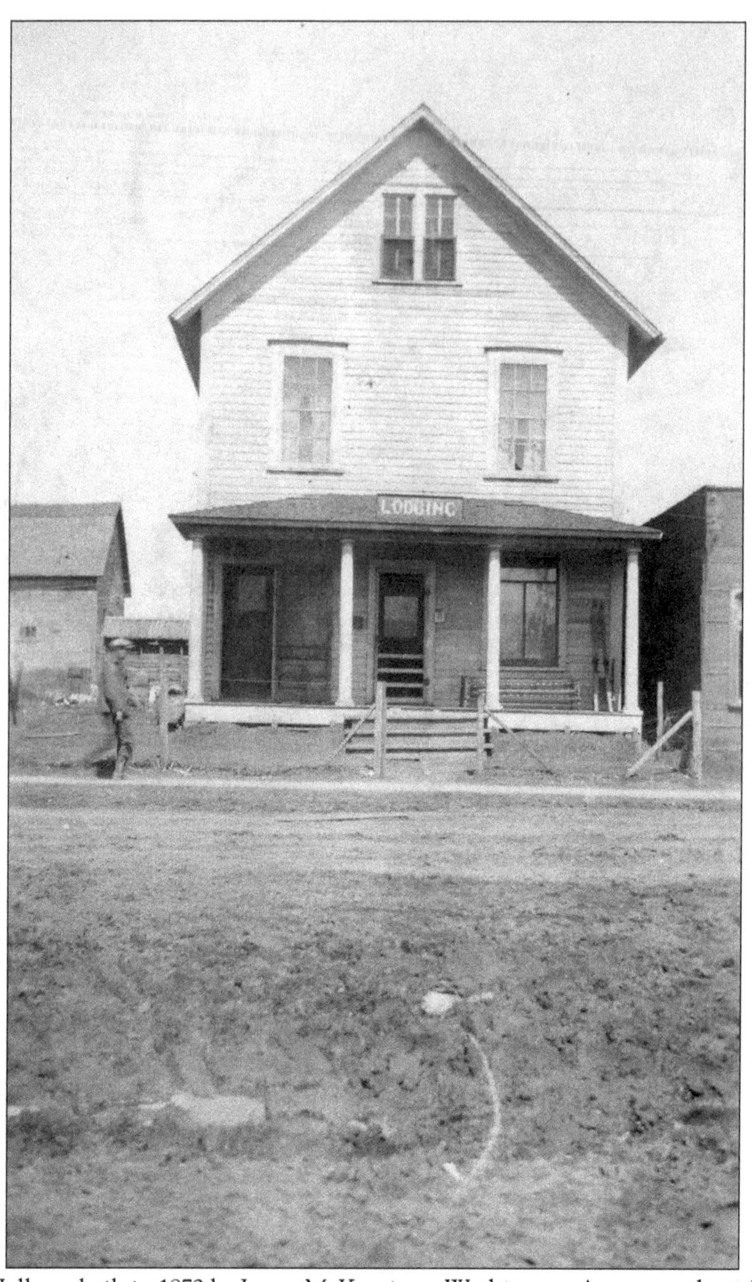

McKenzie Hall was built in 1872 by James McKenzie on Washington Avenue and quickly became the S.N. Horneck & Bowman Store. S.N. Horneck was a pioneer merchant who started his store in a small building and later teamed up with H.A. Bowman. Horneck emigrated here in 1849 and settled in Buffalo, New York, where he engaged in the mercantile business. He eventually came to Detroit in 1873, attracted by the building of the Northern Pacific Railroad. He began business as S.N. Horneck and Company, his associate being his father-in-law, G.V. Mooney. He later went into business with H.A. Bowman, originally from Buffalo, New York, and formed S.N. Horneck & Bowman. Horneck was also postmaster under the term of Pres. Grover Cleveland. This site became Erickson Skelgas in later years and was then moved to 120 East Main Street to house the Lakes Electric Motor Shop.

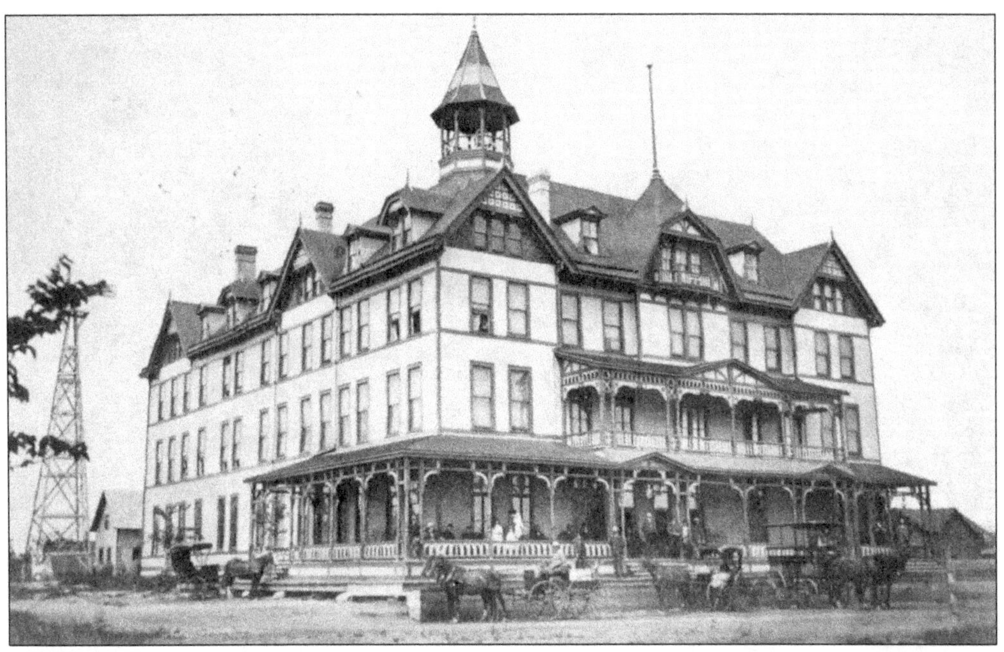

In 1884, E.G. Holmes and J.A. Bowan designed and built the Hotel Minnesota. It was located on the corner of Washington Avenue and Frazee Street, several hundred yards from Lake Detroit. It was a four-story wooden structure with 75 sleeping rooms, a dining room that could seat 100, a billiard parlor, and a large sample room where salesmen displayed their wares. The best years are said to have been in the latter 1880s and early 1890s under the ownership of John K. West. West also conceived of the steamboat line and lock-and-dam system that operated on the string of lakes between Detroit and Pelican. On June 26, 1915, the prosperous hotel became nothing but a mass of charred embers and smoking ruins as the result of a fire that broke out in the laundry room.

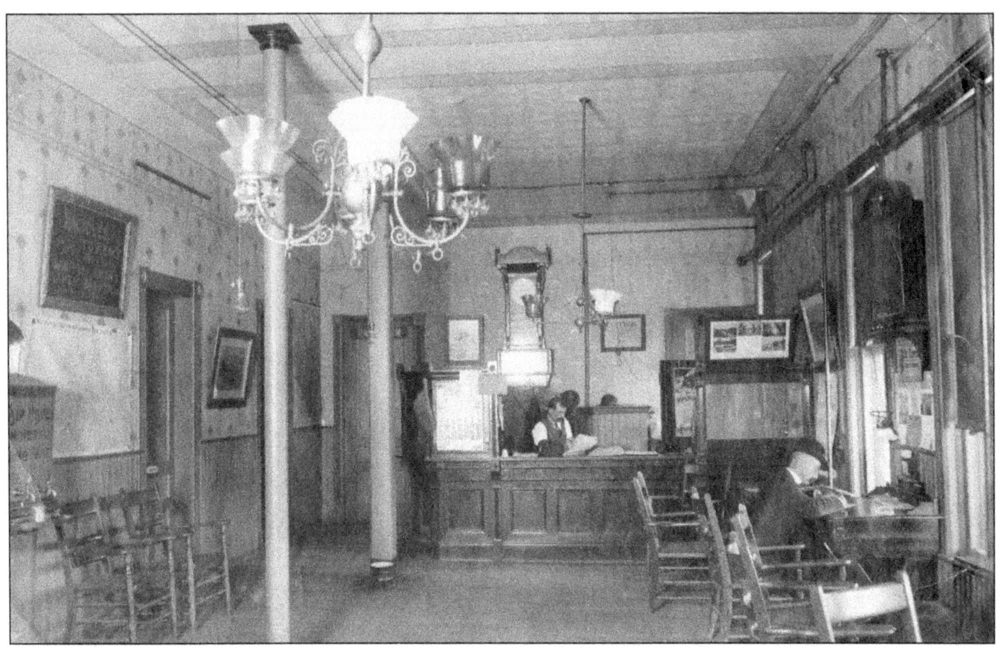

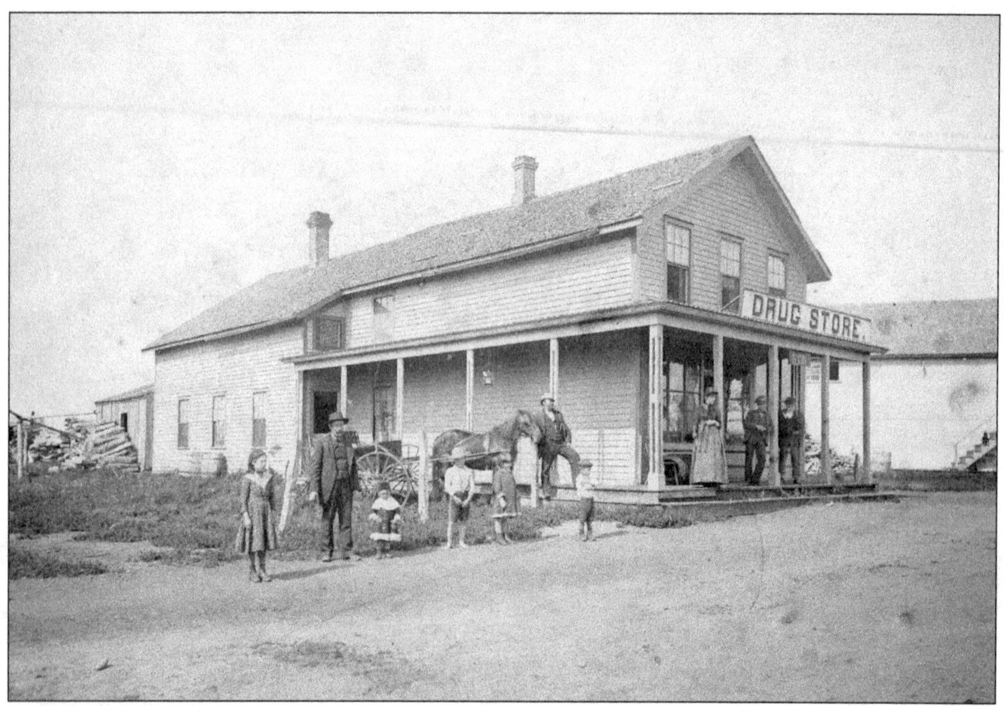

John A. Teague came to Detroit in 1874 and was operating one of its three drugstores by 1885. Theo G. Arzt and Emma K. Ogden ran the other two stores. Teague's Drug Store (top photograph) was located on Pioneer Street and sold patent medicine for all aches and pains, for people or horses. Folks did not go to the doctor very much, but relied on home cures. In 1887, Dave Carson came to Detroit and operated Carson's Pharmacy (below) located on the northeast corner of Washington Avenue and Front Street. He manufactured and sold many "valuable medicines." Drugstores, such as Teague's, were the favorite gathering spots of old-timers to swap stories and learn the news of the day.

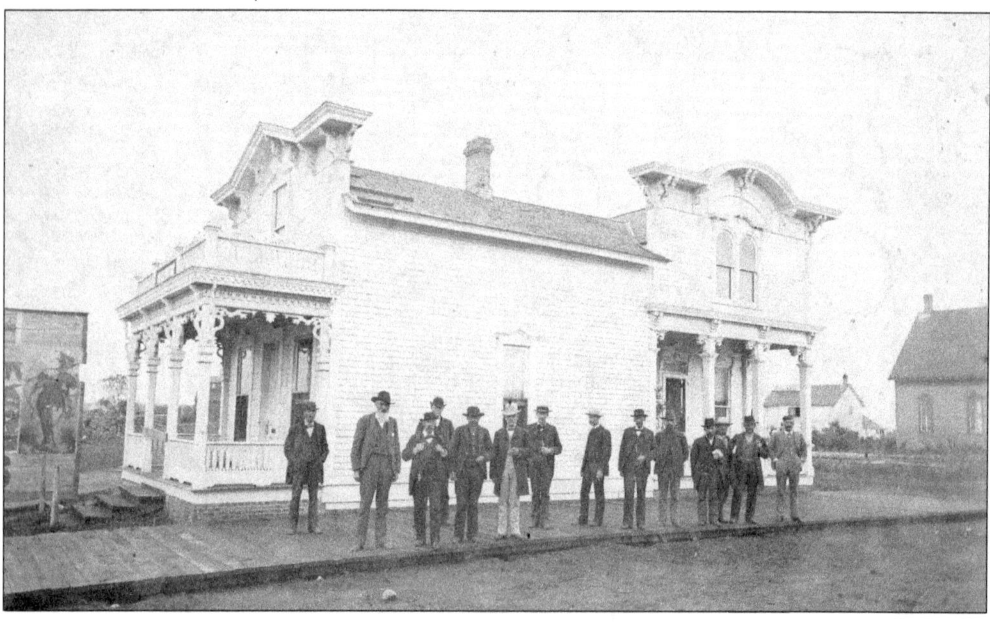

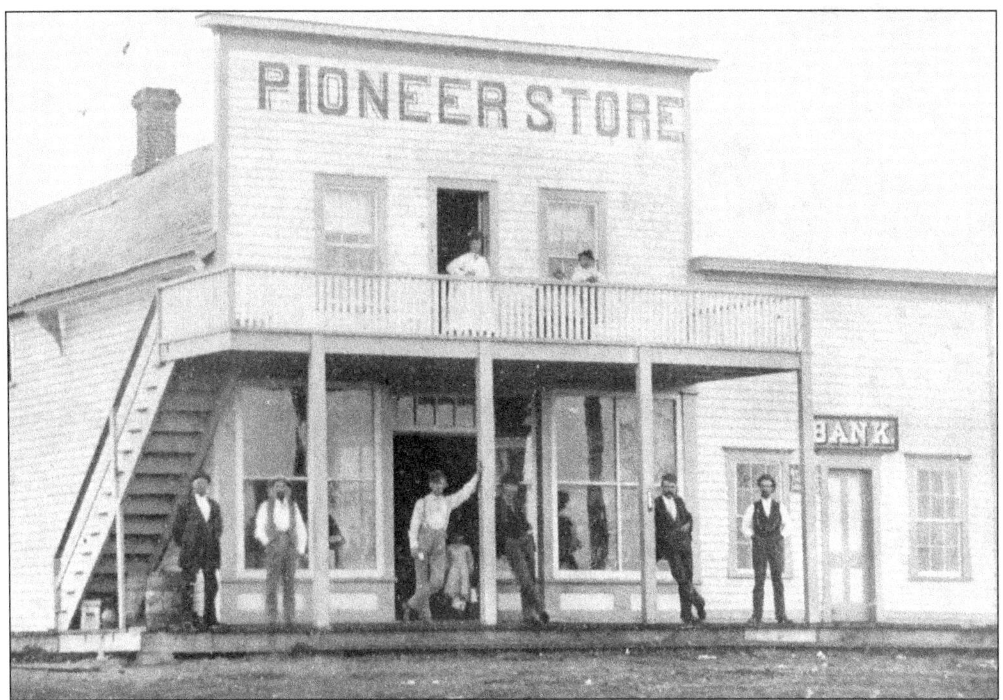

The first store in Detroit, the Pioneer Store, was located next to Teague's Drug Store and owned by E.G. Holmes and John Harding Phinney. Phinney was very prominent in all social and public affairs, and engaged in various branches of trade until he was elected sheriff. Phinney held various county, village, and city offices and took a leading role in Detroit's development during its pioneer period.

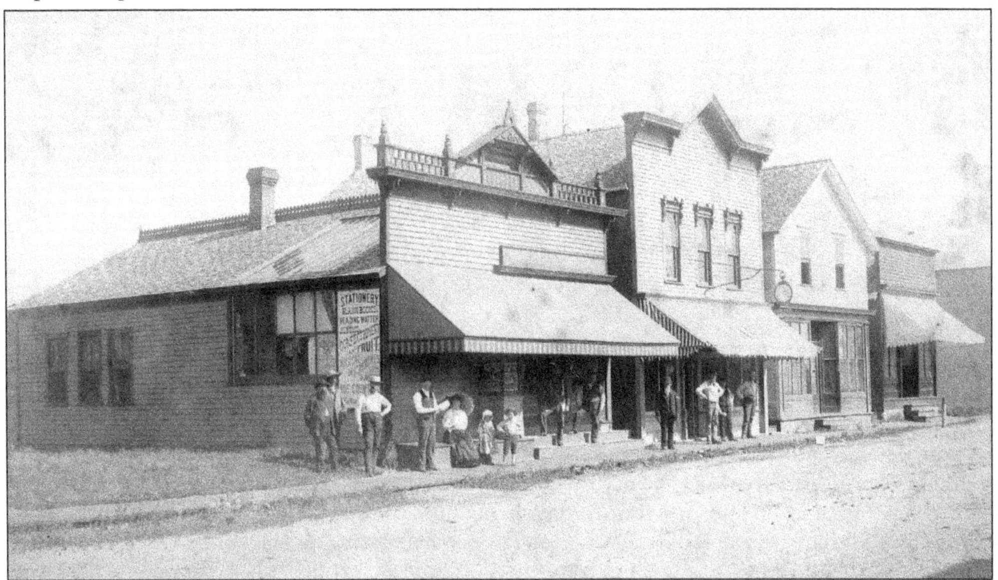

The east side of Washington Avenue held such stores as the Reybergh Gun Shop, the Kuchinbecker Store, Porters Meats, and the Ryerson Building and Studio. R.D. Ryerson was responsible for many of the dramatic photographs of the early fires in Detroit Lakes. In those days, photography was no easy, simple affair, but a rather complicated art.

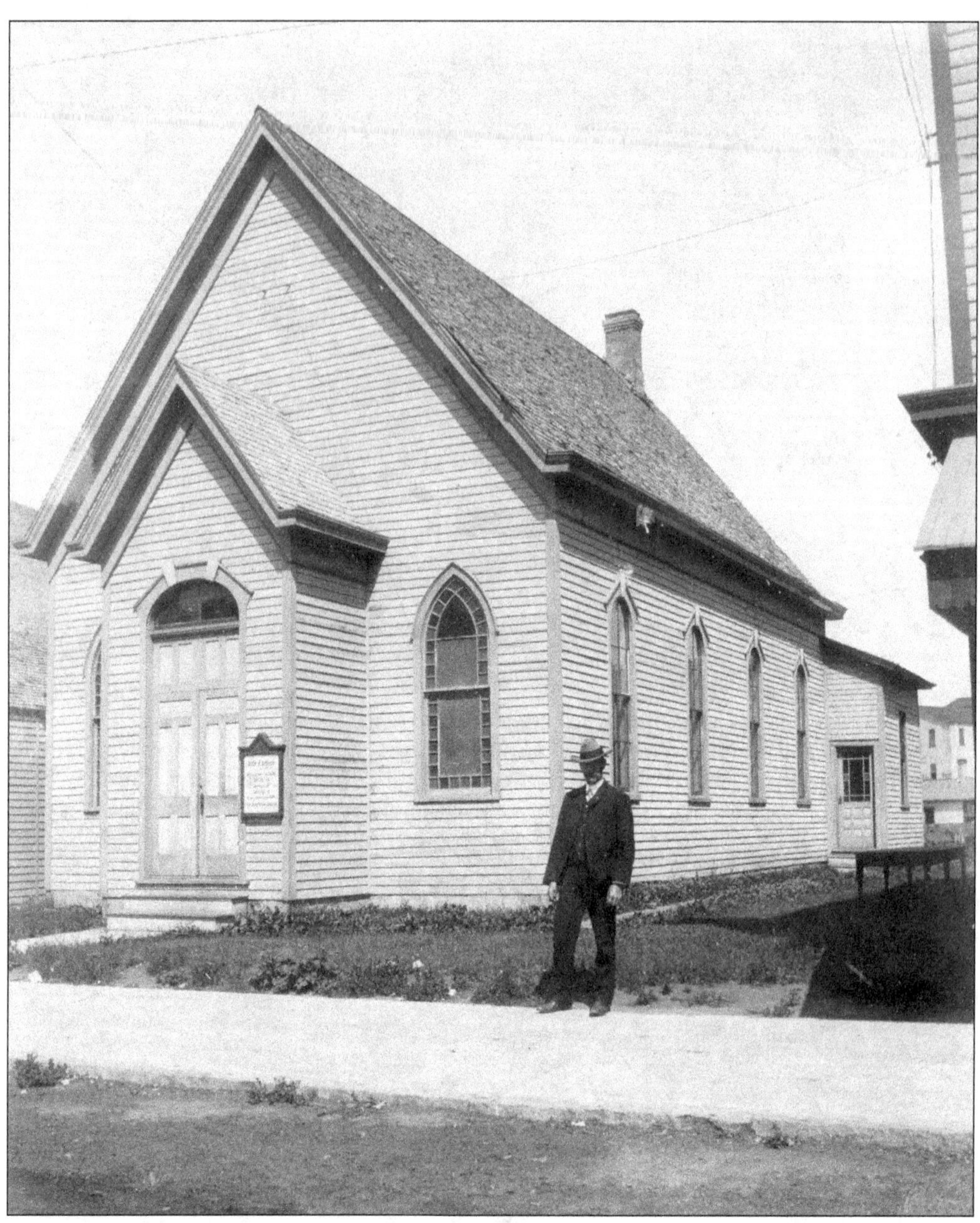

In 1871, when the Methodist Church authorized Rev. James Gurley—a missionary for the Northern Pacific Railroad—to come and minister to their small congregation, there were no churches in Detroit. Their meetings were held in homes, hotels, and halls. The Baptist and Congregationalist churches were organized the next year. Rev. Gurley stayed until 1873, when the Methodist Episcopal Church was organized. The Congregationalists had just completed their church and asked the Methodists to share services. The Methodist Episcopals, under the leadership of J.W. Cornish, felt they could build a new frame church in the center of town at 807 Washington Avenue. The dedication was held on June 29, 1879 and their first parsonage was built between 1897 and 1899 at 1016 Washington Avenue, where the Catholic rectory now stands. Rev. Earl and Margaret Burns were the first residents. Pictured in the foreground is Dr. Leonard C. Weeks, a prominent physician in the city and a Methodist parishioner.

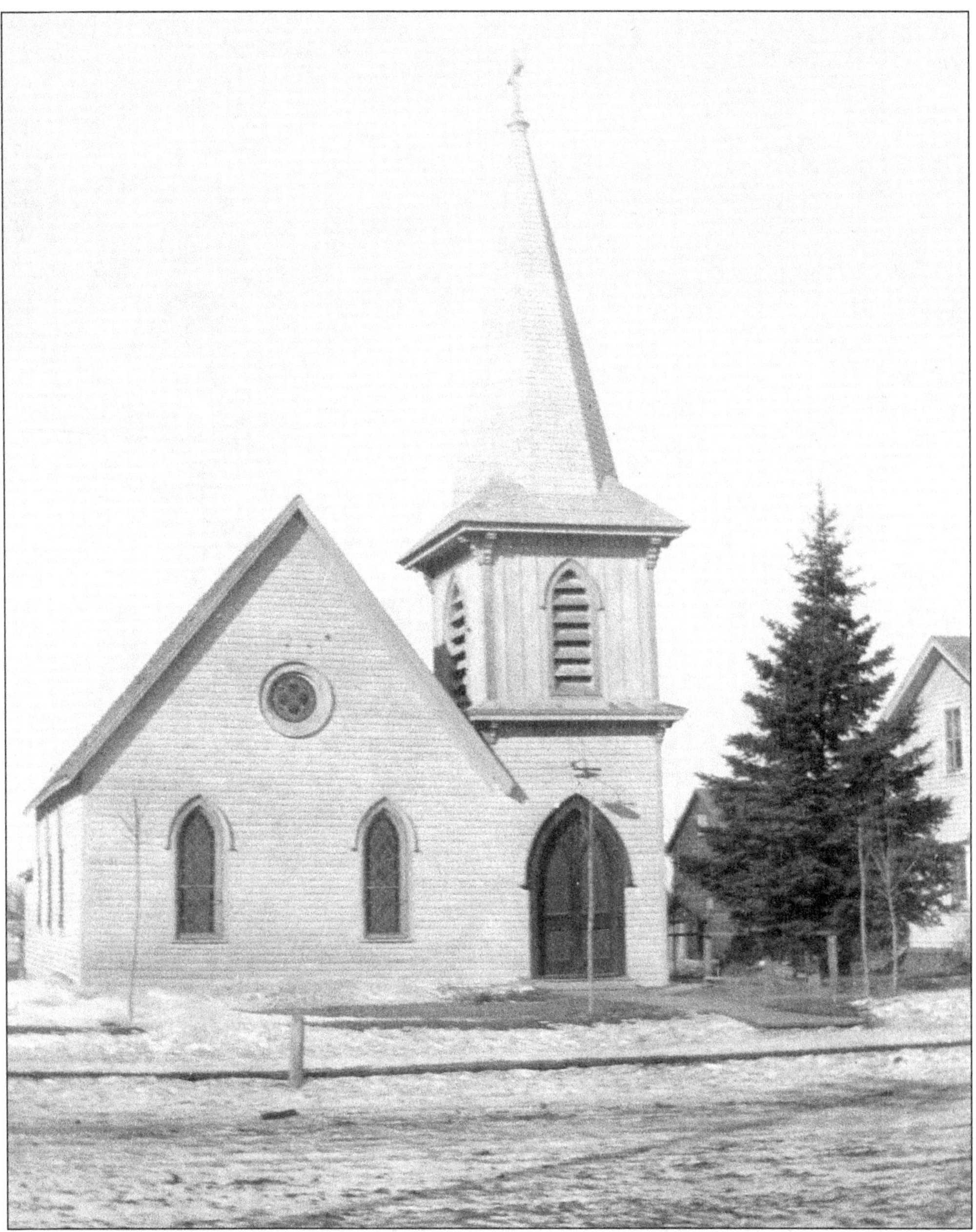

The Episcopal Church was the fourth church to organize in Detroit. The services from 1872 to 1883 were held in the Tyler's Hotel, Peake's Hall, the Holmes Opera House, and the early Baptist, Congregational, and Methodist churches. When Rev. R.M. Johnson became the first resident pastor in 1882, he began work to build a church. The church was located west of the first Congregational church on the hill where Washington Elementary School was. During these times, the hill was referred to as "Gospel Ridge." On April 4, 1883, the bell was hung in the tower, and on May 6, the first services were held in the new building. On September 16, 1885, Bishop Whipple, during his last visit to Detroit Lakes, consecrated the church as St. Luke's Episcopal Church. In 1891, it was decided to move the church to a location near the courthouse, and on November 22, Archbishop Appleby and Bishop Gilbert conducted the first service.

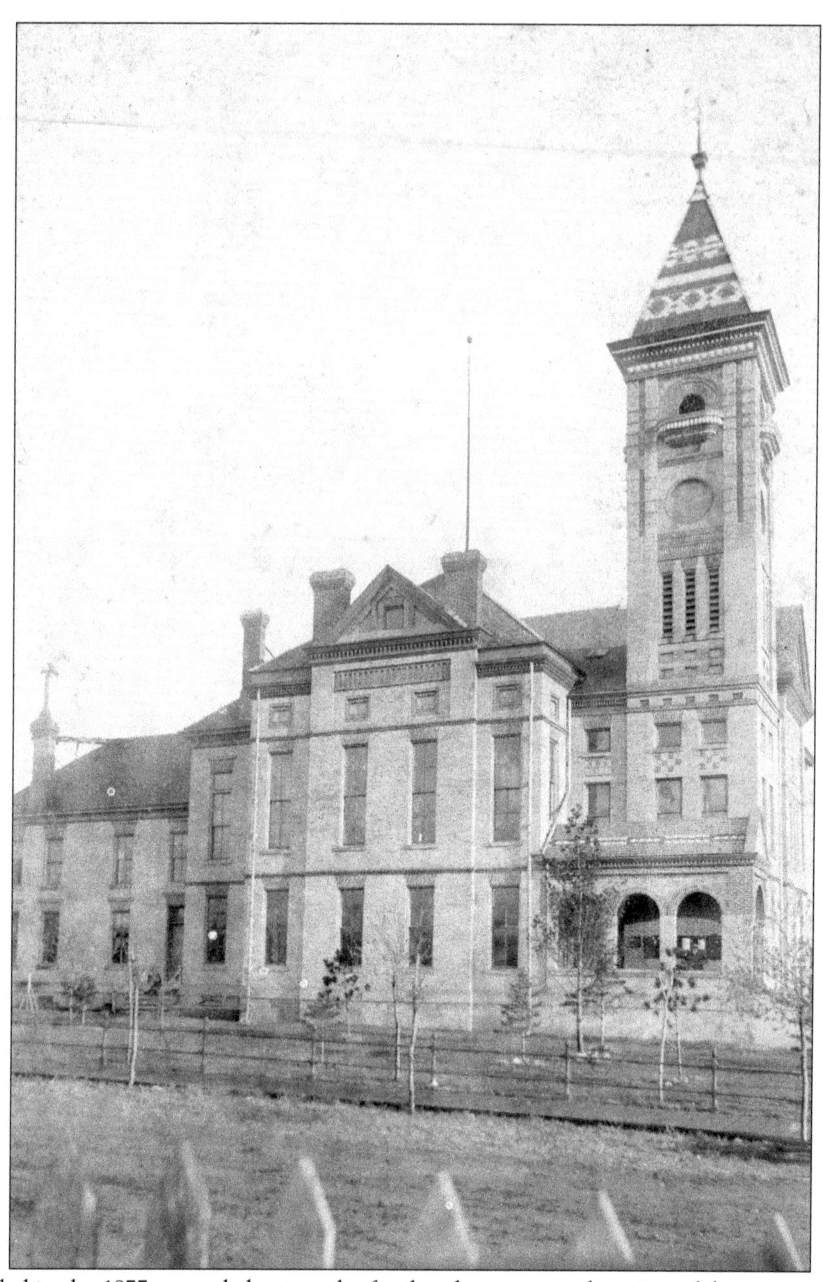

As decided in the 1877 general election, the final and permanent location of the county seat was Detroit. The Township of Detroit, according to a previous agreement, paid the rent annually for a building used by the county officers that was owned and occupied by G.C. Nunn. There was a strong wish on the part of the people living north, east, and south from Detroit—and more particularly on the part of the people living in the village—to clinch the location of the county seat by building a courthouse and jail. Not until 1884 did the resolution pass with the help of E.G. Holmes. There was not much opposition to the jail proposition, but a storm of protests came from Lake Park over the courthouse, and an injunction suit commenced but was later set aside. T.J. Martin and Marcus Shaw built the foundation of the courthouse and jail, and A.A. Whittemore constructed the building. The building was completed and dedicated on May 30, 1885.

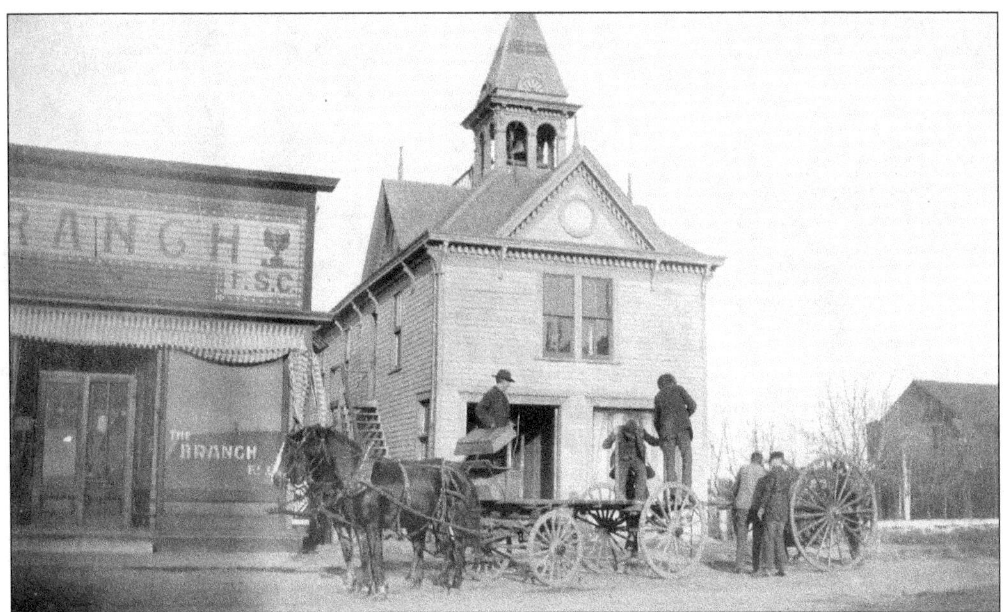

City hall was built on the north side of Pioneer Street between August and September 1885. It was located with other buildings, across from where the Graystone is and where the westbound lane of Highway 10 is found. The village council purchased the land from E.G. Holmes for $200. An architect from St. Paul named Bassford drew up the plans, and A.A. Whittemore was awarded the contract for the work. The building was lost in the fire of 1914.

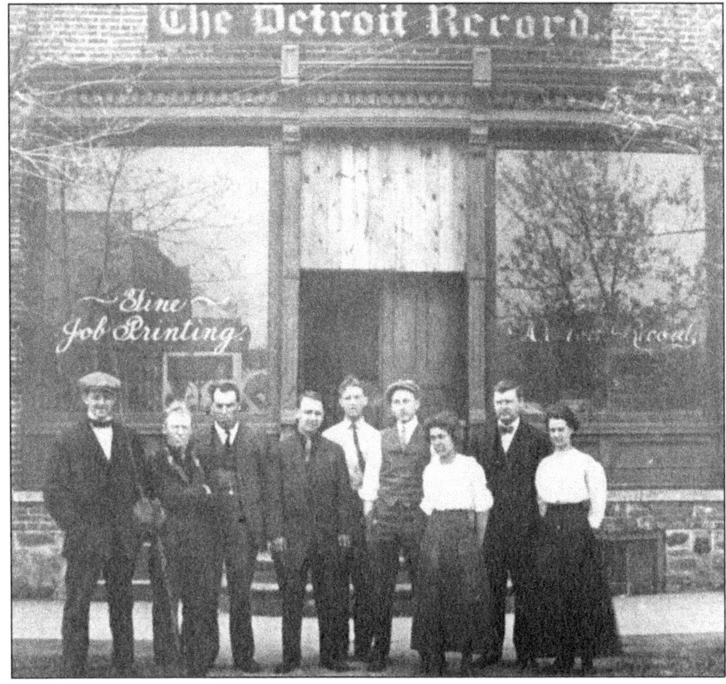

Many early newspapers were published in Becker County and Detroit Lakes. The *Record* (pictured), the county's pioneer paper, began at Ottertail City and moved to Detroit on May 18, 1872. M. Kihn began the *Detroit Quiver* in November 1907. It was changed to the *Detroit Herald* in 1911, the *Detroit News-Tribune* on April 3, 1924, and the *Detroit Lakes Tribune* on November 4, 1926. The editor at the time was William F. Ball, and E.G. Holmes was the proprietor.

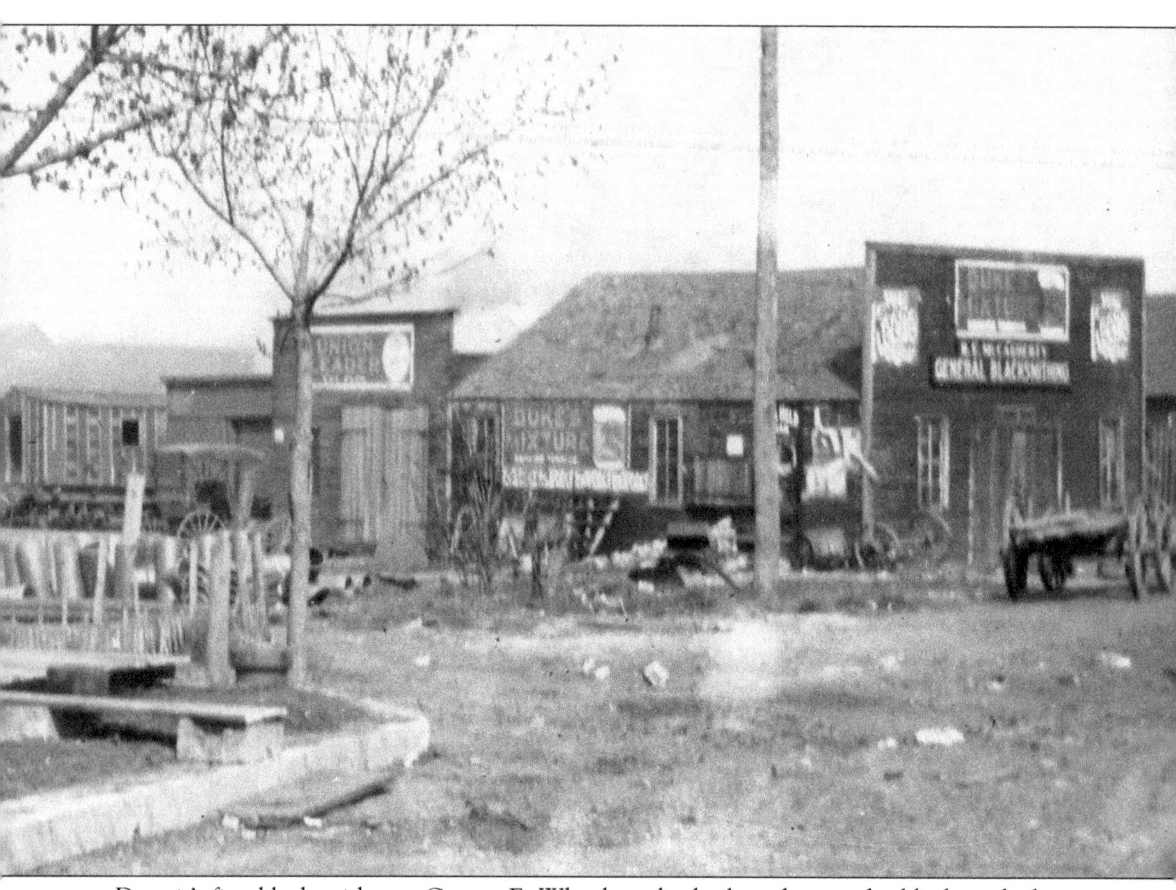

Detroit's first blacksmith was George E. Wheeler, who built and opened a blacksmith shop in Tylertown on August 3, 1872. Some other early blacksmiths were John Nelson, W.M. Leaming, O.J. Olson, Robadau and Spicer, and Dan Still. They were all busy workmen, and the sound of their hammers shaping out red-hot horseshoes could be heard throughout the day. If anything around the home was broken, it was taken down to the blacksmith shop. They were described as hardworking, tobacco-chewing "he-men." Sometimes the *Detroit Record* took a good-natured poke at the blacksmith: "The blacksmiths are now feeling good, the state of the roads requires a large amount of work on the [shoes of] farmer's teams." Pictured above is M.C. O'Kelly's blacksmith shop, which burned down in the fire of 1914. O'Kelly had moved to Detroit from Iowa and followed his vocation as a blacksmith.

Two

Cultural Growth 1890–1900

By 1890, Detroit was firmly established around the Northern Pacific and Soo Line Railroads, with the business district stretching at least four blocks in either direction of each track. The "competition" between the north and south sides of the village had begun, with bankers and businessmen vying for the best spot. Pioneer Street (which has now been overtaken by the Minnesota State Highway 10 bypass) and Washington Avenue served as the main commerce corridors of the city. Grant and Main Streets' proximity to the tracks, and their easy access to freight and delivery, helped them become the working centers of town, with lumber mills, blacksmiths, livery stables, mills, and breweries. The edges of town, at Frazee Street and what is now Highway 34, were slowly being developed, with a road established from Detroit to White Earth. The first roads extending to the lakeshore, Washington Avenue and Summit Avenue, were also constructed at this time. Boardwalks allowed people to make their way from the train to Detroit Lake and onto a steamboat bound for Shoreham, which took only one hour. Horse-drawn taxis, from places like Hotel Minnesota on the corner of Washington Avenue and Frazee Street, aided in this increased tourism. E.G. Holmes built a small electric station behind the Blanding-Norby Department Store on what was known as the Holmes Block and endeavored to have electric streetlights downtown. A water and sewage system was developed, and the Pokegama Springs Bottling Company began marketing the groundwater from Detroit as the purest in the region. The Pioneer Settlers Union, originally formed in 1882, became more active, and in a forward-thinking action started to gather stories about the early years of the county, including the city of Detroit. The city jail and county courthouse were operational, allowing for a "civilized" lifestyle to develop in Detroit. By the end of the 19th century, Detroit was a bustling city of 2,060 residents.

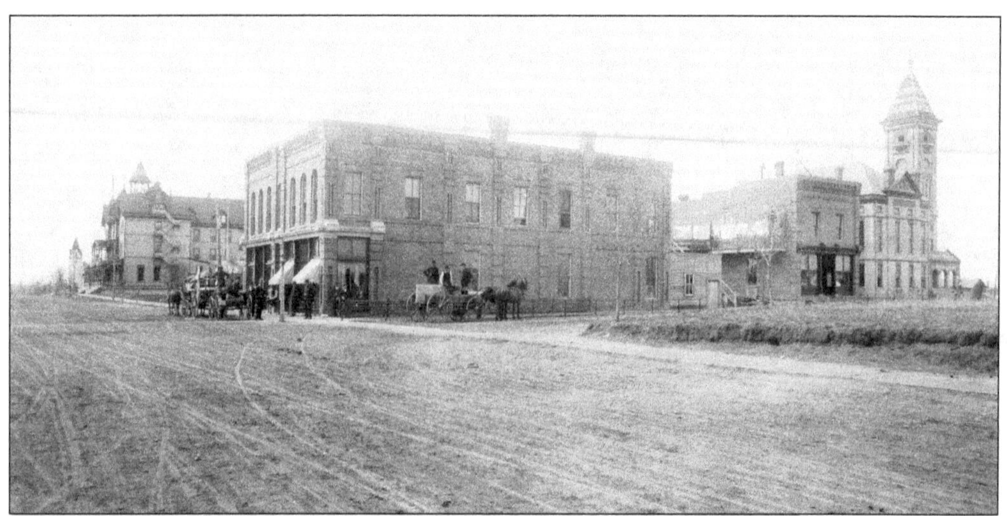

The view above is looking south on Washington Avenue. In the distance are the early Catholic church, the Hotel Minnesota, and the building that housed the Gopher Grill, now the Main Street Restaurant. At the right is the old courthouse and the office of the *Detroit Record*. The empty lot at the right became the site for Schaffer's Ready-to-Wear.

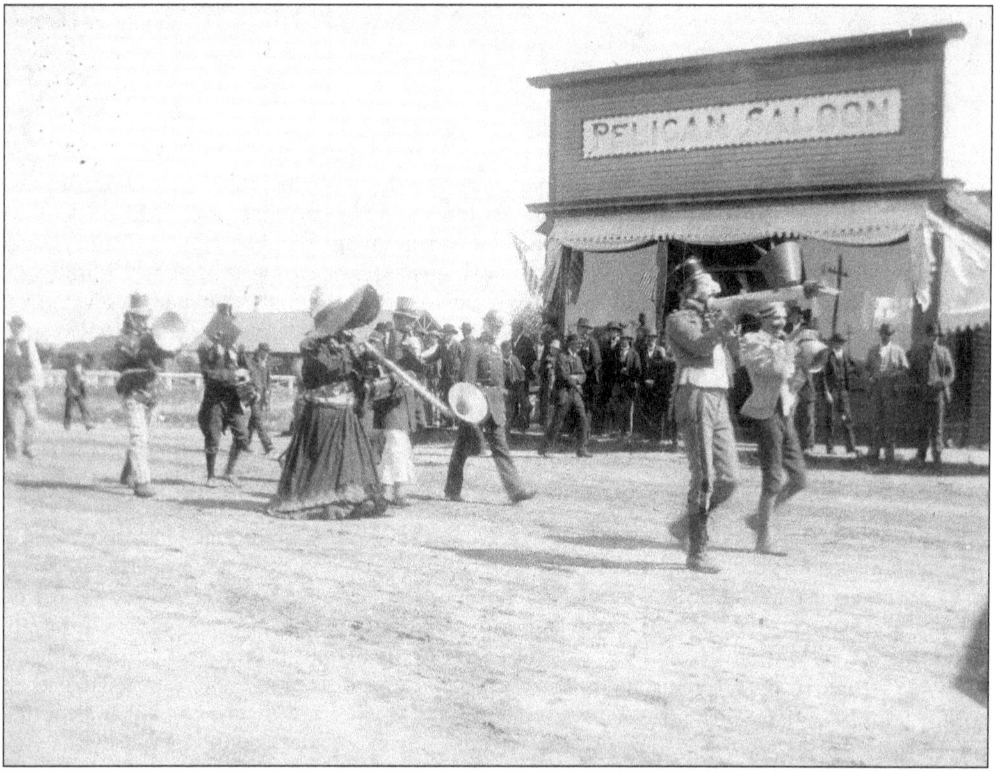

The Pelican Saloon opened in June 1894. It received its name when a large white pelican was placed over the doorway, but the ownership of the bird came into question when it mysteriously disappeared out of the Hotel Minnesota. Between the time the saloon opened and the next week, the pelican switched hands three times, but found its way back to the saloon. The Pelican was torn down in 1905 to make room for the depot.

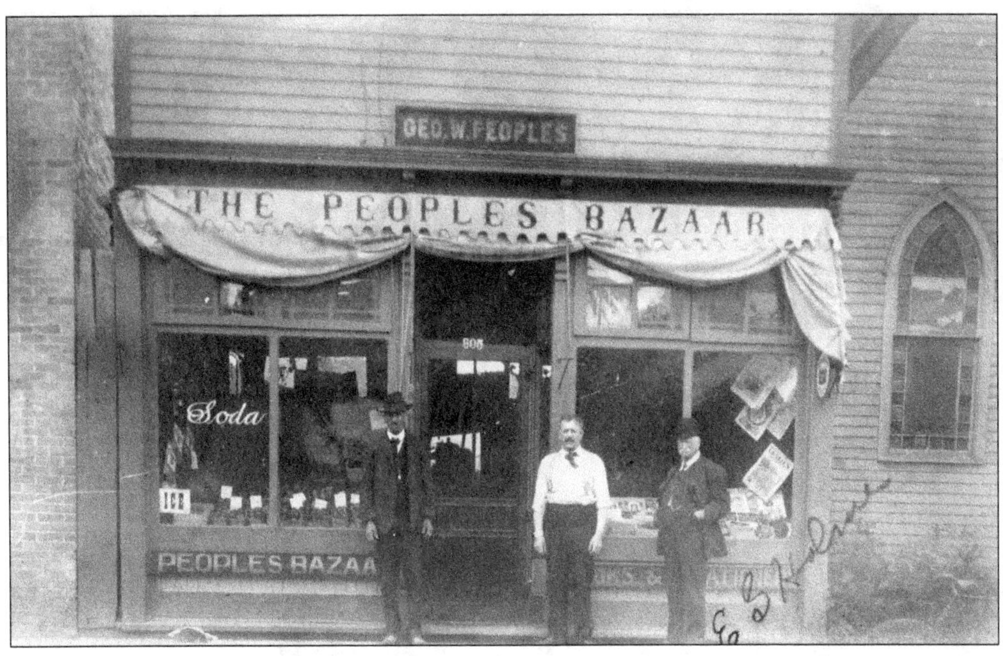

George W. Peoples came to Detroit in 1883, and was first employed by Col. George H. Johnston and James Turnbull. He eventually struck out on his own and opened a book and stationary store. Not only was he a merchant, he was also a member of the council and city board, a charter musician of the city band, a member of two leading fraternal organizations, and a center fielder on the baseball team. When Peoples was a member of the school board, the decision to construct the Holmes School and the Washington School buildings was made. The Peoples home, located at the corner of Washington Avenue and Willow Street, is shown below around 1898.

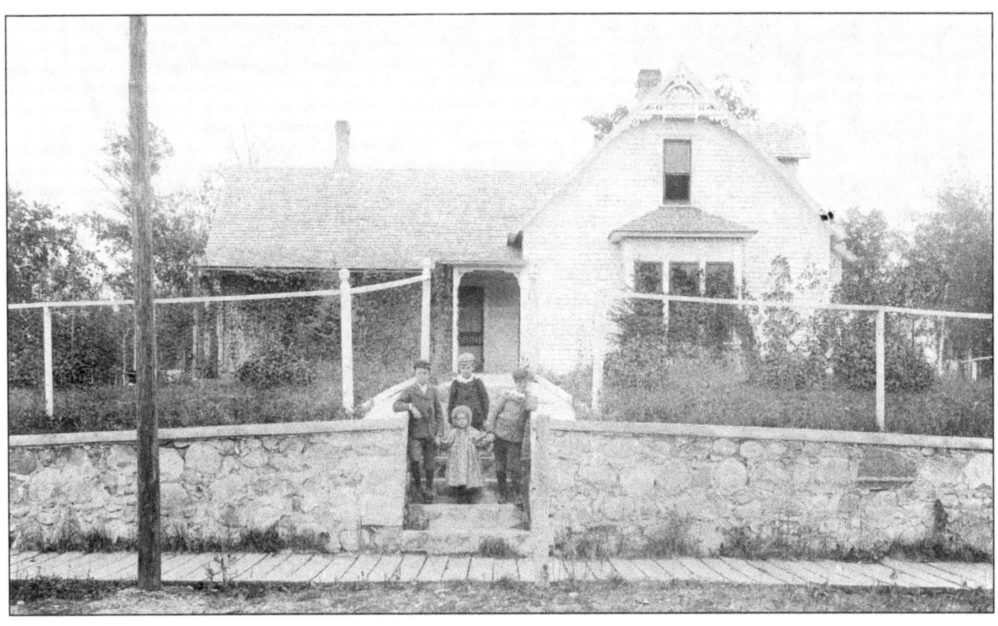

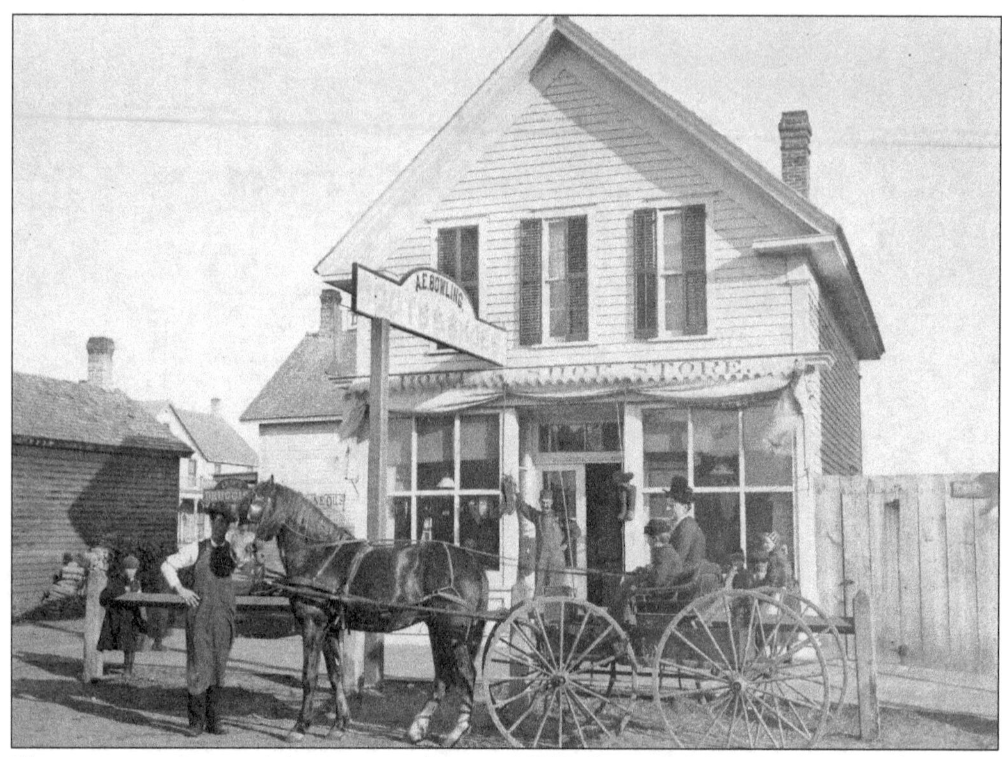

There were two boot and shoe stores in Detroit: M.V.B. Davis and A.E. Bowling. Bowling came to Detroit from Michigan with his young wife on April 15, 1895, and soon made a small fortune as a boot and shoe merchant by opening the Bowling Shoe Store, located on the north side of the Northern Pacific tracks on Washington Avenue. He made boot pacs and shoe pacs as well as handmade boots and shoes to size. The soles were put on with small wooden pegs, and the cobbler would sit all day and peg away with his small hammer. Bowling was also president of the village council in the 1880s.

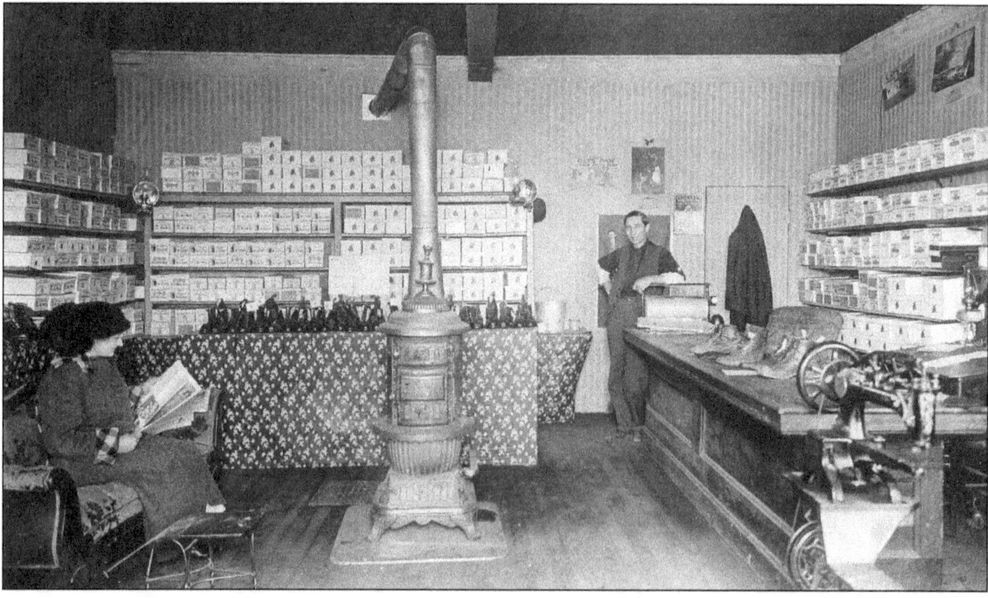

Early post offices were informal central locations where settlers could get their letters. The post office in Detroit moved many times. Starting out in 1871, it was located in the Tyler Hotel, but when the town site was laid out west of Tyler's, the post office moved to the Lakes Hotel. The post office was again moved to a building located at 505 Washington Avenue, and for some time it was located in a building at 717 Washington Avenue. In 1892, they moved south of the tracks to 902 Washington Avenue. In August 1934, a new building was erected at the corner of Lake Avenue and State Street before finally ending up at 250 West State Street in 1967.

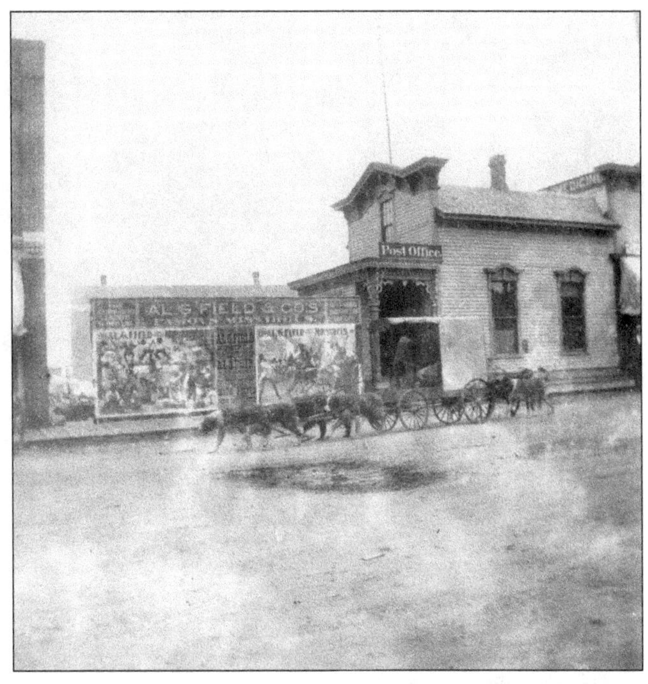

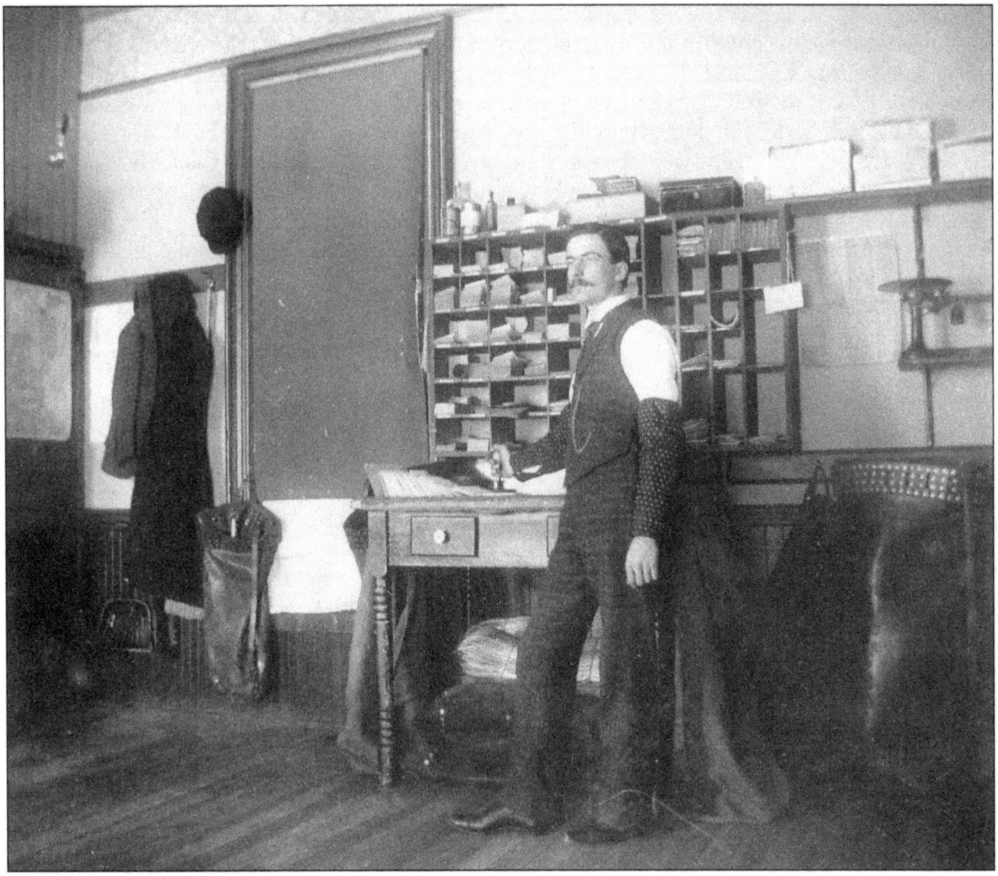

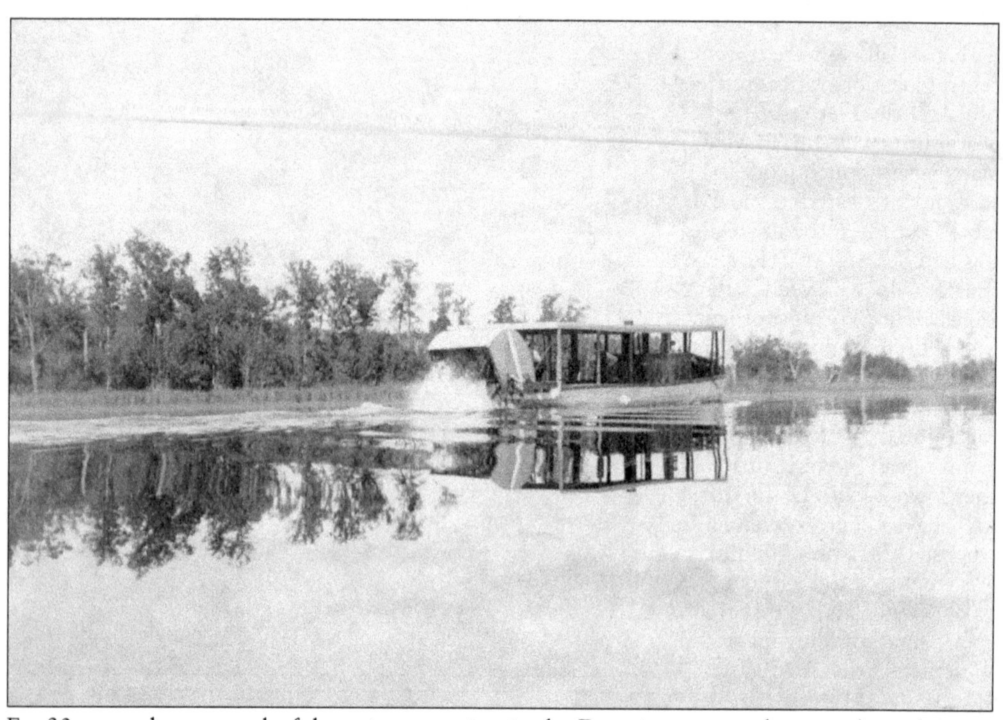

For 30 years, the most colorful tourist attraction in the Detroit area was the steamboat that ran from Little Detroit Lake to Pelican Lake. In 1888, the Pelican Valley Navigation Company was formed with John K. West as president. West was also called the "Father of the Detroit Lakes tourist industry." In March 1889, Blanding and Smith were contracted to build steamboats for the company. The first pair of steamboats on the river and canal system was the *Lady of the Lakes* (pictured on the next page) and the *Robert Fulton* (pictured above). The first steamboat on Detroit Lake was the *Minnie Corliss* (pictured below), which was launched at the foot of Washington Avenue on April 30, 1889. It was 70 feet long, 16 feet wide, double-decked, and could carry 200 passengers. John H. Smith was the captain.

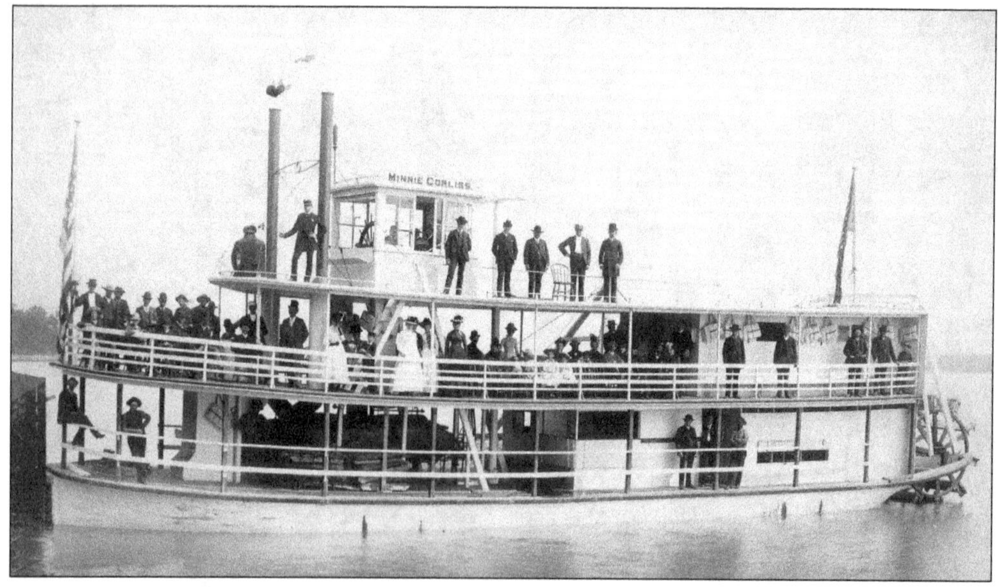

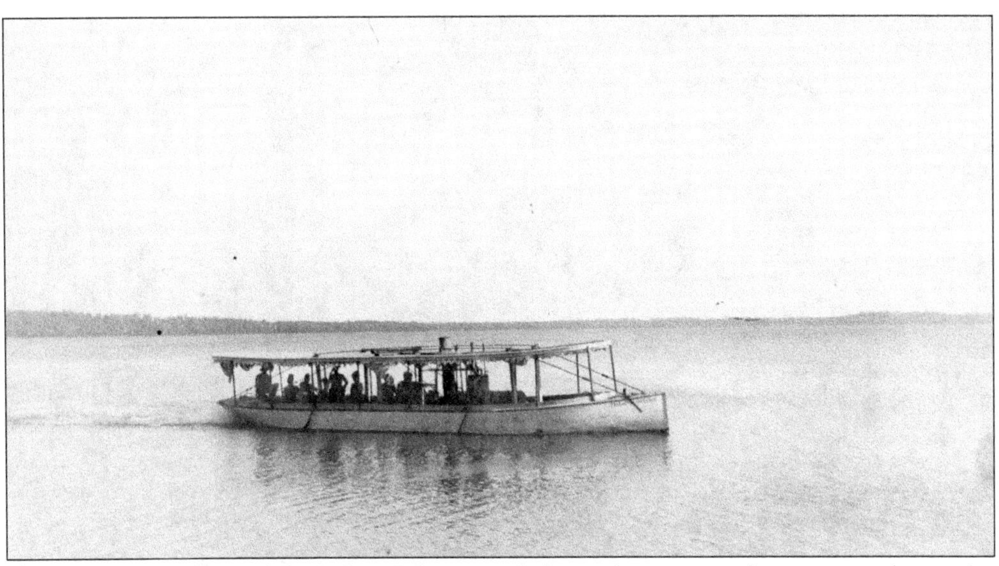

The *Lady of the Lakes* and the *Robert Fulton* provided steamboat service for tourists and were also used to haul wood from the Shoreham area after the tourist season was over but before the lakes froze. The *Lady of the Lakes* was 54 feet long, carried 12 passengers, and had two engines. For the 15 years he operated the boat, Albert Johnson, the engineer, never missed a train connection and never had an accident. For many years, the steamboats provided the only means for summer tourists to reach their homes on lakes below Detroit. Pictured below is the steamboat landing at the foot of Washington Avenue.

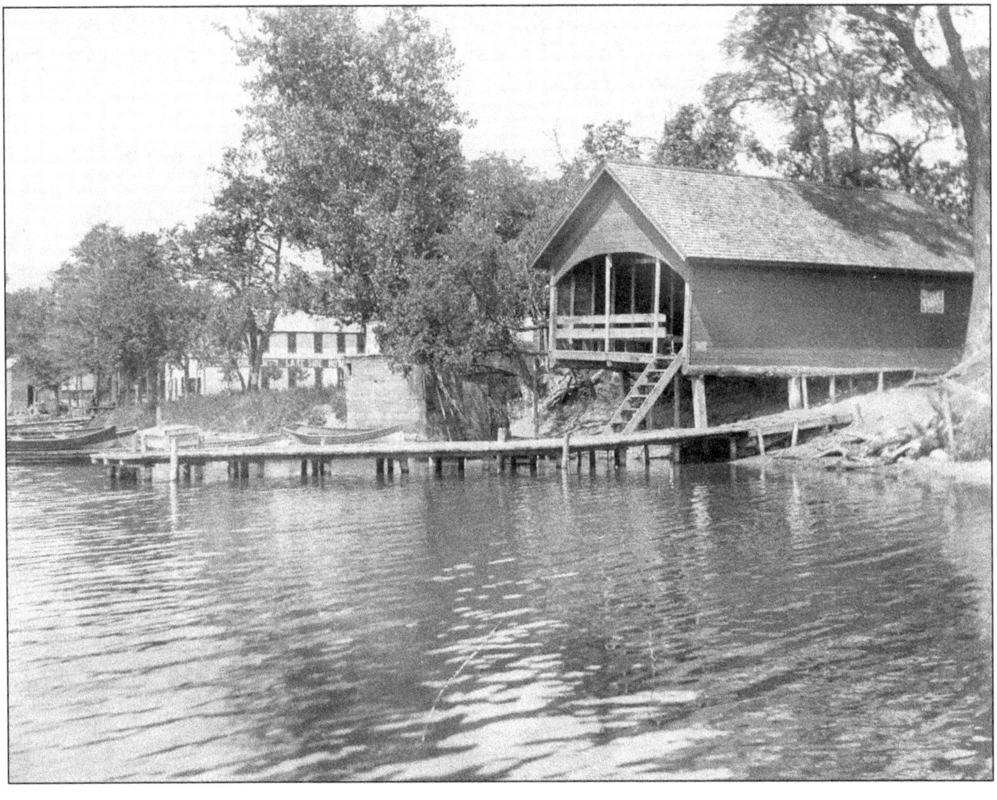

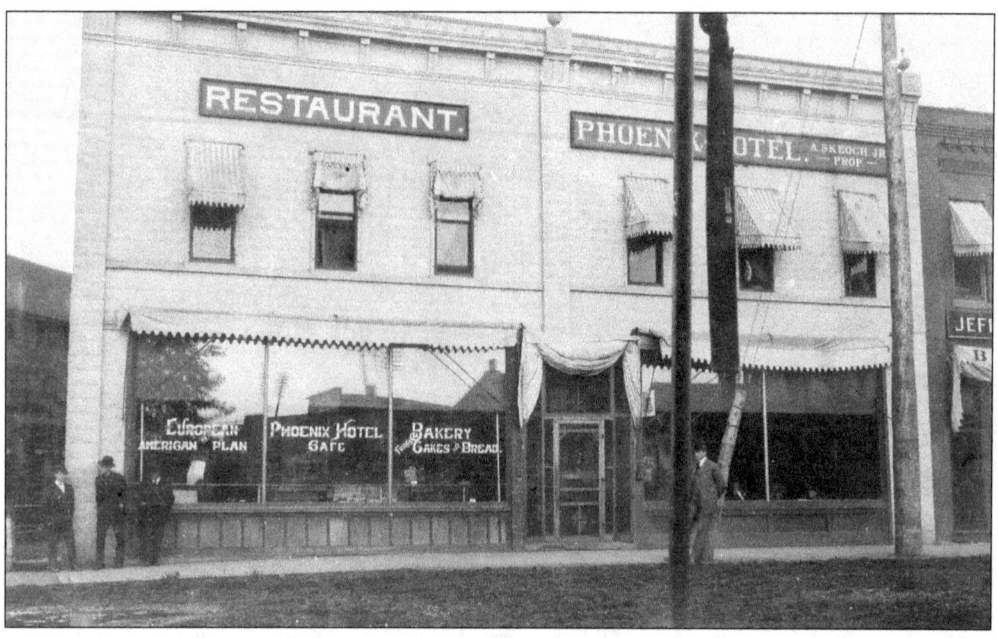

Anthony Skeoch ran the Phoenix Hotel (above) and bakery (below) and was one of the best-known and most popular businessmen around. He came from Fargo in 1893 and partnered with his brother Albert in the restaurant business. During his residence of about 13 years, he became a very popular citizen, taking an active interest in public matters and serving as a member of the city council. The Phoenix Hotel eventually changed hands and was renamed the Colonial Hotel. Later operators were John Harding, Ed Conley, and Stewart Doyle. It was remodeled in 1945 but was destroyed by a fire that killed two men on January 20, 1955.

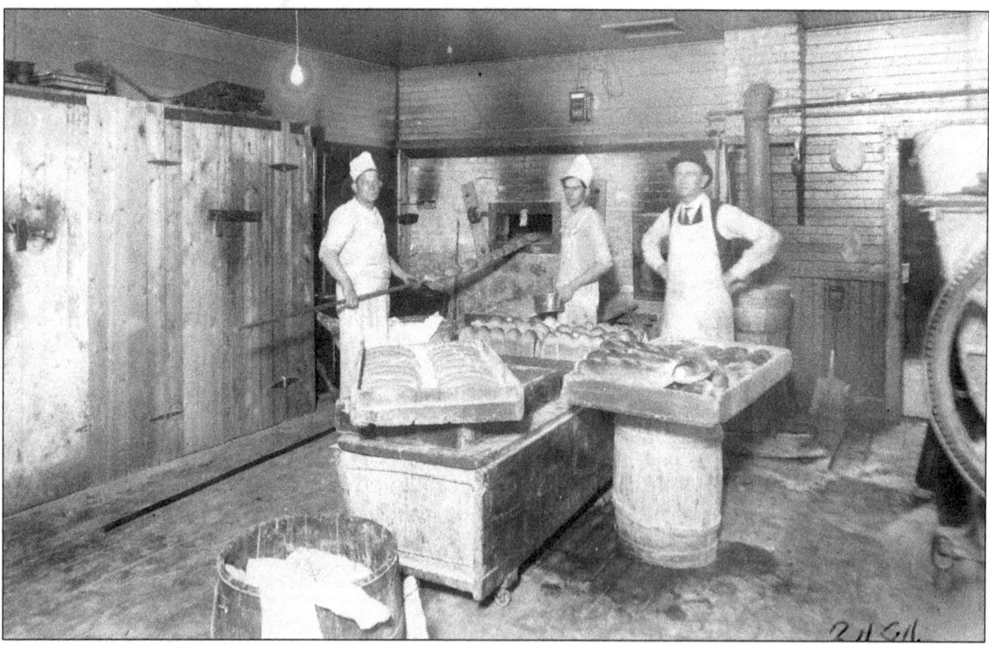

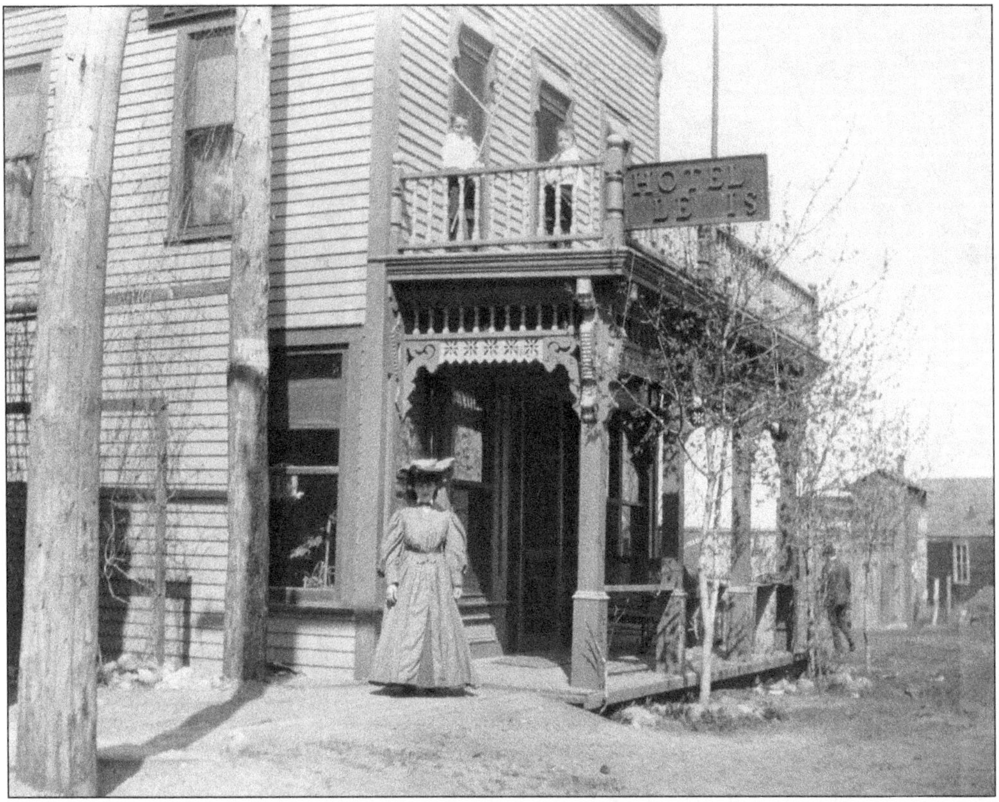

The Lewis Hotel was built in 1899 and located on Front Street behind the First National Bank. D. Samuel Lewis originally used this building as a violin construction and repair shop. He also made tables, clocks, and cabinets. In the upper part of the building, there was a tea shop that was operated by his wife, Mary. As the town grew with the tourist boom, so did the demand for accommodation. Since their current building was not big enough, the Lewis family moved another building onto their lot and connected the two. The hotel had 28 private rooms, a large dining room, and lobby. The lobby was furnished quite simply, with taxidermy animal heads and cream pitchers mounted on the walls. Mary's collection of dishes, pictured below, was later donated to help start the Becker County History Museum.

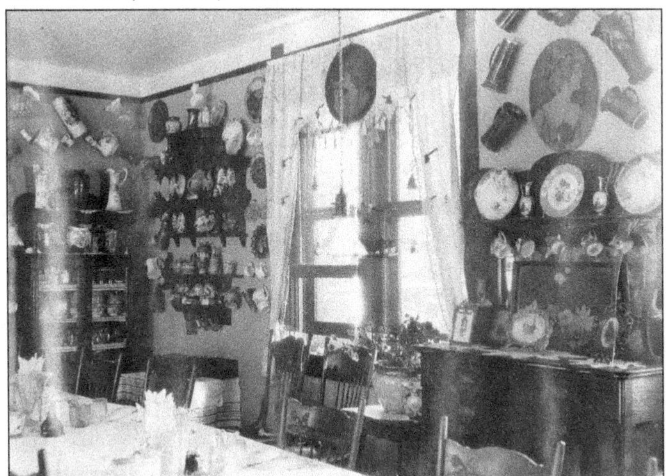

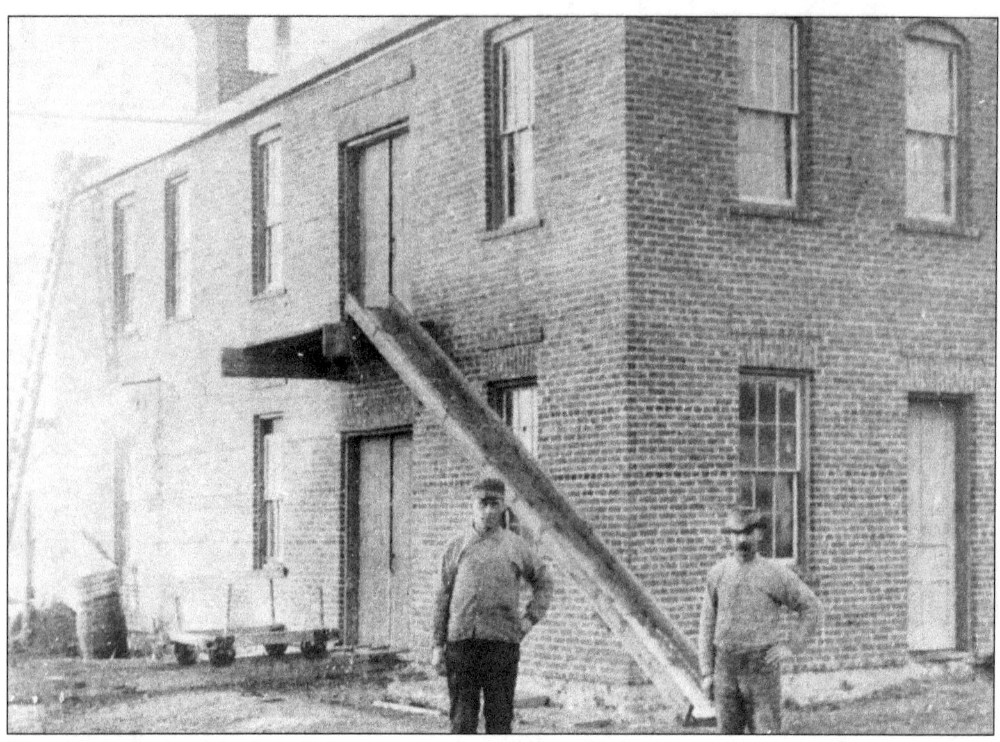

The J.H. Sutherland Ax-Handle Factory was built and established in 1885 by Judge J.H. Sutherland. It was constructed of native brick, had a sawmill attached, and was run by steam power. It manufactured elm and oak yokes and single trees for horse harnesses. This factory supplied the Northern Pacific Railroad with all kinds of handles for its workers. Ward Connell was the engineer, and Tubbs and Bill Yerks were mill workers.

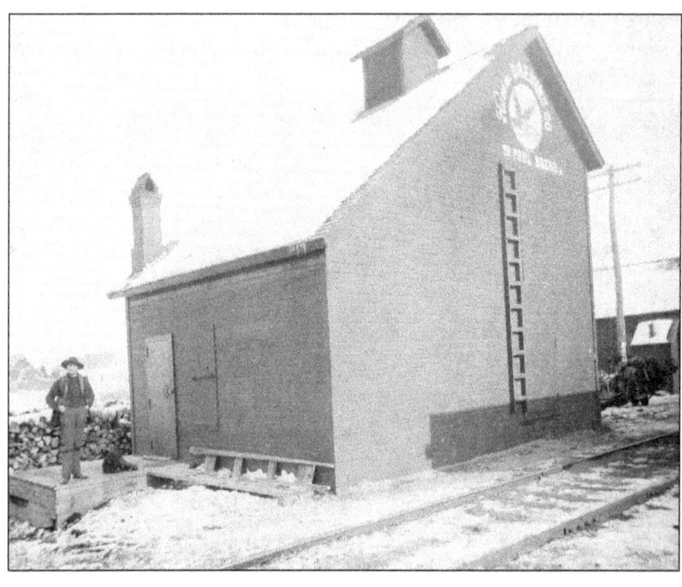

Hamm's Beer Warehouse was located on the north side of the Northern Pacific Railroad tracks on Lake Avenue near where Berg Auto Electric (later Napa) once stood. Its location was conducive to receiving shipments from the T. Hamm Brewing Company. Theodore Hamm and A.F. Kellar started Hamm's in 1865, and by 1886 it was turning out 40,000 barrels of beer, making it the second largest in the state.

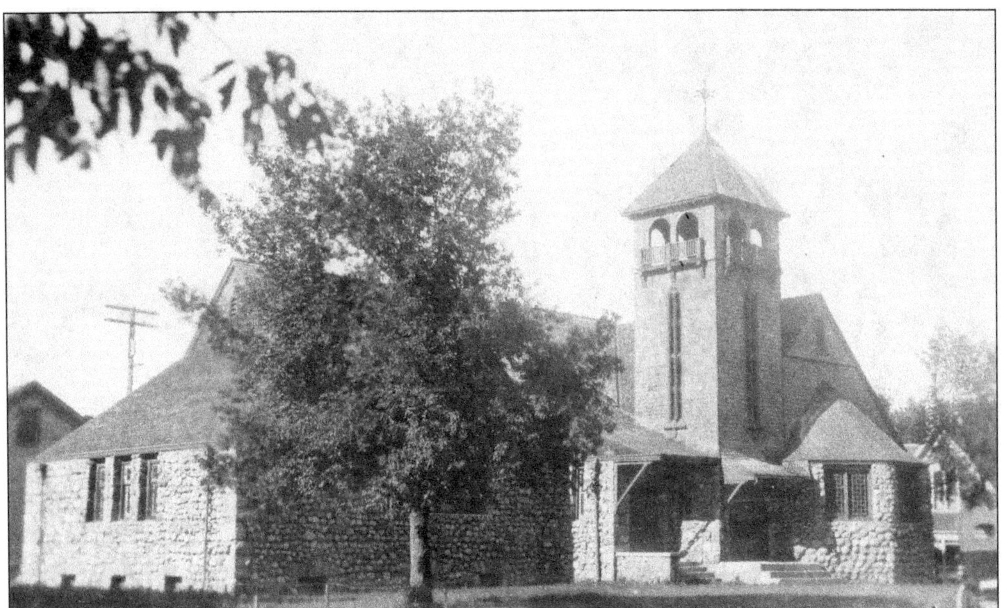

The First Baptist Church was organized on July 20, 1872, at the McKenzie Hall. Soon after, it started building a new church that was ready for occupancy by Christmas. It soon became a popular community center and was used for concerts and other get-togethers. Eventually, a new church was needed. After a donation of land and money from E.G. Holmes and the Jeff Irish families, the first service was held on October 22, 1893.

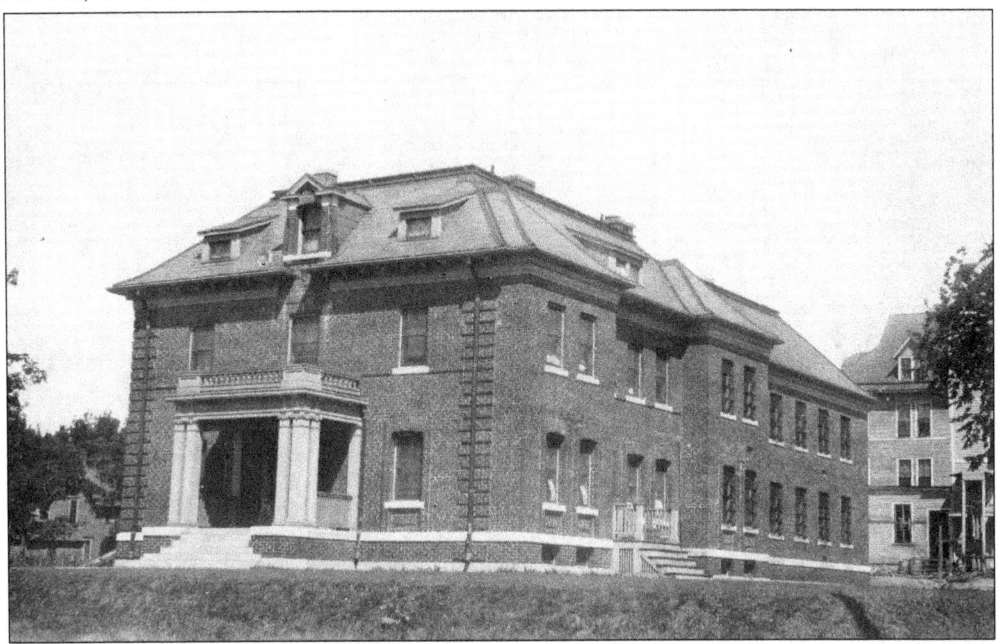

John H. Phinney was one of the pioneer settlers of Detroit. Soon after arriving, he engaged in business with E.G. Holmes. He was elected in 1880 as sheriff of Becker County and served three consecutive terms, or six years. In all matters of public interest and in the improvement of the city, he always took an active part and was a man of strong convictions. Pictured is the sheriff's office, residence, and county jail.

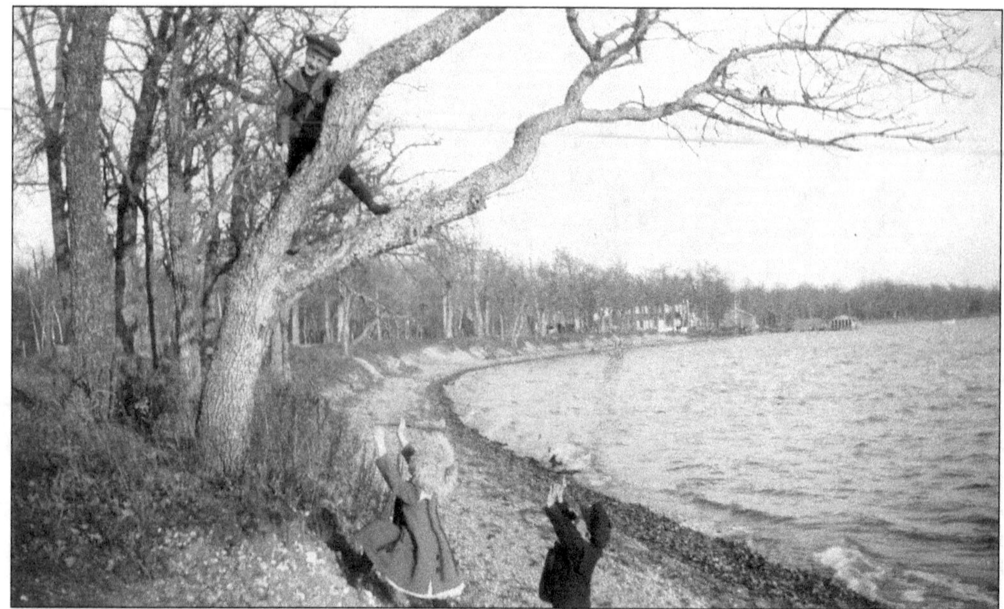

In the early days, Detroit was jokingly called "Swamp Town," "Sloughville," and even "Mudville," because there were so many sloughs and swamps right in town. The area south of Frazee Street to the lake was one vast tamarack swamp. The appearance of the city today is a dramatic testimony to the work of the early businessmen who envisioned a busy city with wide, clean streets and avenues leading all the way to the lake.

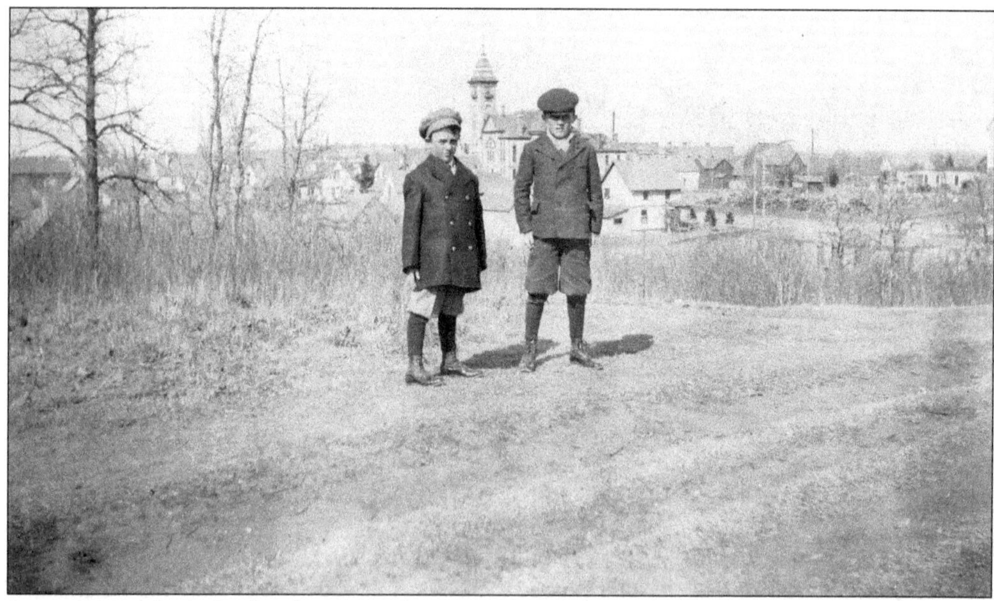

Samuel F. Fox built the first house on the present town site of Detroit Lakes. The log cabin, built in the spring of 1870, was located on what is still known as Fox's Hill (above), just southwest of the courthouse. He and his family lived there only three years, and his cabin was torn down in 1885.

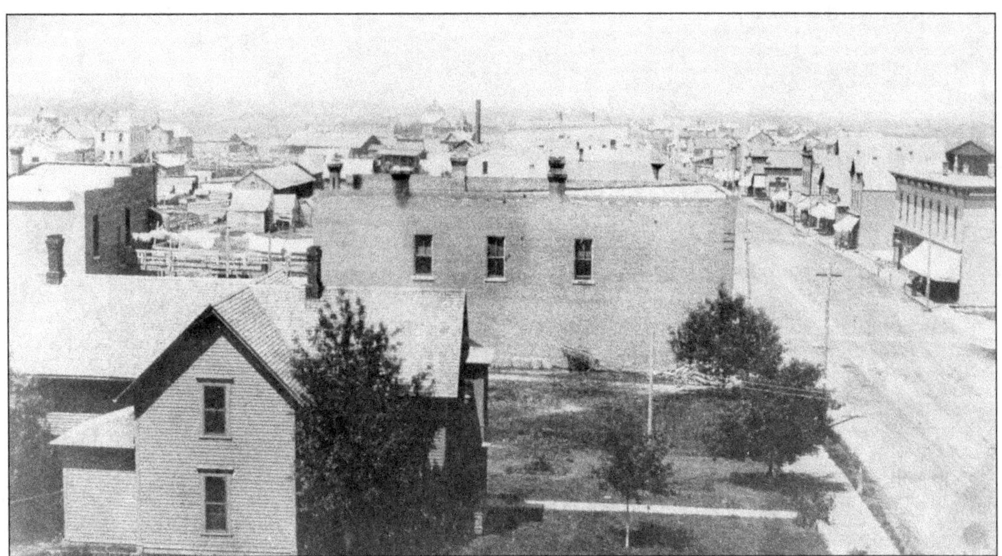

The 1890s were the days of wooden sidewalks. One wooden sidewalk extended all the way down the west side of Washington Avenue to the lake. At times, the spikes used in fastening the planks to the runners would work up far enough to catch the woolen braid on the inside hem of a woman's skirt and rip off a long piece.

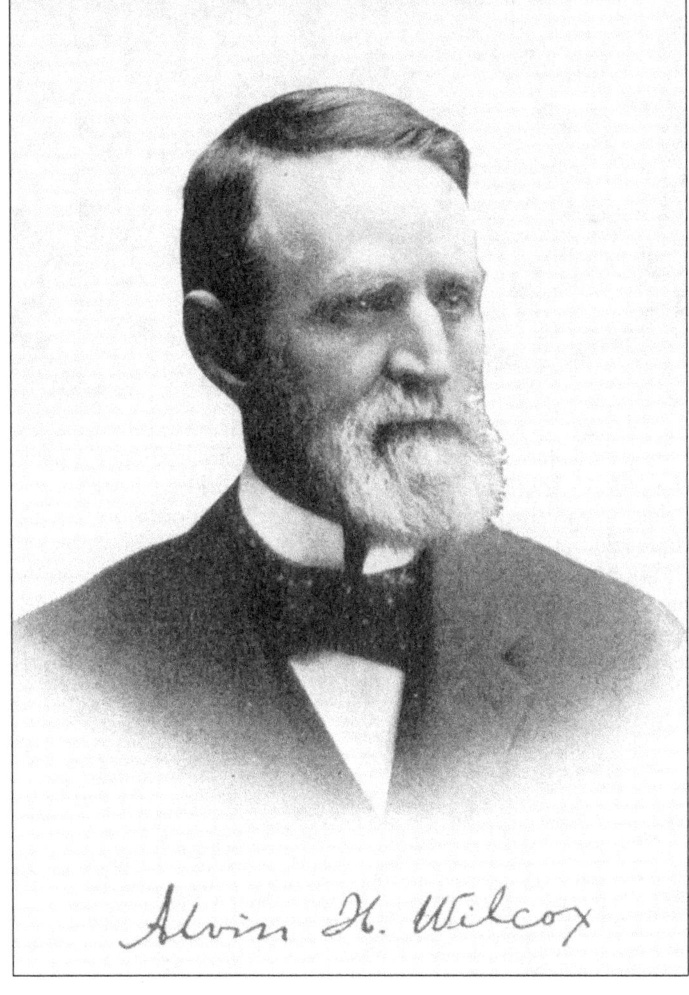

Alvin H. Wilcox was made US deputy surveyor of 13 townships, including Becker County. In 1872, he surveyed the city of Detroit. Later in life, he was vice president and stockholder of the Wilcox Lumber Company. Along with Mrs. Jessie West, he also edited A *Pioneer History of Becker County*, which covers all developments of the area and can currently be purchased at the Becker County History Museum.

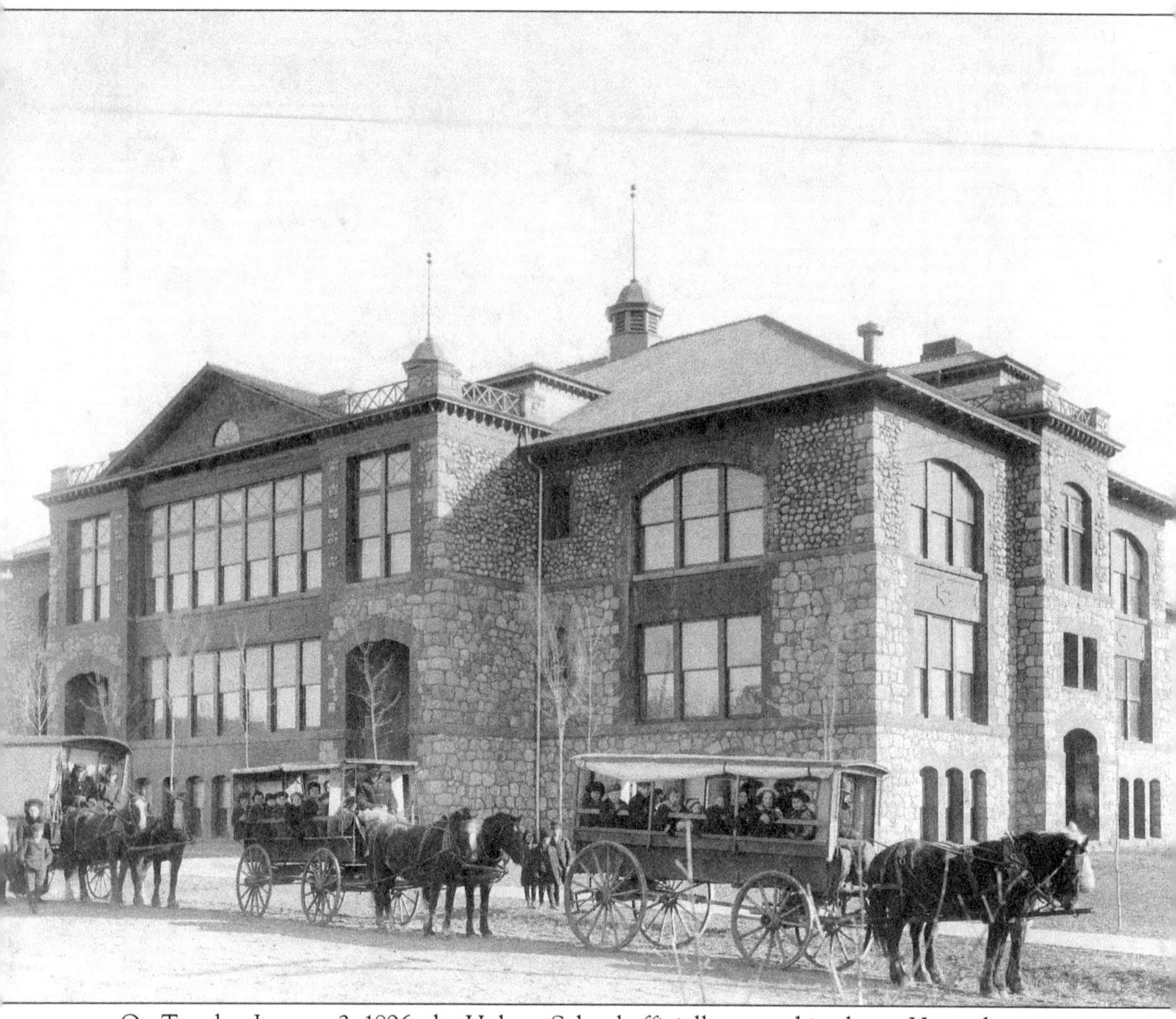

On Tuesday, January 2, 1896, the Holmes School officially opened its doors. Horse-drawn carts, the school's transportation, picked up the children since most of their parents worked in the fields early in the morning and used their transportation to get there. The Holmes School had three additions. The first addition was built in 1895, the second was added in 1909, and the final addition was built in 1939, adding a small stage and a new auditorium. The school received its name from the "Grand Old Man" of Detroit Lakes, E.G. Holmes. In October 1980, the Holmes School went up in flames, and it took 75 firemen to extinguish the fire. The only addition that was saved was the 1932 addition and the bell, which had fallen through seven floors and landed in the basement.

Three
A New Century
1901–1925

At the turn of the 20th century, Detroit was booming, and the city experienced more building during this time than in any other. Cement sidewalks and granite curbing was laid in the business district of Washington Avenue, from the Northern Pacific railroad to the Hotel Minnesota. A new railroad depot was constructed in 1908, giving passengers a more comfortable place to spend their time and also providing a park for leisure time outdoors while waiting for their train. Chautauqua assemblies were held on the park grounds off Summit Avenue. An American adult education movement of the late-19th and early 20th centuries, Chautauqua brought entertainment and culture for the whole community, with speakers, teachers, musicians, entertainers, preachers, and specialists of the day. Municipal utilities, replacing the private offerings of E.G. Holmes, were established and expanded. In 1914, the city of Detroit suffered its most devastating fire, which began in Rahm's Livery Stable on State Street near the current location of the post office. This fire engulfed the downtown, which lost 26 buildings. A year later, the Hotel Minnesota, considered the jewel of Detroit tourism, also burned. As a result, new building codes were established and brick became the preferred construction material. The Graystone Hotel was constructed over the winter of 1915 and 1916, under what locals referred to as a "circus tent," to accommodate the visitors who would have previously stayed at the Hotel Minnesota. Also during this time, the city and county learned to value their freedoms when they sent hundreds of their sons and daughters off to war. In 1924, a formal Becker County Historical Society was established from the remnants of the Pioneer Settlers Union, and the search for a museum space began in earnest. Small cabin resorts abounded and the leisure appeal of the lakes continued to grow. By 1920, the population of Detroit had grown to 3,426.

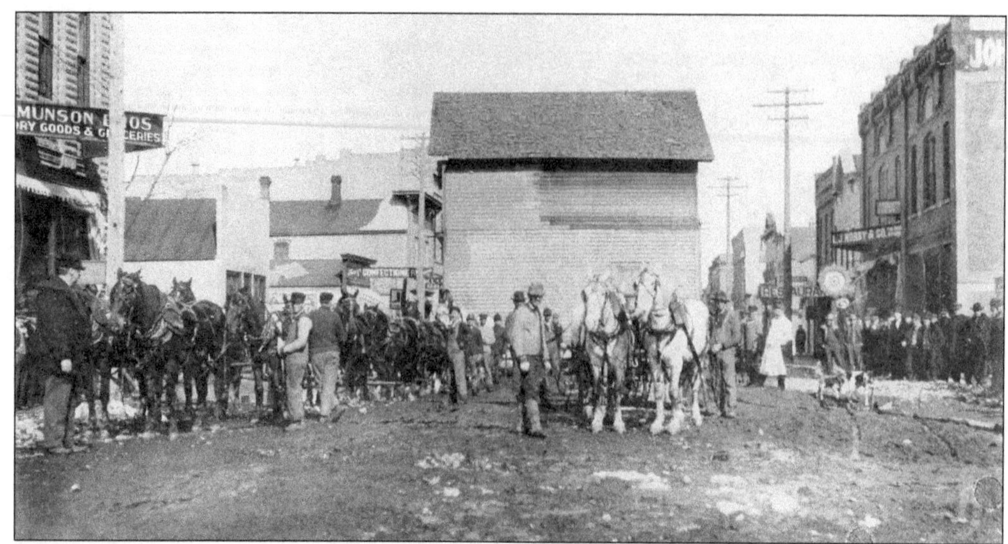

With its growth, the city had to adjust to the needs of its businesses. Here, Dave Carson's store was being moved from the northeast corner of Washington Avenue and Front Street to 212 East Frazee Street to make room for new construction. Harry L. Johnson used his horse team and skids to move the building. The streets of Detroit were still muddy and filled with refuge, all signs of a city on the brink of "civilization."

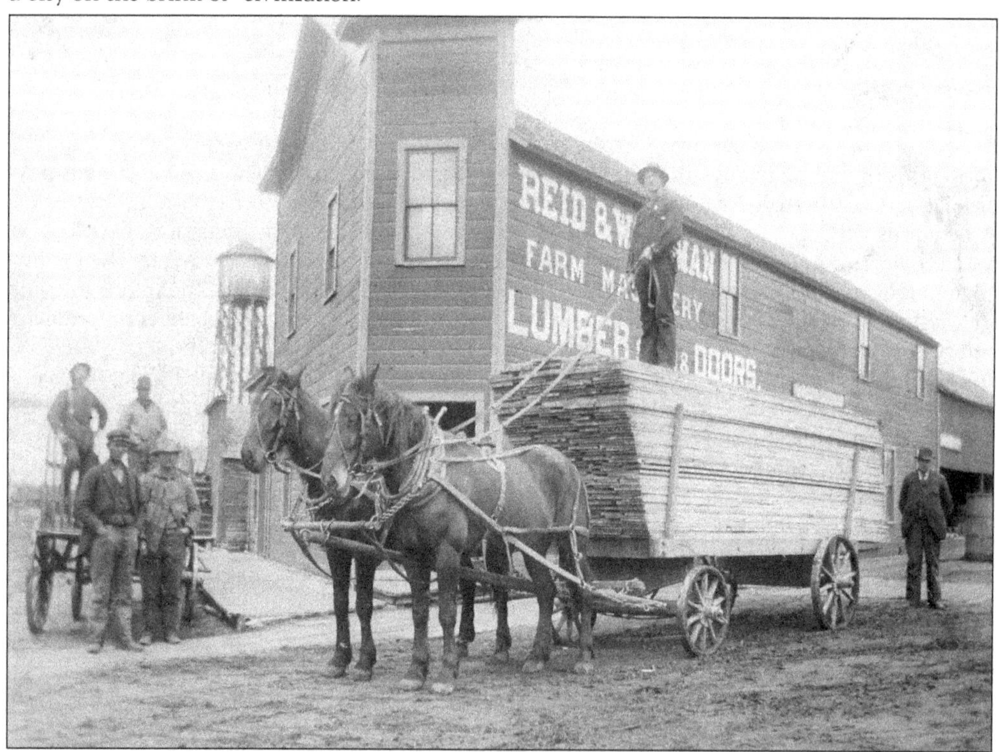

William Henry McCart was a pioneer drayman of the city. He operated a dray in Detroit for 56 years, starting with his father and then venturing into the trucking business on his own after four years. McCart was one of the first in town to use motor trucks instead of horses and wagons in the dray business. The wagon in the photograph is carrying 9,400 pounds of lumber.

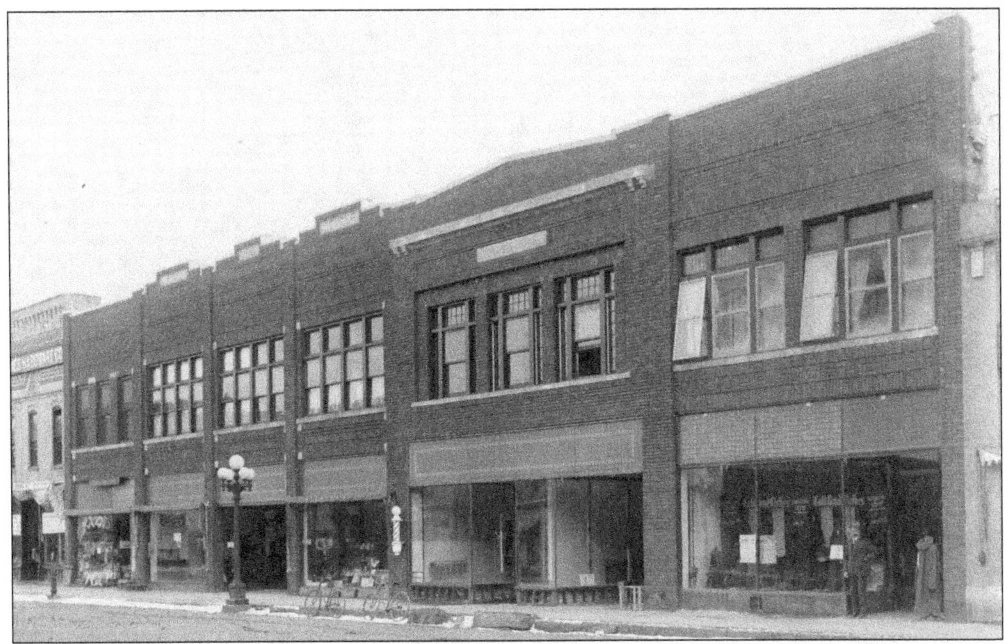

The John H. Smith Company started in 1887. Smith later partnered with Albert Blanding and E.G. Holmes to form Blanding and Smith. In 1898, they parted ways, and Smith moved across the street into a new building. Blanding then partnered with Lewis J. Norby, forming Blanding-Norby Company before splitting in 1906. Norby then moved across the street, buying Smith's building and opening L.J. Norby Company. In the bottom photograph, Geo Hamilton, Judd Wood, and Arthur Blanding are inside the store. The Blanding-Norby Company had a pneumatic cash carrier system installed throughout the store, so only one cashier, located upstairs, handled the money.

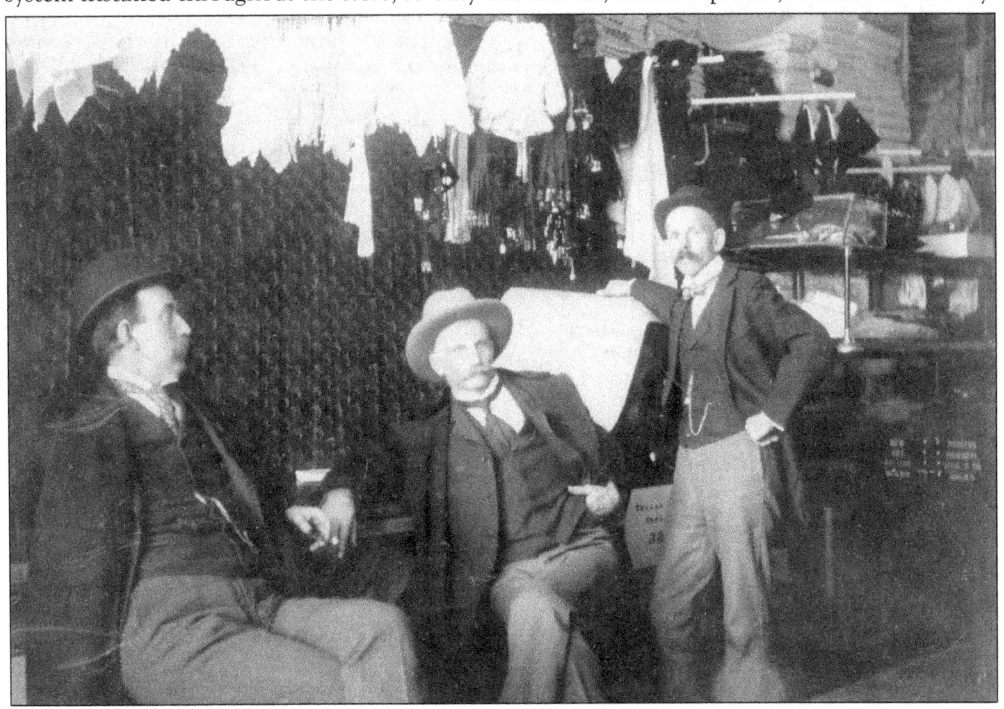

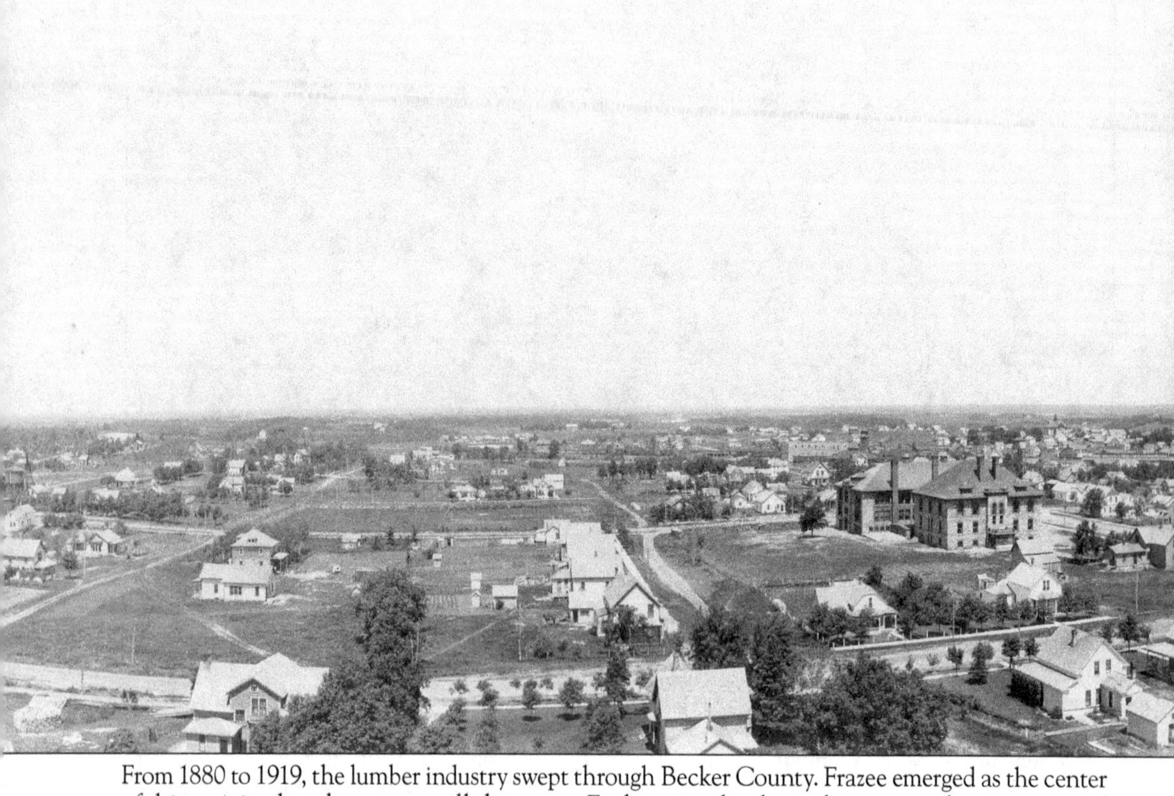

From 1880 to 1919, the lumber industry swept through Becker County. Frazee emerged as the center of this activity, but there were mills here, too. Each spring, lumberjacks came to the city to spend their paychecks. Historians estimate that in those years, the lumber firms cut down a total of 500 million feet of pine, mostly tall, straight Norway pine—which took at least 1.5 million trees—and an additional 125 million feet of oak timber. In addition, area farmers cut an estimated one million

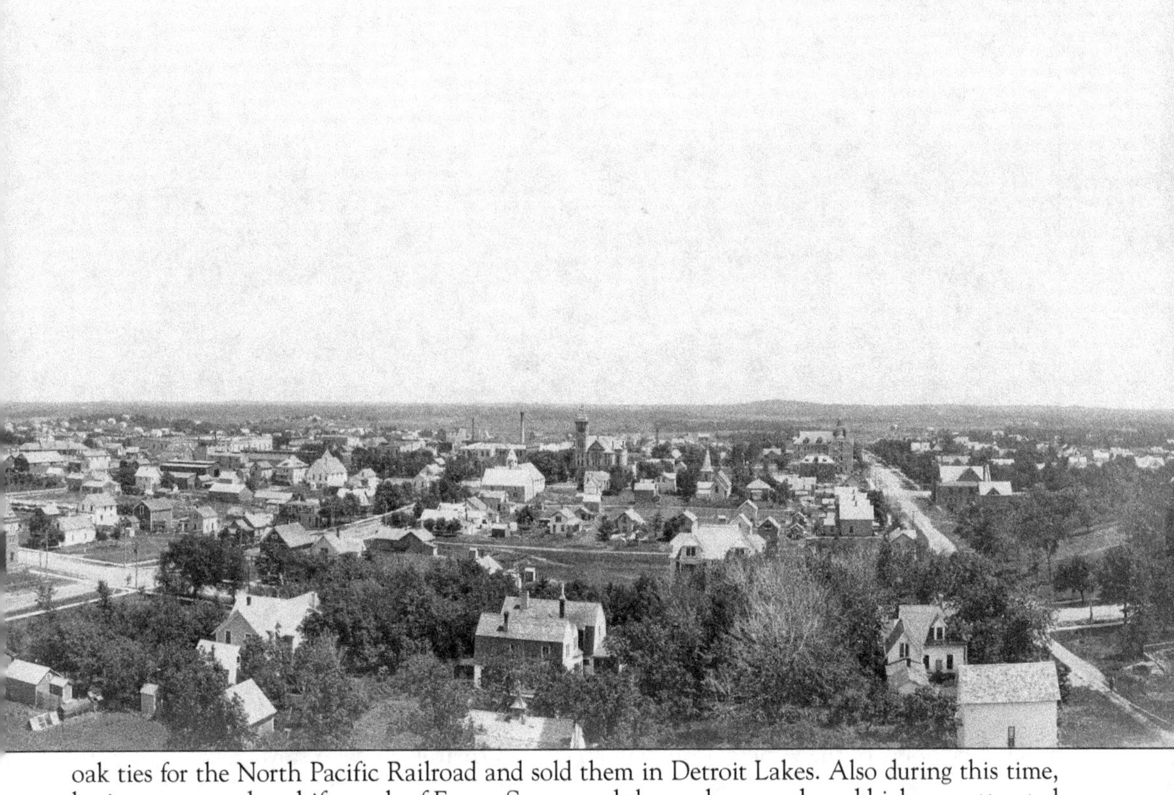

oak ties for the North Pacific Railroad and sold them in Detroit Lakes. Also during this time, businesses started to shift south of Frazee Street, and the work on roads and highways attracted people here to take advantage of the natural resources and fine shopping. This photograph shows Detroit's main streets looking north, with the Holmes School at left center.

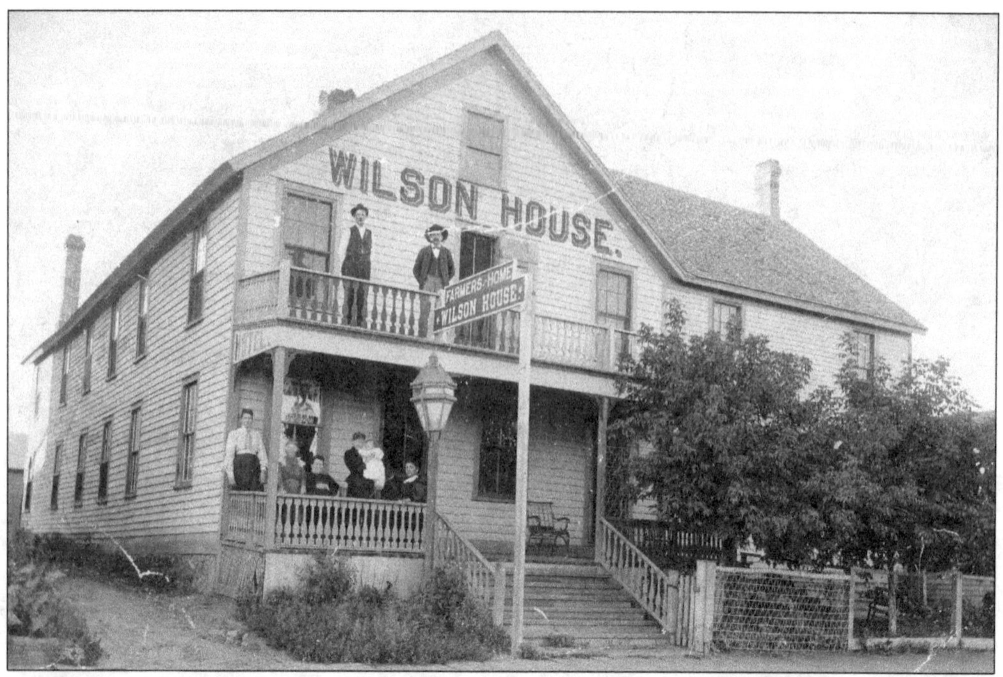

The Wilson House stood between Davis and Washington Avenues on the north side of Main Street. It was owned and operated by George Wilson and was later sold to E.L. Jordon, father-in-law of Bert Clement, chief of police. The guest registry at the hotel listed many stagecoach passengers. Some of the American Indian chiefs and their wives who stayed overnight were Hole-in-the-Day, Obe-mway, Wak-kah-nu-go-guns, Little Wolf, Musk Rat, and John Badboy, all members of the White Earth Nation.

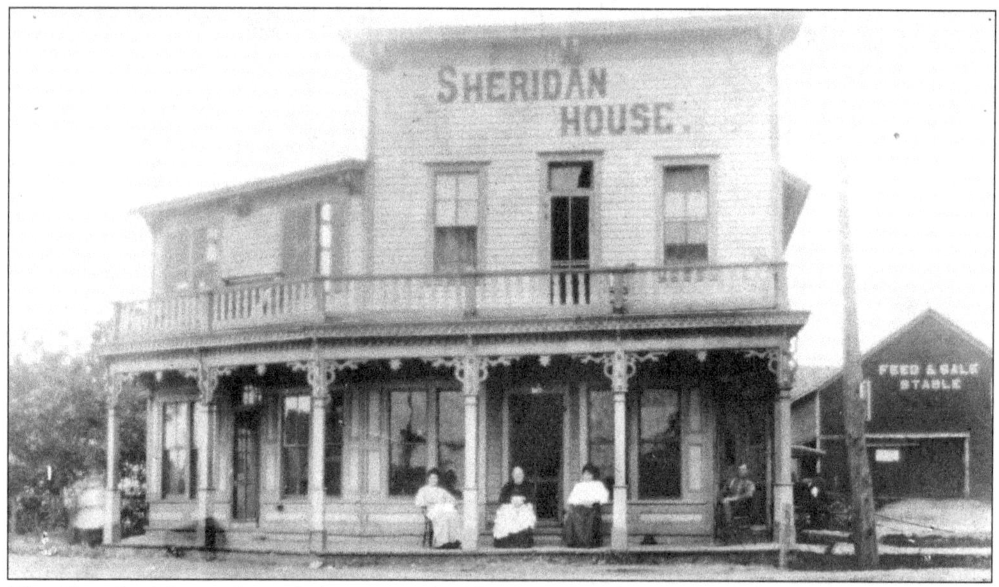

The Sheridan House, formerly known as the Northern Pacific Hotel, was located on Front Street behind Gamble's Store. The fire that consumed the Sheridan House in 1914 was the worst to ever hit Detroit. It began in the upstairs office of the Rahm Livery Barn and was not contained until 26 buildings were destroyed.

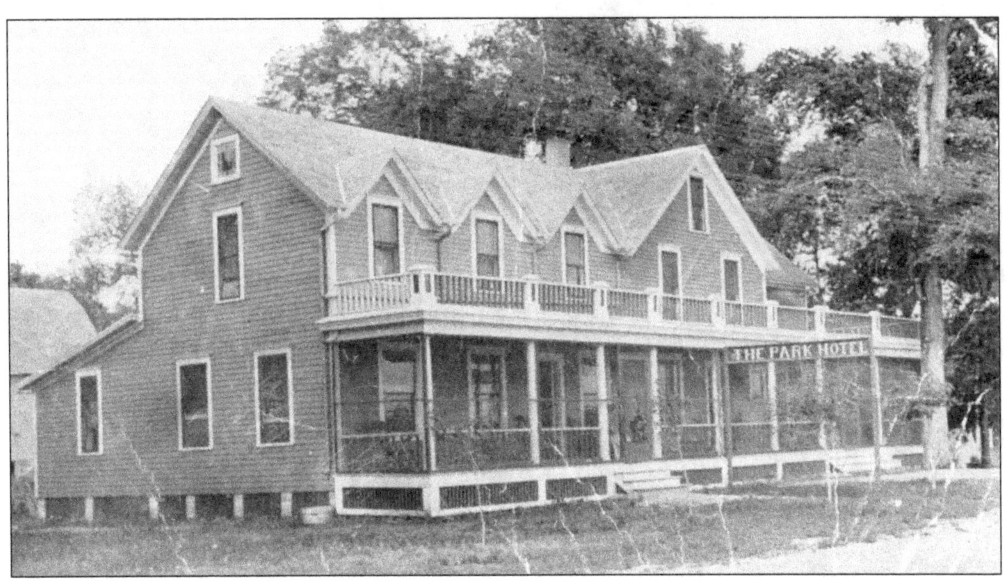

Mr. and Mrs. Fred Weiss erected the Park Hotel on the lakeshore at the foot of Washington Avenue. In 1916, a fire consumed the Park Hotel, but Weiss persevered and built a larger and better building. Being located on Detroit's busiest thoroughfare, the Park Hotel "provided all the conveniences of a city residence and the pleasure and restfulness of a summer hotel." It was later sold to Harry P. Woodhouse, Weiss's son-in-law from Medicine Hat, Canada, and eventually the building was turned into the Elks Lodge before being torn down in 1977 to make room for the swimming beach water slide, a tourist attraction.

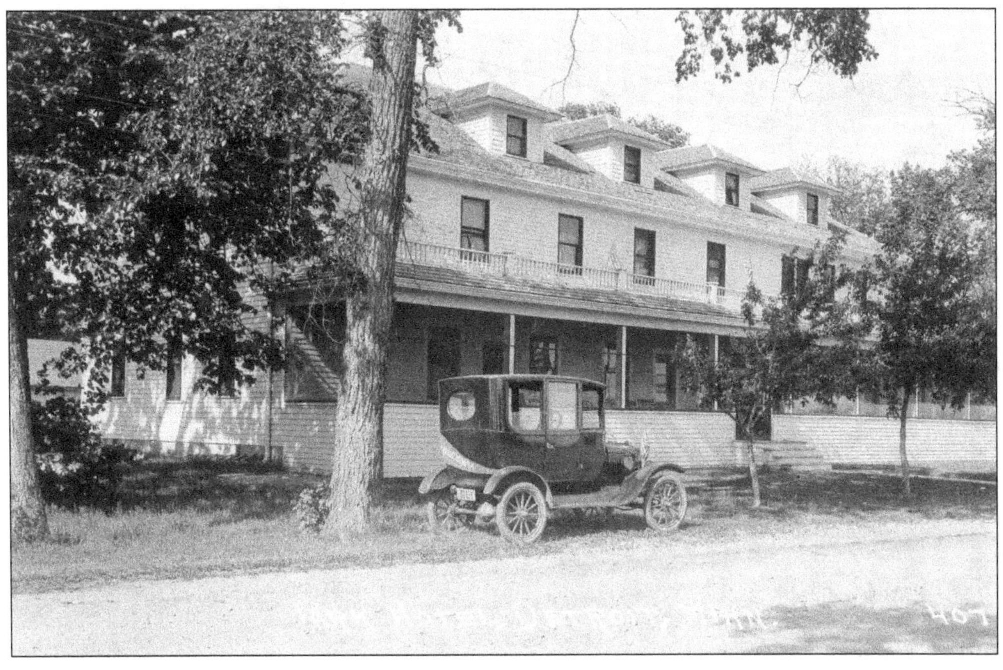

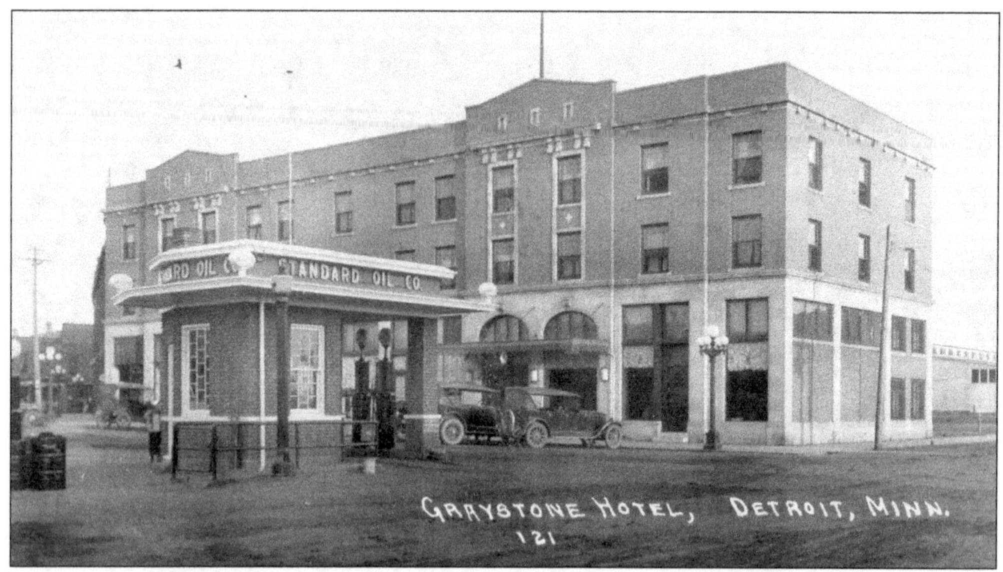

The Graystone Hotel was an unusual blend of a city hotel and rural resort, offering modern lodgings with access to the area's abundant natural attractions. One of the guiding forces behind this hotel was E.G. Holmes, who reestablished the Hotel Minnesota Company and sold stock to raise capital for his endeavor. Edward F. Broomhall from Duluth was chosen as the Graystone's architect. The big improvement to the hotel was that it was built to be fireproof, and in its initial planning stage the local newspaper stressed this fact. Not long after construction, Holmes became its sole manager. At some point between 1917 and 1927, the building that was attached to the east side of the Graystone began serving as an annex, housing individuals who were in town for extended stays.

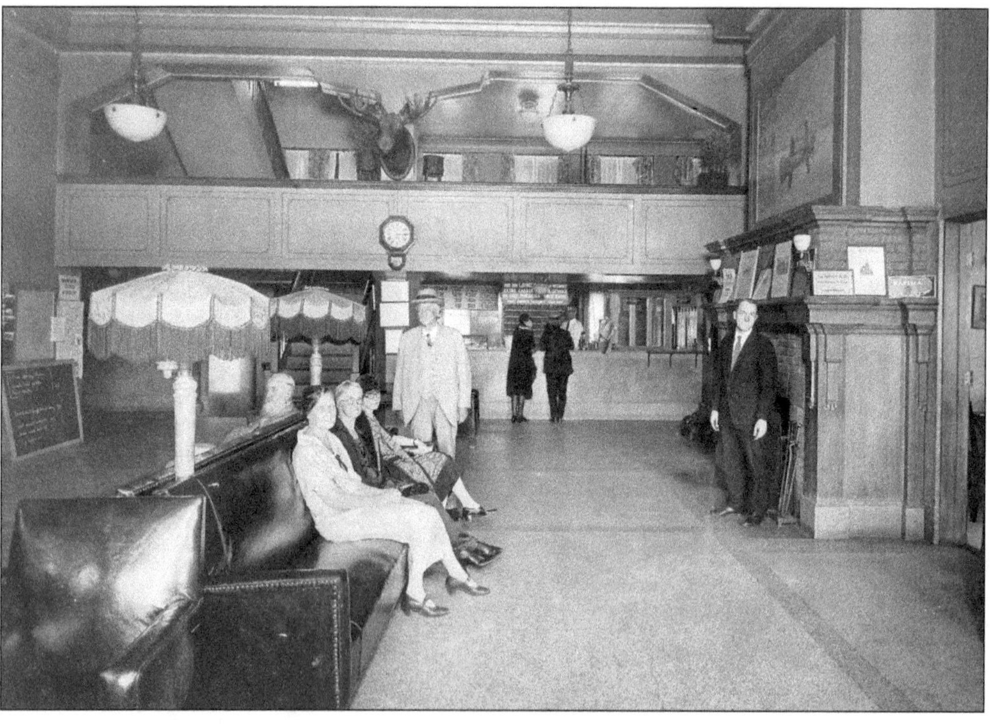

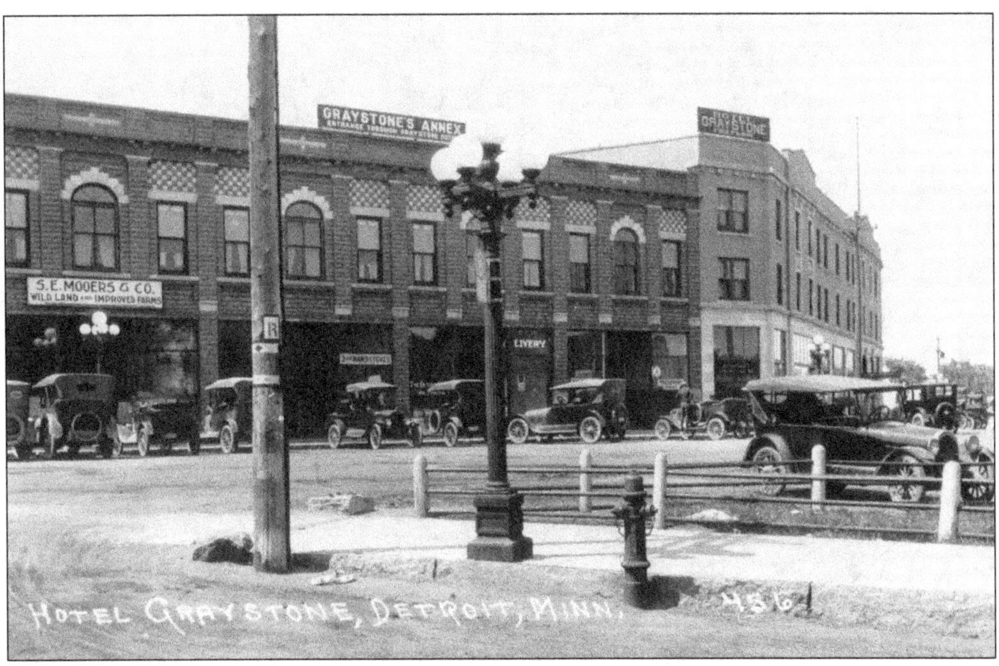

The Graystone was promoted as one of the finest hotels, and the Graystone Café was touted as having "the best food in Minnesota." What set this hotel apart from the others was its focus on tourism, not on traveling merchants and other business-oriented individuals. Although the original plan of the building had been scaled back, the finished hotel was still an impressive facility, containing 60 rooms on the second and third floors, most with baths. The lobby featured a terrazzo floor and marble wainscoting. A dining room, writing room, barbershop, manager's office, and café occupied the first floor. The exterior of the building was made of Bedford stone on the first floor and local cement brick for balance.

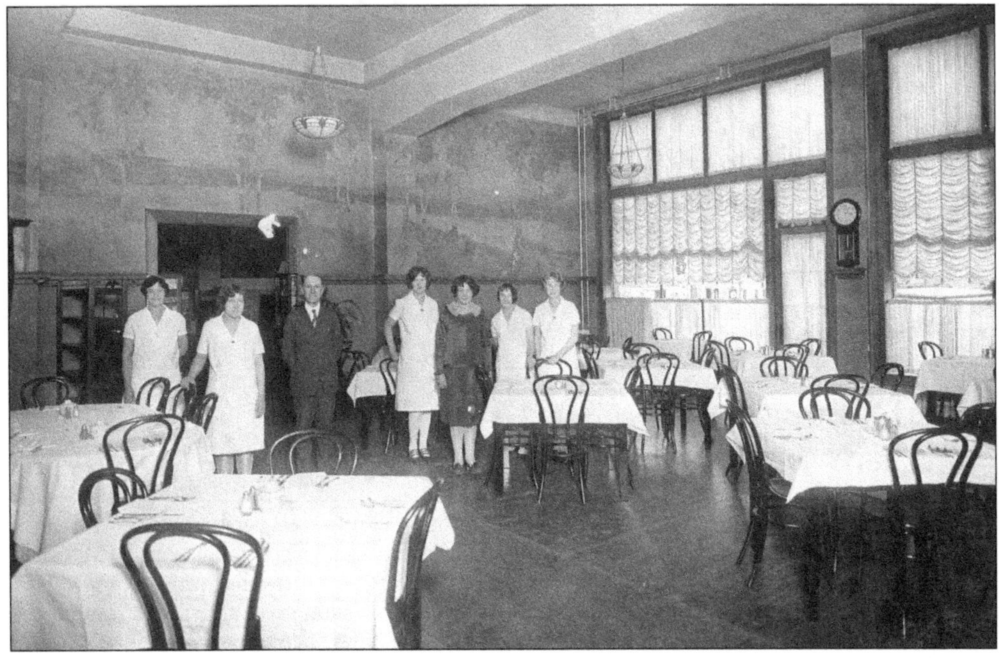

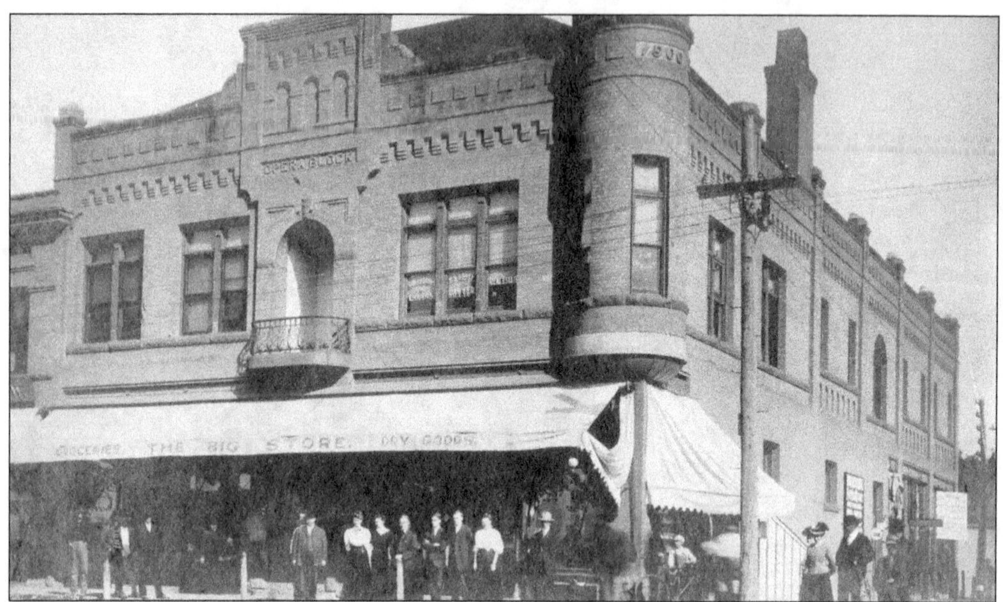

The Blanding Opera House, located on the south side of Front Street across the street from the Lewis Hotel, became a center for all gatherings, such as operas, dances, plays, political gatherings, lectures, and graduation exercises. In 1896, the movie *The Passion Play* was shown by Harry Martell with his cinematograph, as it was called. The opera house was 44 by 73 feet and had a seating capacity of 500. Built by Henry Dix Blanding Sr. and Charles Dix, the opera house burned in 1914. Reportedly, a child ran into the Blanding Department Store and shouted, "The opera house is on fire!" Mr. Blanding replied, "Close the door and let the damn thing burn; it never made any money anyway!"

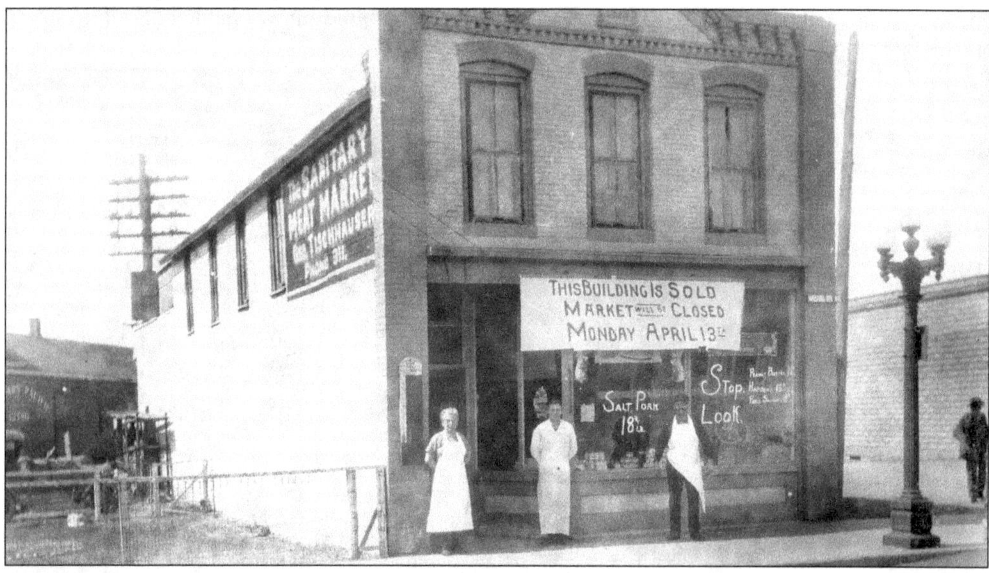

George Tischhauser operated Sanitary Meat Market until it changed ownership in 1914. The new owners were G.J. Hagen, his son Ed Hagen, and A.H. Burgess. G.J. Hagen came from Twin Valley and brought 12 years experience in the butchering trade with him. The other two gentlemen had been making Detroit their home for some time. In 1916, Tischhauser was arrested for having 24 prairie chickens in his possession, a violation of the gaming laws at the time.

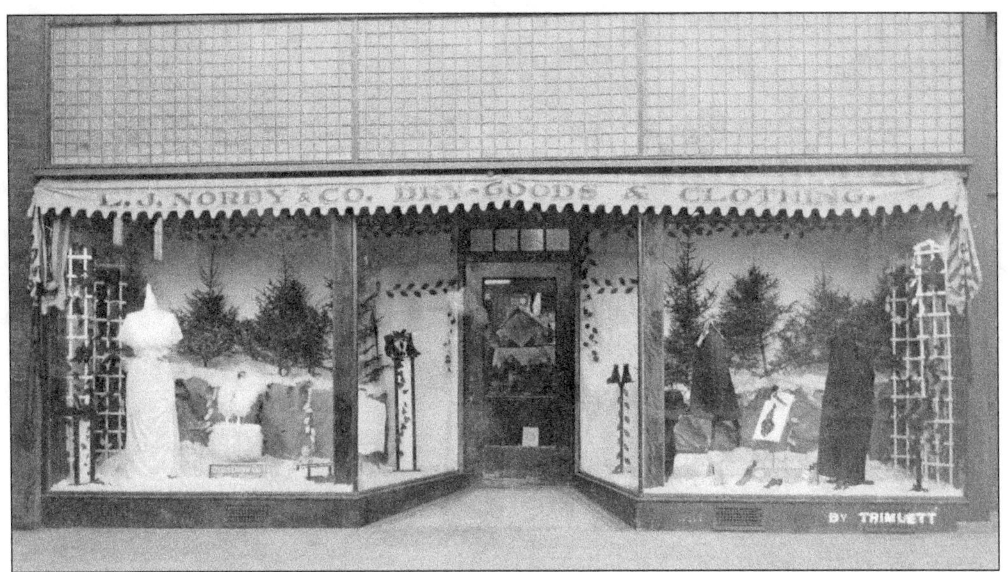

In 1906, Lewis J. Norby established Norby's Department Store, having previously been associated with the Blanding-Norby Company until he ventured out on his own. By 1914, Norby's had expanded to 75 feet. Today, Norby's is a two-story building whose brick facade conceals three earlier structures. One of the earliest structures was built as the Independent Order of Odd Fellows, who continued to meet there until they built a new hall.

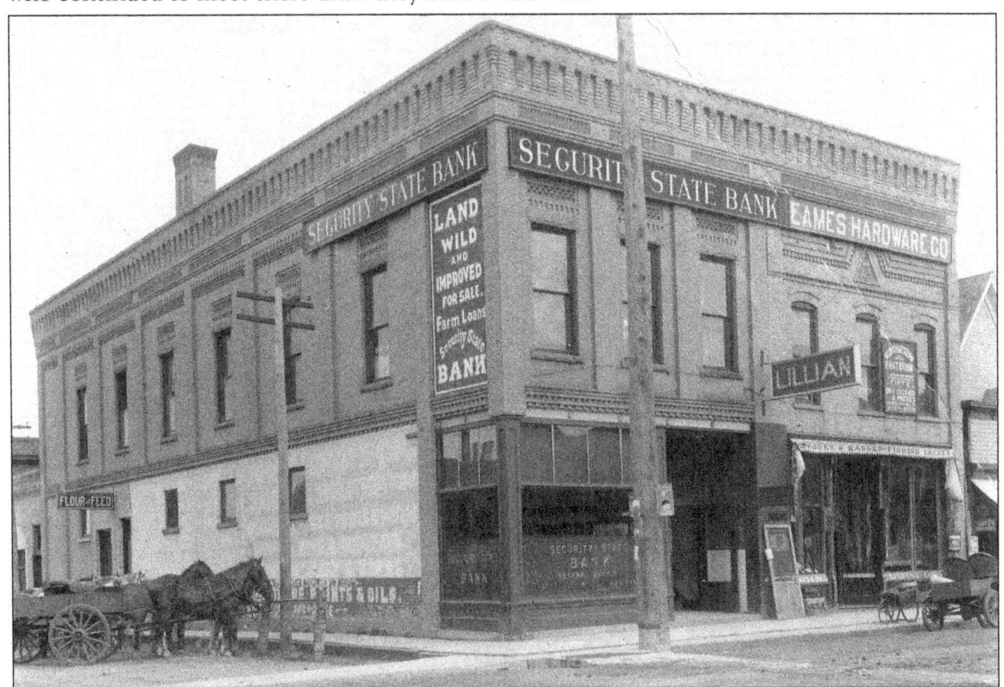

Security State Bank was organized on May 3, 1909, at 801 Washington Avenue, where Beug's Ace Hardware is located today. On November 3, 1914, the bank moved to its new location at 800 Washington Avenue and Front Street, eventually closing in 1929. The building had many other occupants, such as Buckman's clothing store, a hardware store, a shoe store, and professional offices. By 1950, the building was a J.C. Penney department store.

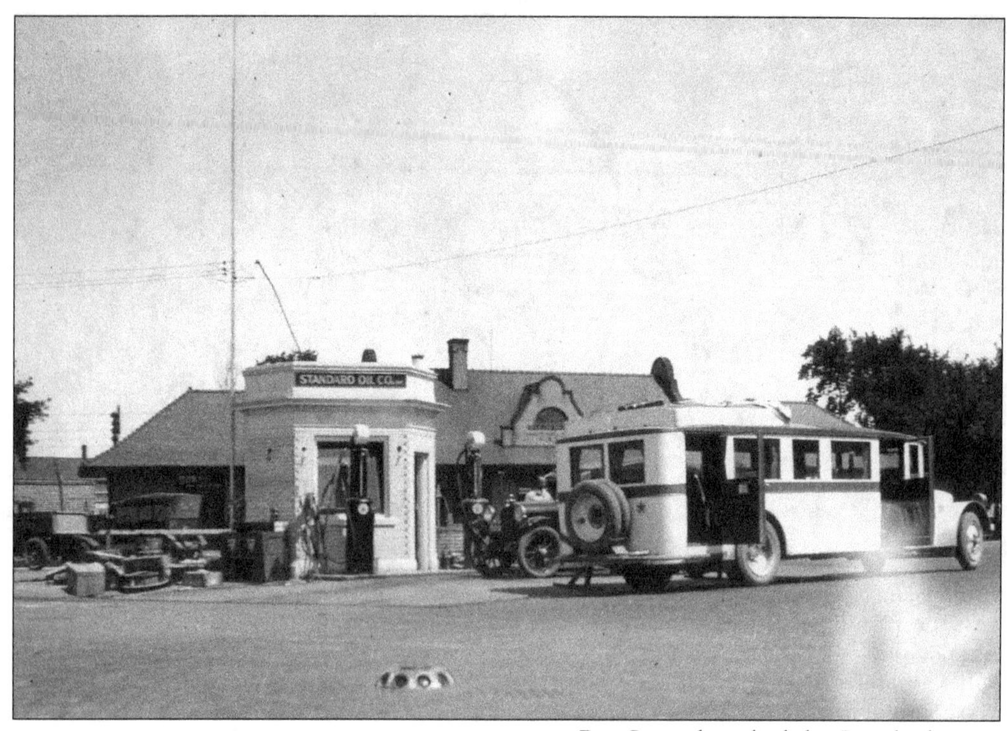

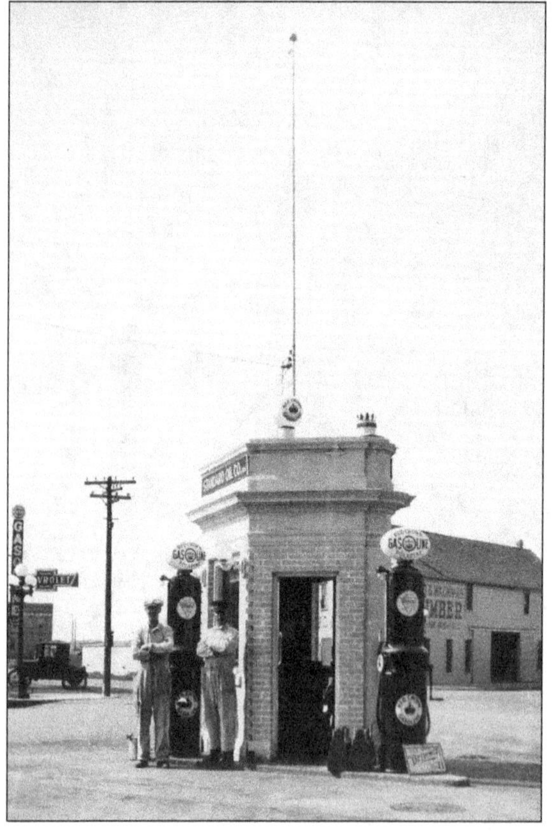

Roy Sauer described the Standard Oil Company station as "the greatest promotional thing Detroit Lakes has ever had." Located just north of the Graystone Hotel, it was dubbed "The World's Smallest Station" by Robert Ripley in his column, "Believe It or Not." Enga Maria Nelson was the designer of this three-and-a-half-foot-by-four-foot station, which featured a winding stairway that led to a 10-by-15-foot basement, where there was a restroom and storage spot. Roy Sauer, his father, and brother all managed the station and tried unsuccessfully to buy it from the Standard Oil Company. After the Sauer brothers entered the service, the Standard Oil Company was left without an operator, so they sold it to the City of Detroit for $500 and it was torn down to make way for a traffic safety island.

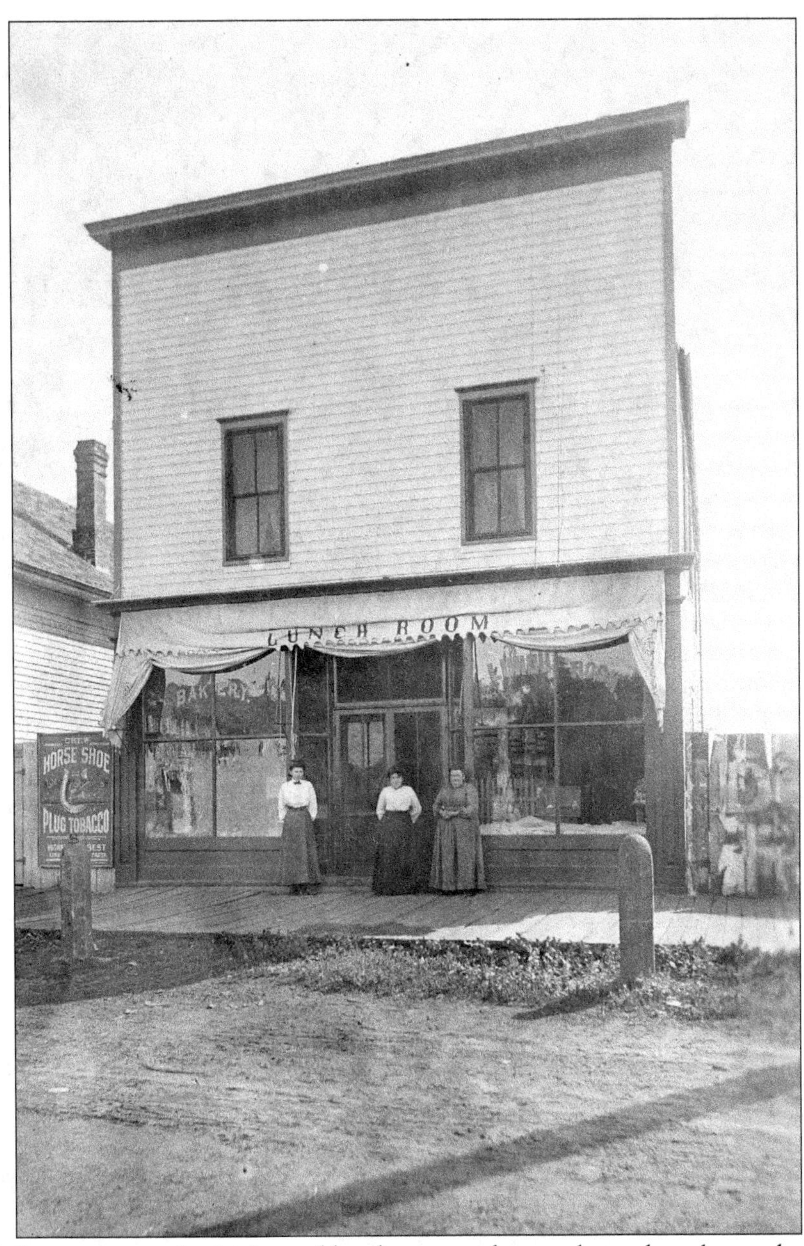

Millane's Store was a confectionery and lunch counter that was located on the north side of the Northern Pacific Railroad tracks at 611 Washington Avenue. The owner and operator, Mary Millane, came from Ireland in 1871 to settle in St. Cloud, Minnesota. She married Edward Millane in 1881, and the couple made their home in Sauk Rapids before coming to Detroit in 1894. It is unclear when the Millane Store opened, but it was sometime after they made their home here. They sold cigars, tobacco, and stationery and also rented out rooms when needed. In the photograph above are Mrs. Jim Keyes (Mary and Edward's daughter), Mary Cook, and Mary Millane. Mary passed away in 1910 from an automobile accident that was called the most distressing motor accident in Becker County. The car that Mary Millane was riding in flipped over, pinning her to the ground. The 12-year-old boy who was driving was protected by Mrs. Millane and survived the accident.

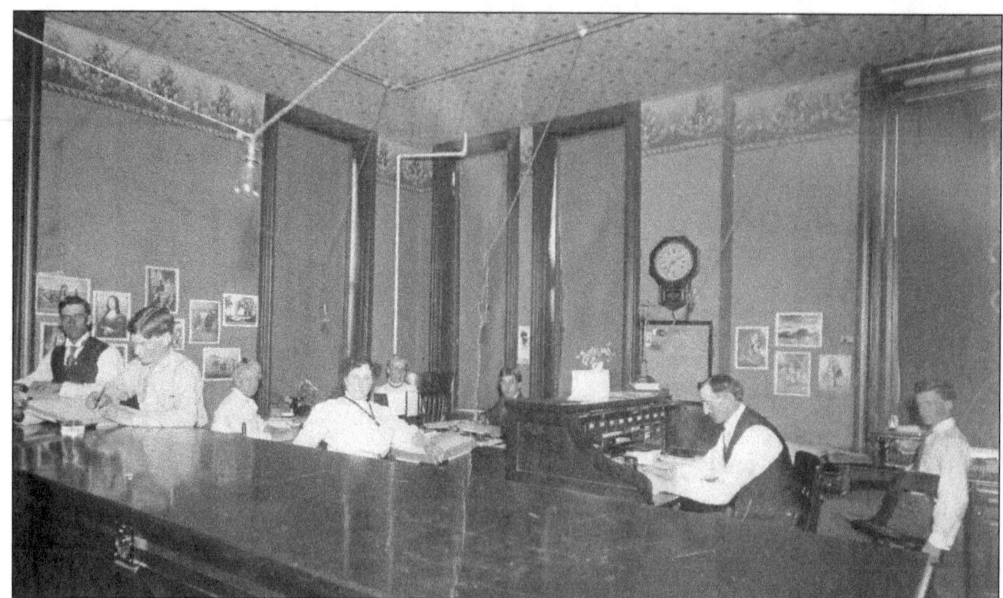

These images show the interior of the Becker County Courthouse. One of the earliest lawsuits held in the courthouse includes a case involving Harvey Jones, who was arrested for administrating family discipline with an ironwood sapling. He was tried before Squire McGrew and a jury of 12 men, who found him guilty. His sentence was 30 days in the Otter Tail City Jail. The commitment papers were given to Capt. F.K. Small, who made arrangements with John O. French, one of three constables. While en route to jail, Jones asked to consult with an attorney. French left his overcoat unattended when he went for a drink of water, and after a few miles down the road Jones argued that French had no authority to take him to jail. Upon finding that French did not have the papers in his coat anymore, he had no choice but to let him go.

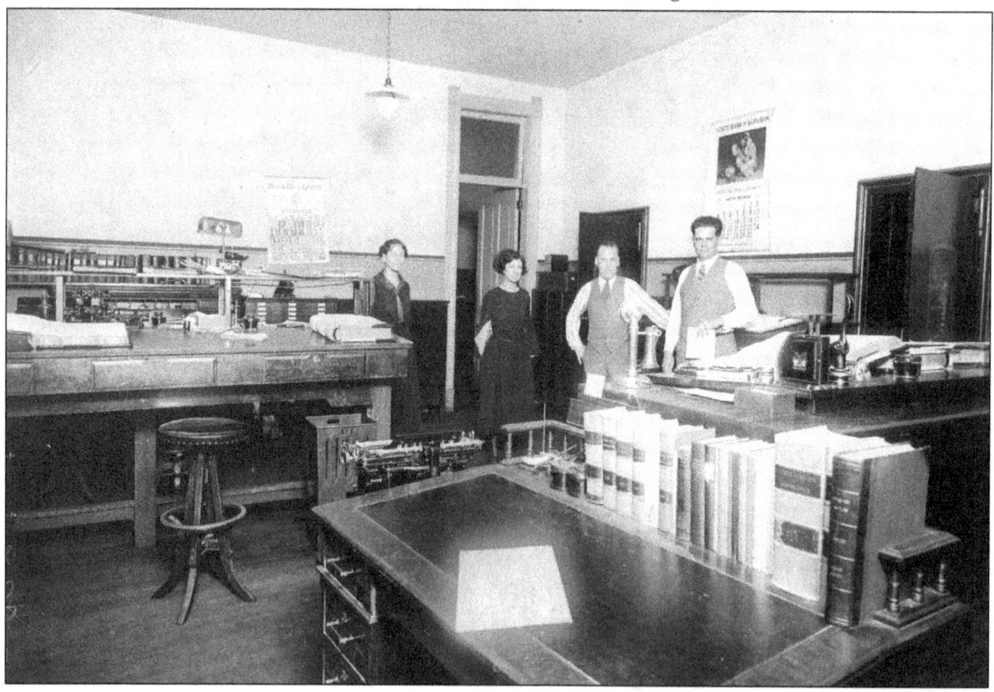

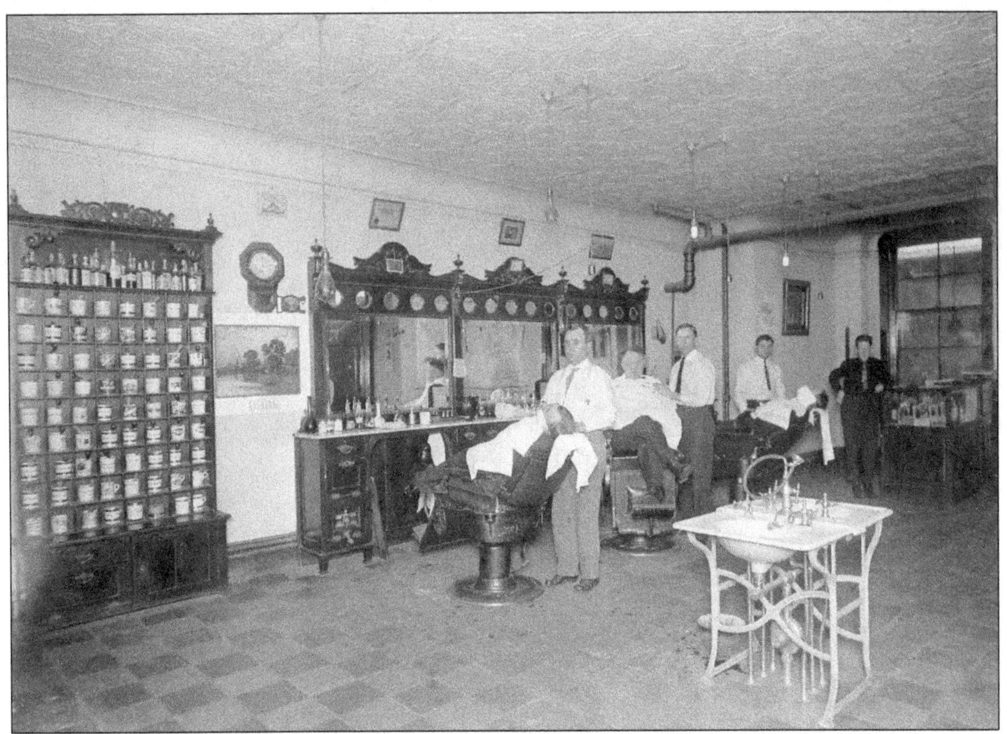

The best-known barber in the early days was George C. Bush. His shop was located on Washington Avenue, a block south of the opera house block. It was the place where one found out the "who's who" in the village of Detroit and the latest news on sports and politics. Bush served several terms as president of the village council and as county sheriff.

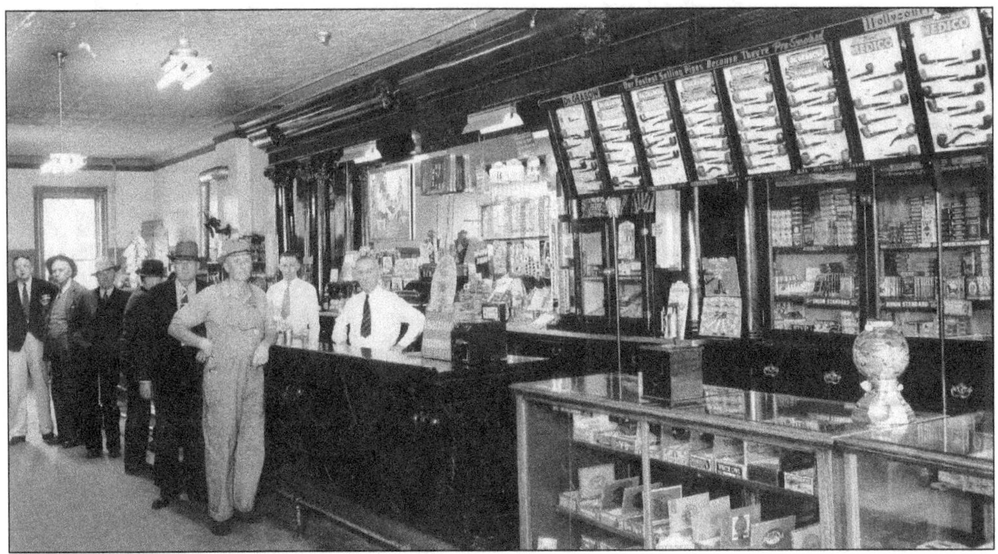

Courtright's, located at 713 Washington Avenue, was owned and operated by Frank S. Courtright. Advertising described the soft-drink parlor as an "up-to-date thirst parlor for discriminating people," which also happened to carry the finest lines of imported and domestic wines and liquors. One interesting fact was that he offered automobile delivery to any part of the city.

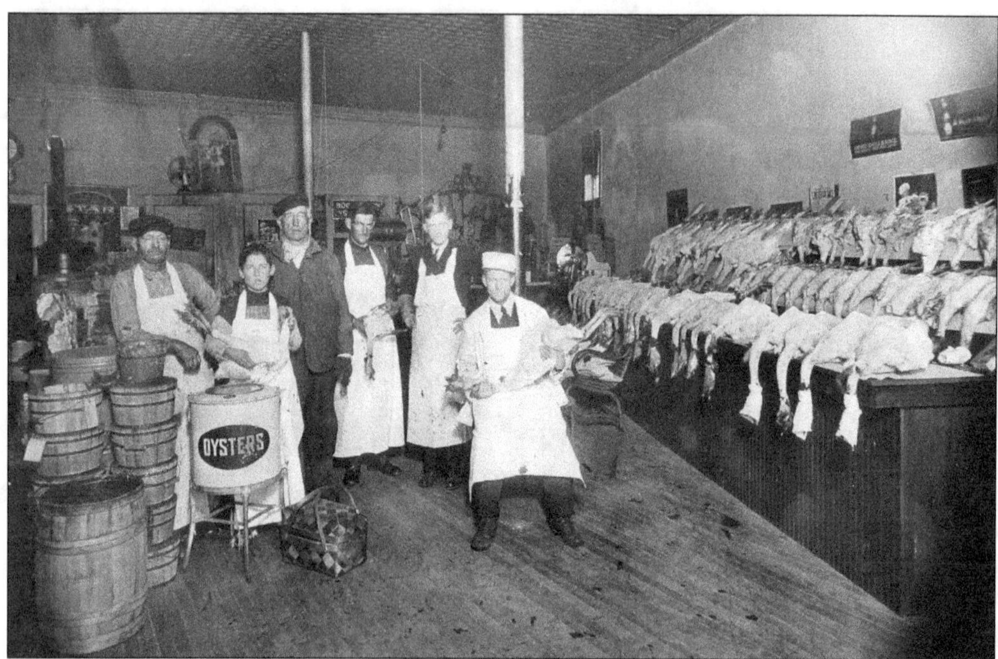

Ed Hagen first operated Hagen's Meat Market in 1912 under sole ownership, but in later years he partnered with Dennis Hagen. They were located on Washington Avenue and Main Street. In 1933, they moved to the north side in a building formerly occupied by Bilstad Hardware Company and later by Swanson's second ax-handle store.

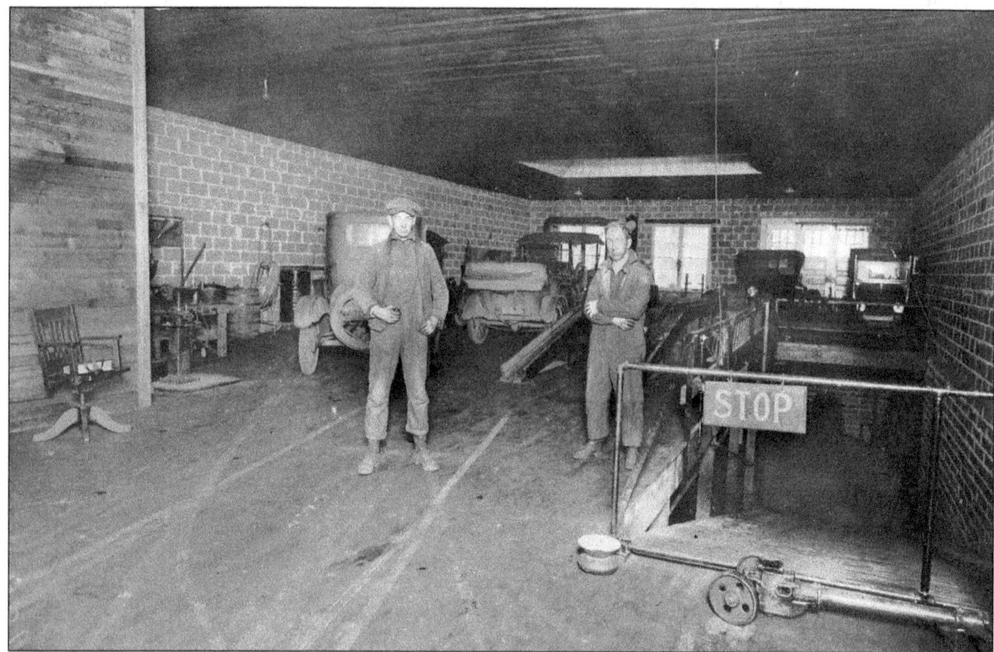

Peoples Garage was owned and operated by George W. Peoples. Built in 1922, it was located opposite of the courthouse with its entrance facing south, directly toward the north entrance of the courthouse. The garage was one-story in height and built of local hollow cement blocks and cement brick. Peoples mainly worked on Dodge automobiles.

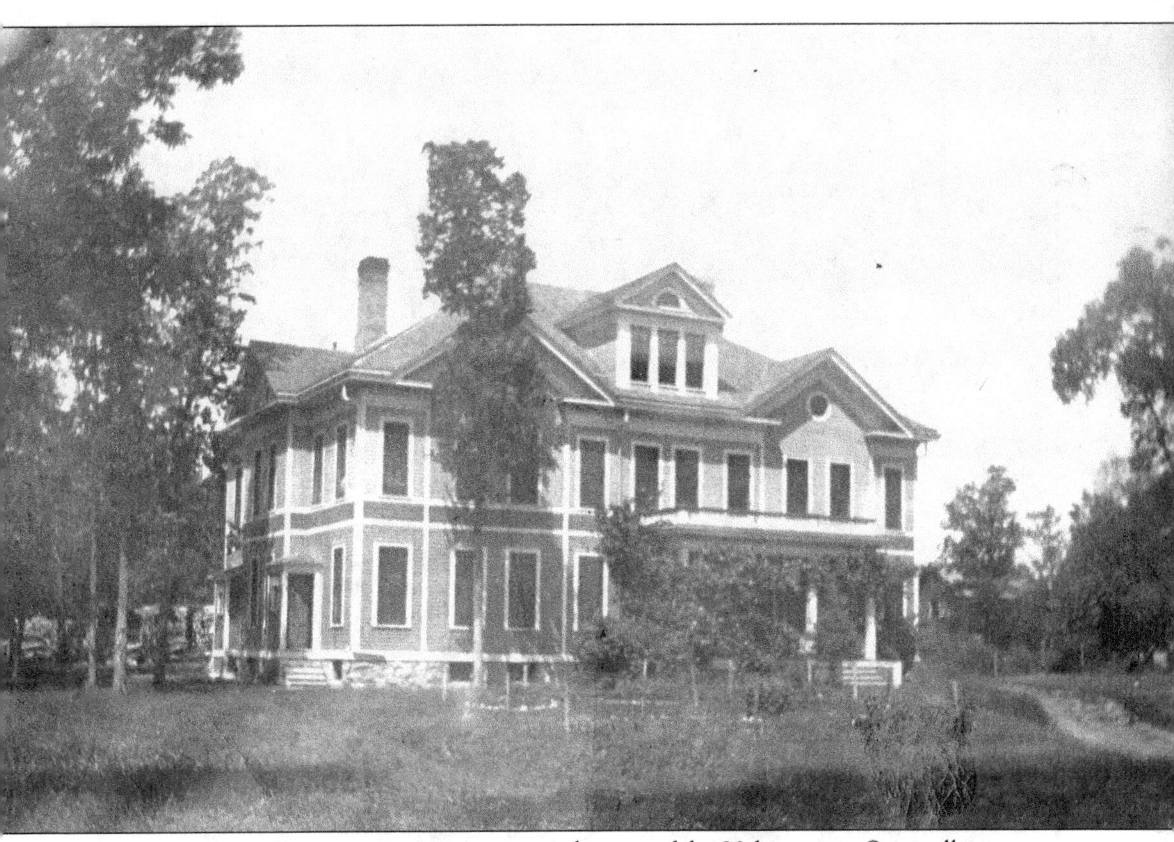

Infirmaries were a common presence in towns at the turn of the 20th century. Originally set up as hospitals to treat the low-income sick, these buildings later became poorhouses for the destitute, much like state hospitals for the mentally ill. Residents were referred to as "inmates," and staff were called "overseers." The environment at times was more like that of a prison than a social service. However, they did provide a necessary service to the community. The original Becker County Infirmary building burned on March 13, 1900. At that time, the building was situated near the Eininger Camp cabins. John Dexter, the overseer, quickly removed the 15 inmates to the barn that was located nearby. Dexter, unable to get the phone to work, mounted his horse and rode into town to sound the fire alarm. A new building was constructed at the fairgrounds, which was considered a good and convenient site on account of its tillable ground, used for growing vegetables to feed the inmates. The infirmary, constructed in 1900 by Brainerd Manufacturing Company for $2,500, was situated on a beautiful wooded ridge facing Detroit Lake. The property consisted of a brick basement and two stories of convenient apartments for male and female occupants. In 1936, it was leased to a private operation before closing in 1940. In later years, it was used as a 4-H clubhouse.

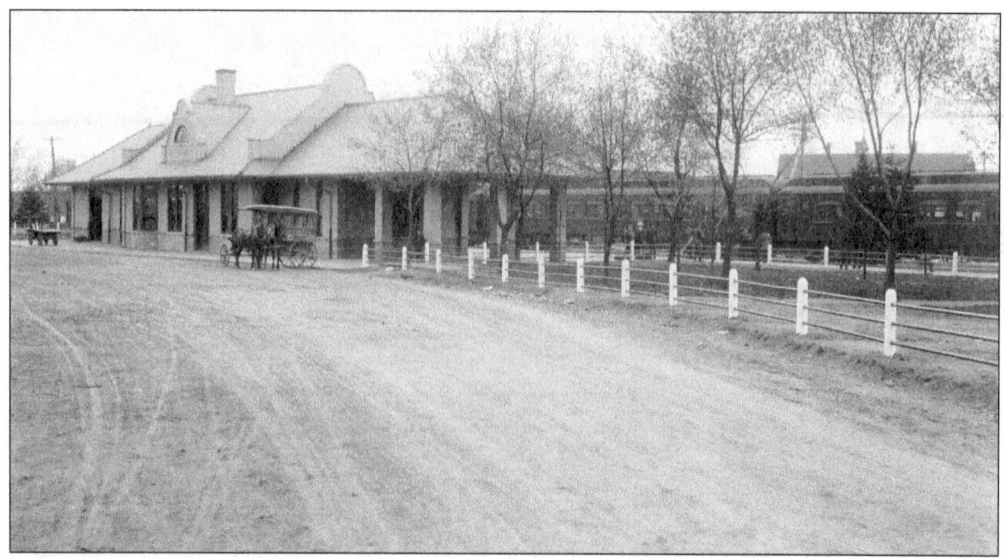

Completed in 1908, the depot was located on the northern edge of the city's original business district. The depot measured 110 by 36 feet and, as originally constructed, had a 36-by-36-foot waiting room with an 18-foot ceiling, a ladies waiting room, a men's smoking room, a ticket office, a baggage room, and bathrooms. The building was visually prominent and serves as one of the best-preserved examples of railroad architecture in northwestern Minnesota today.

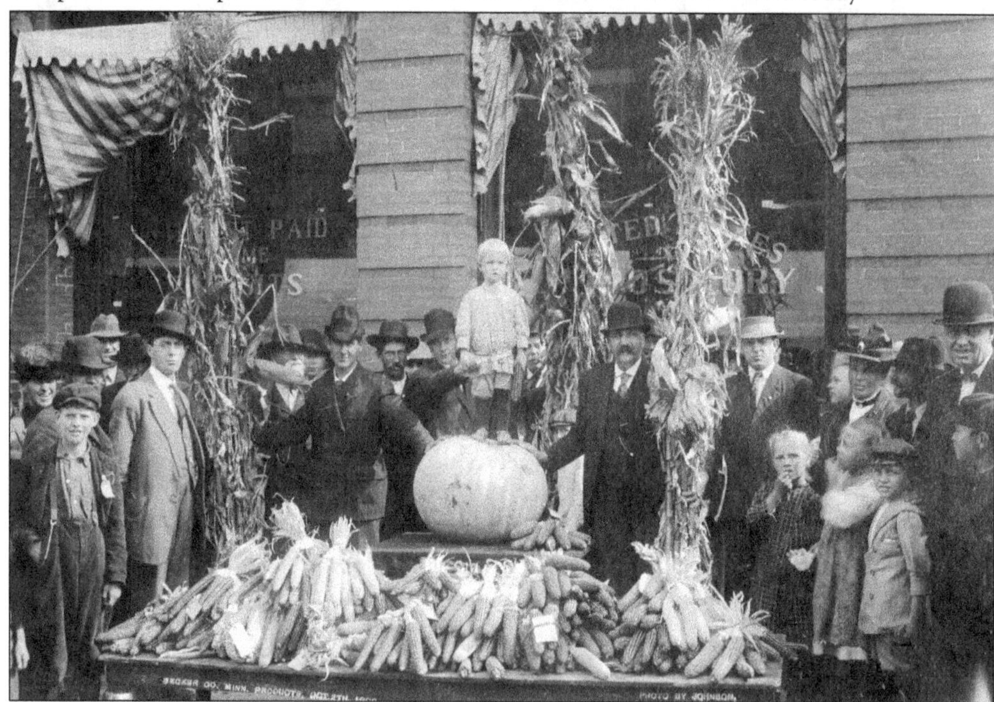

In this 1909 photograph of the first Becker County Corn Exhibit, the corn stalks on the sidewalk were freestanding at 14 feet high. An enrolled member of the White Earth Band of Ojibwe on the White Earth Reservation raised the squash, which weighed 115 pounds and was six feet in circumference. This photograph was taken in front of the First National Bank in Detroit. All vegetables were raised in 1909 in Becker County, Minnesota.

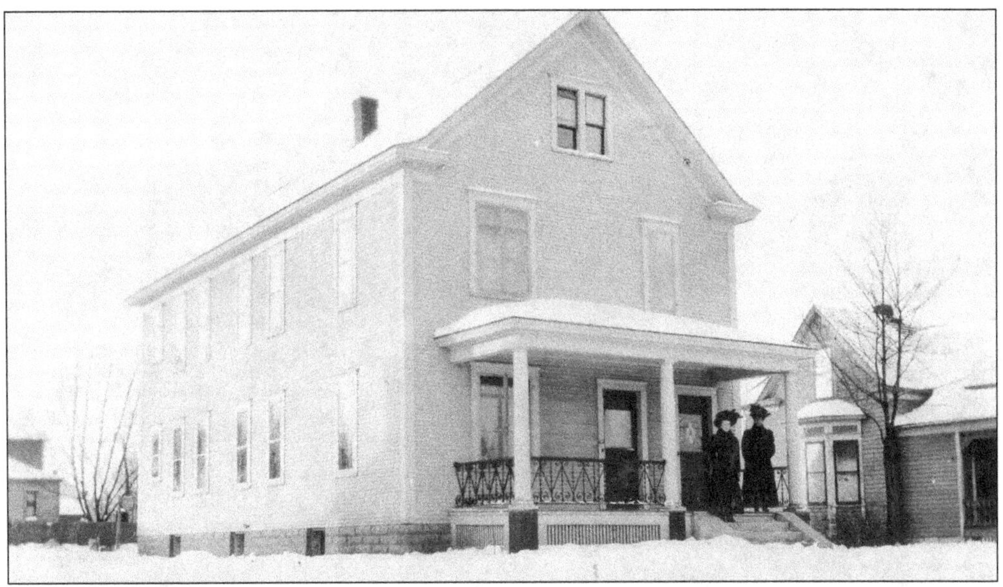

Dr. Leonard C. Weeks, or "Old Doc Weeks," was one of Detroit's pioneer physicians. He took care of his patients in the upstairs room of his home, pictured above, located south of the Congregational Church from 1896 to 1905. He built and equipped a hospital at what is now 207 East Frazee Street (pictured below) before closing it in 1909. The county infirmary served as a hospital until Weeks reopened his community hospital in 1919. In 1928, the American Legion post tried unsuccessfully to get voters to approve a Becker County hospital. However, they did secure stock subscriptions and completed the new hospital in 1929 with the help of the Businessmen's Club. In 1939, the Sisters of St. Benedict at Crookston assumed the bonded debt and converted the hospital into what is now known as Essentia Health St. Mary's.

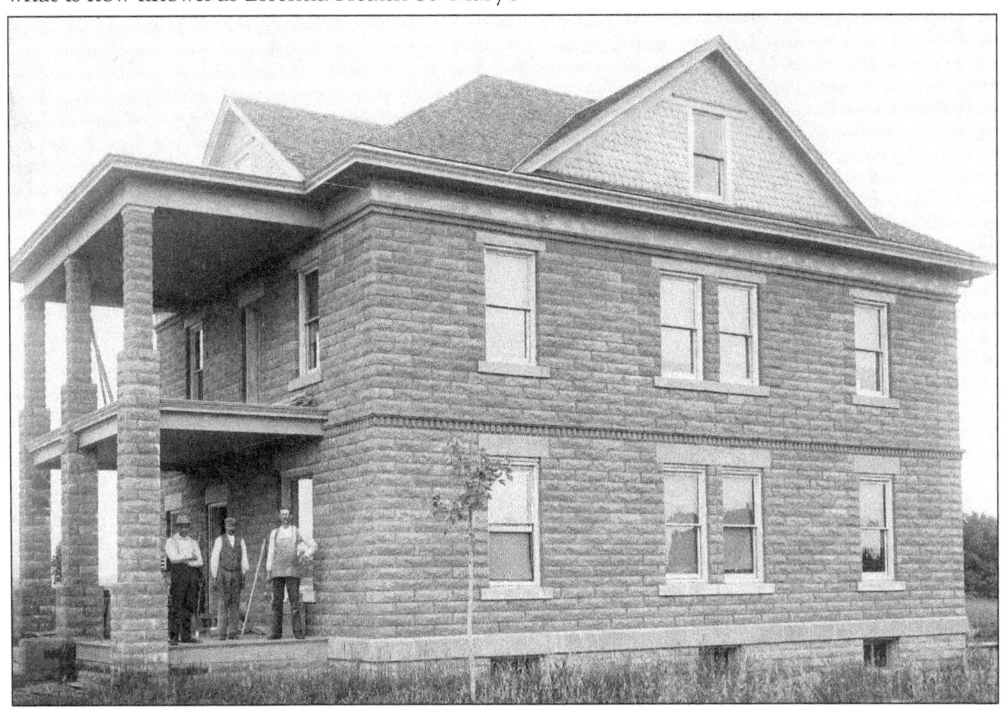

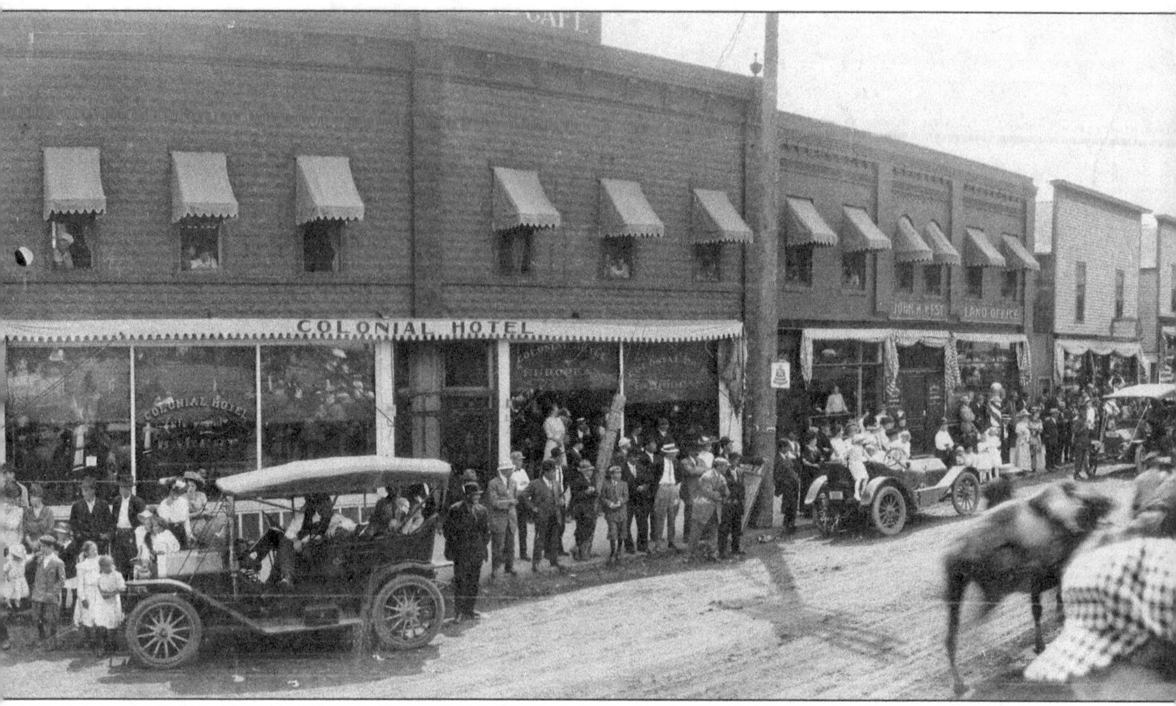

On June 24, 1912, the Gollmar Bros. Circus came to town. Within a few hours, they were setting up. Visitors were given the run of the grounds as they watched all the employees erect the tents and feed the animals. The grounds were probably visited by a few hundred people, many of them coming from surrounding villages. At 10 o'clock, the parade started, and every man, woman,

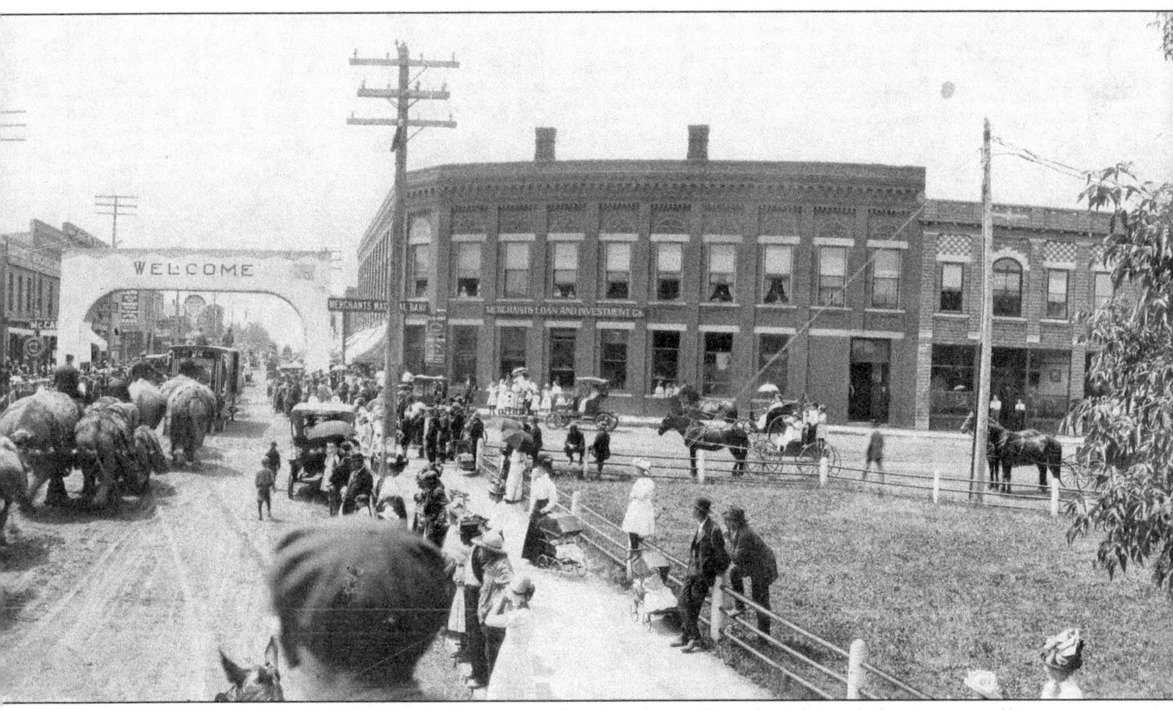

and child from the surrounding country seemed to be there. Four bands and the steam calliope furnished the music, and by two o'clock the trumpet sounded the grand entry, where nearly 3,000 people collected under the big top. This is Washington Avenue looking south from the Northern Pacific Railroad tracks.

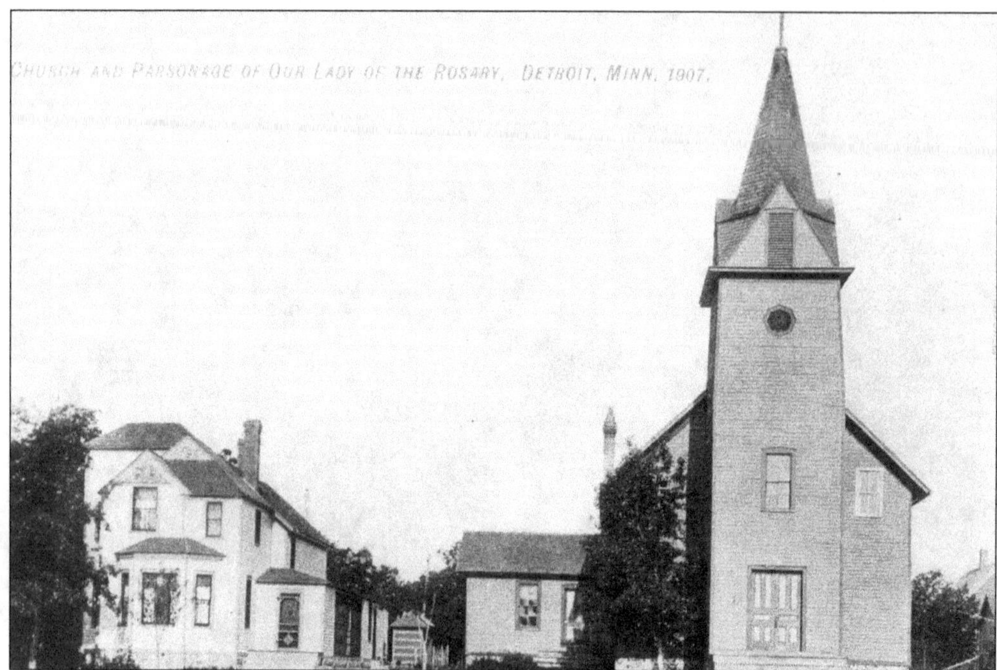

In 1871, Father J.B.M. Genlin of Canada established the Holy Rosary Catholic Church, and Samuel J. Fox donated the land on which it was built. The first building was destroyed in a windstorm, and the second church was not completed until 1885, only to be damaged in a tornado. In May 1892, the parish was incorporated under the name Church of Our Lady of the Rosary, and work began on a parsonage. A bazaar was held to purchase a bell in 1903, and the winner, Mrs. Smith, was able to christen the bell in honor of her patron saint, St. Anna. In 1908, the church was moved and rebuilt, and in 1914 the foundation for the present church was laid. The cornerstone was blessed on May 2, 1915.

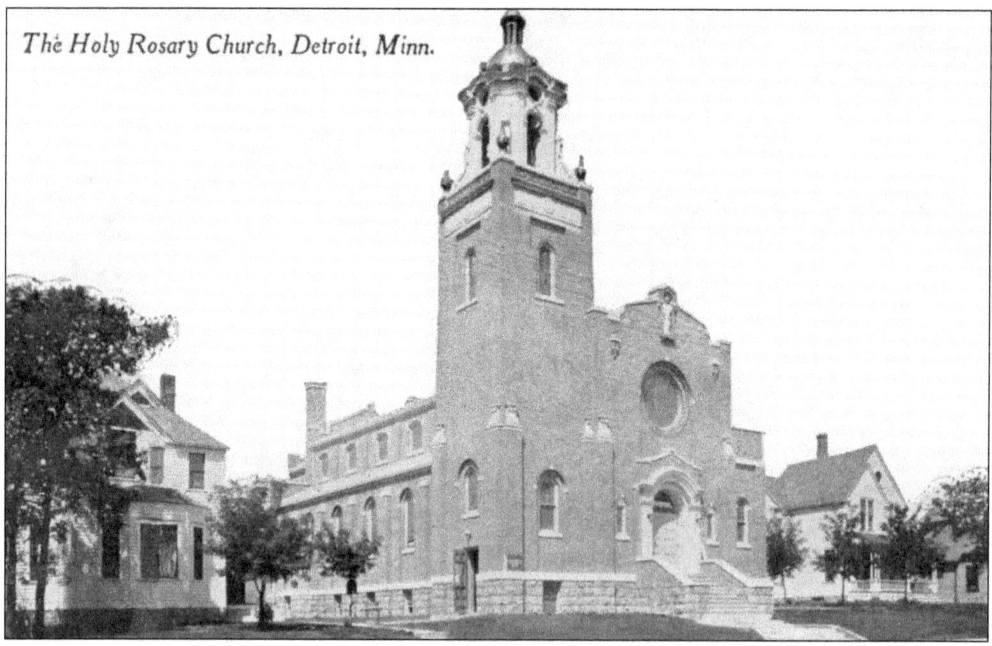

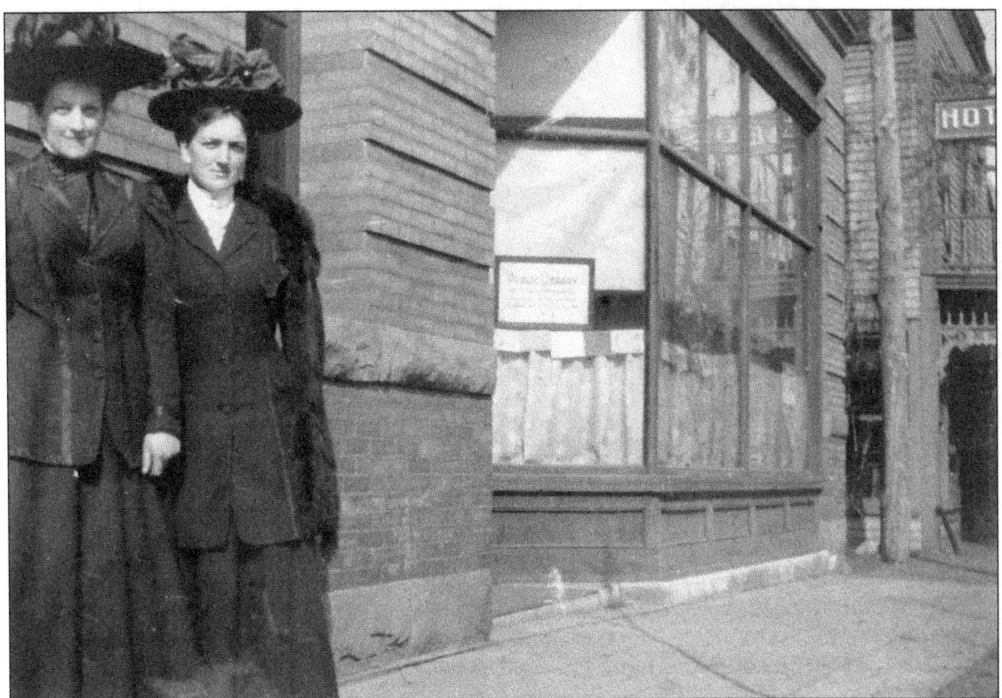

On September 7, 1907, the Library Club took action because they were concerned there were no books available for their children or the general public. The construction of the Detroit Lakes Library in 1913 was made possible through a $10,000 grant awarded by the Andrew Carnegie Foundation. It was agreed that there was to be a cornerstone laid in a wall of the library, so on May 13, 1913, with the ladies of the board looking on, it was placed. Located near the central business area of the city, the library stands as an architectural gem in the community. Architects Edward F. Stark and Louis Claude created the library's unique design. The Detroit Lakes Library has played a significant role in the intellectual and cultural growth of this small Minnesota community.

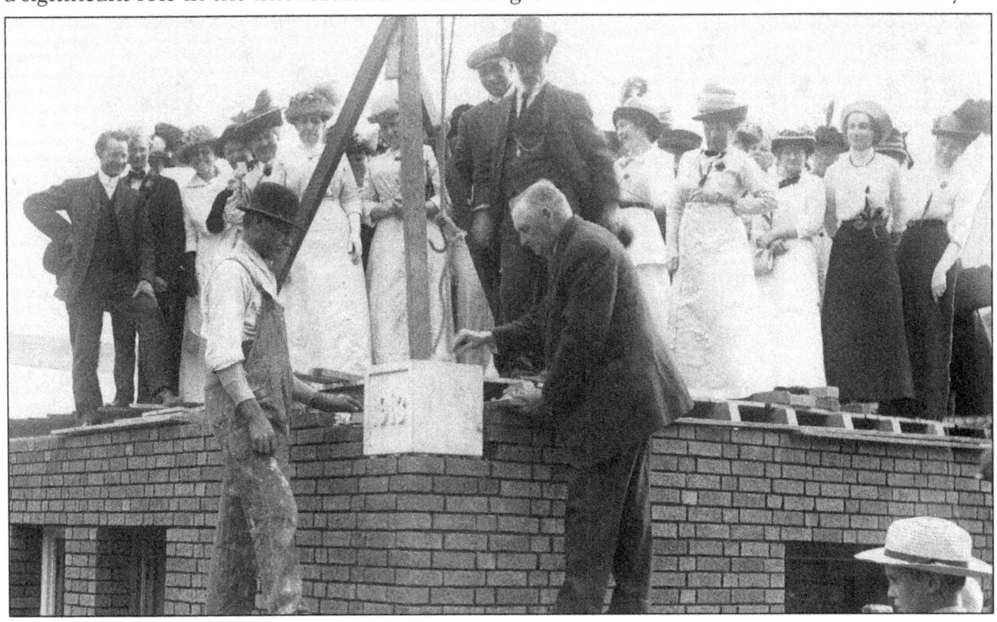

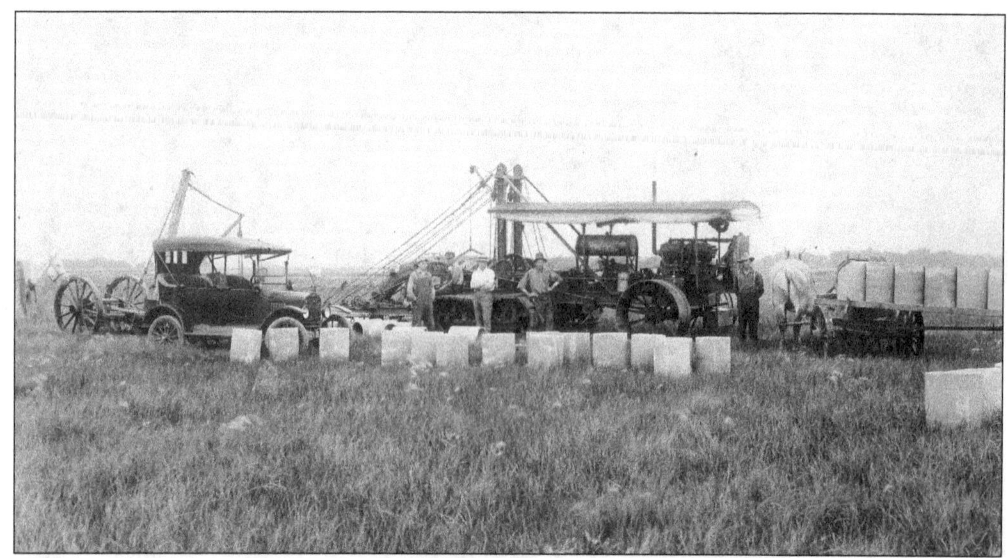

The work of installing a storm sewer in Detroit Lakes to cover the portion of the state that would be paved the following year was finished in 1917. The crew of the Pastoret Construction Company finished up on Holmes Street, between Lake and Washington Avenues. This part of the job was the slowest, as every inch needed to be sheathed in order to hold back the fine sand.

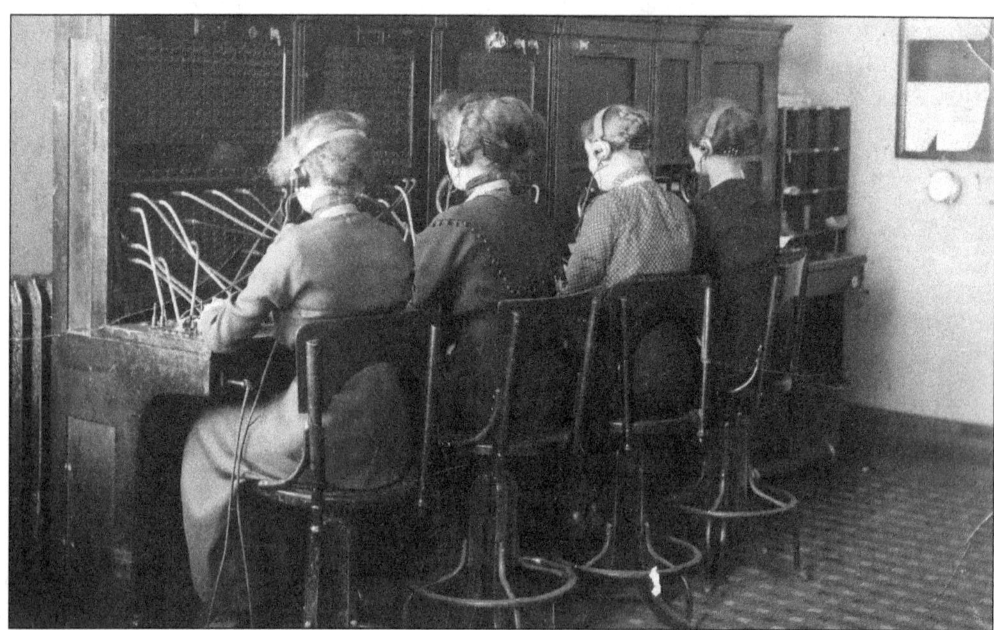

The Detroit Telephone Company organized in May 1895, and Detroit Lakes authorized it to construct, erect, and maintain poles, posts, wires, and other appliances. The job was completed in 1898 with the installation of a switchboard and operator in the basement of the Colonial Hotel. Tri-State Telephone and Telegraph Company purchased the Detroit Telephone Company in 1917 and moved the operation into the Graystone Hotel.

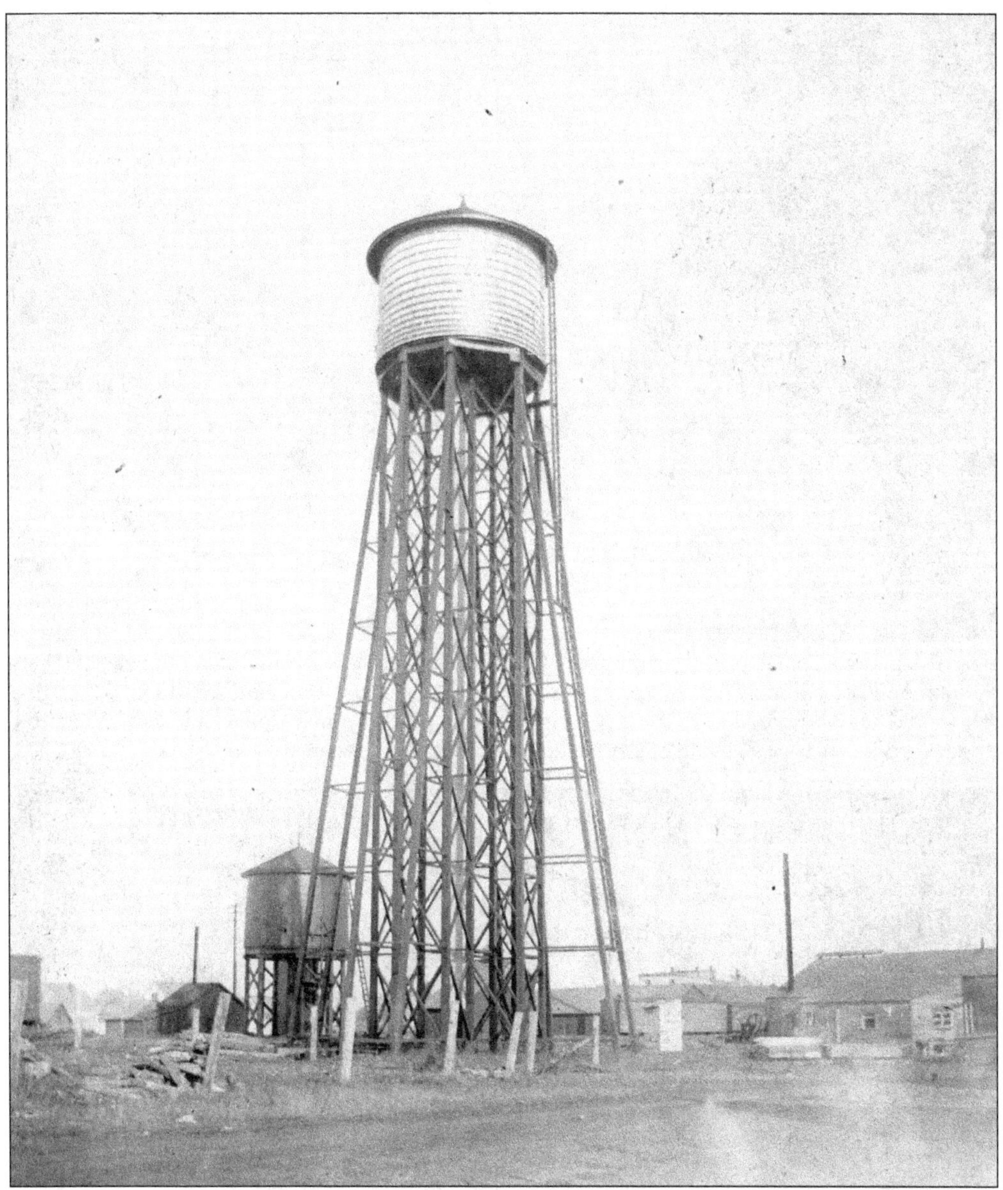

On July 31, 1891, the village council called for a special election for a $10,000 bond to build water works. On September 22, 1891, a contract was awarded for $9,500 to install water mains and hydrants. The original water and light company had used the city's wooden water tower for many years, which stood just west of Reid & Wackman's Lumber Yard. The wooden water tower was pulled down around 1908, and the timbers were used to build the round cottage on West Lake Boulevard. A new steel tower and tank were installed with a capacity of 65,000 gallons. Water mains now extended to the lake, where two electrically operated pumps were installed. The pumps had a capacity of 39,720 gallons per hour, and an intake pump was also extended into the lake. A total of 16 blocks of main and 13 hydrants were installed.

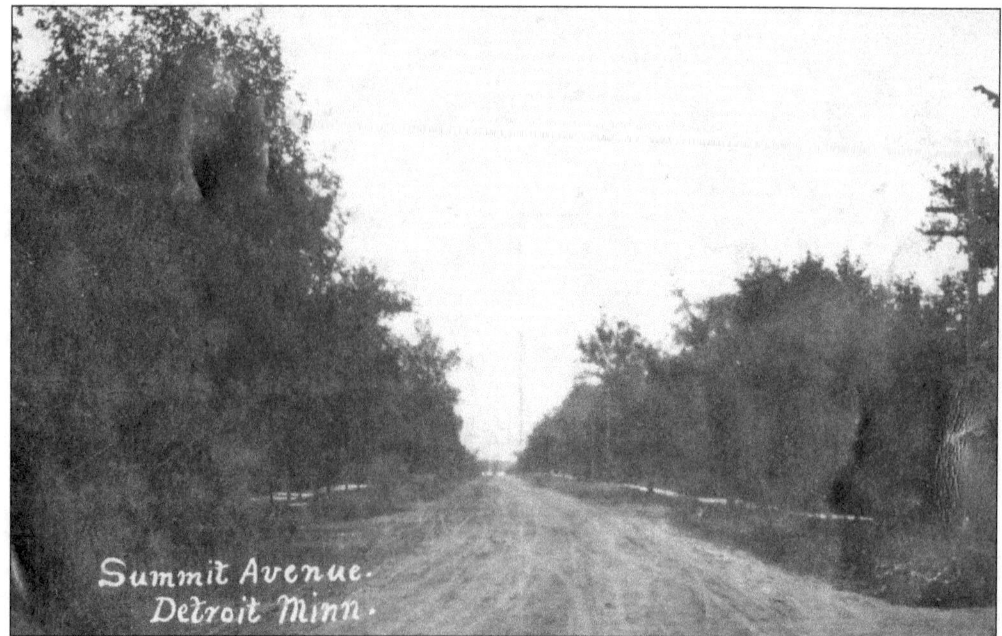

The Chautauqua course brought a number of visitors to the city of Detroit Lakes to hear speakers from around the country. It was held at the lakeshore at the end of Summit Avenue. The value of a good Chautauqua course to the city cannot be computed by mere dollars and cents, but after a poor turnout in 1910, the fate of Chautauqua was put into jeopardy.

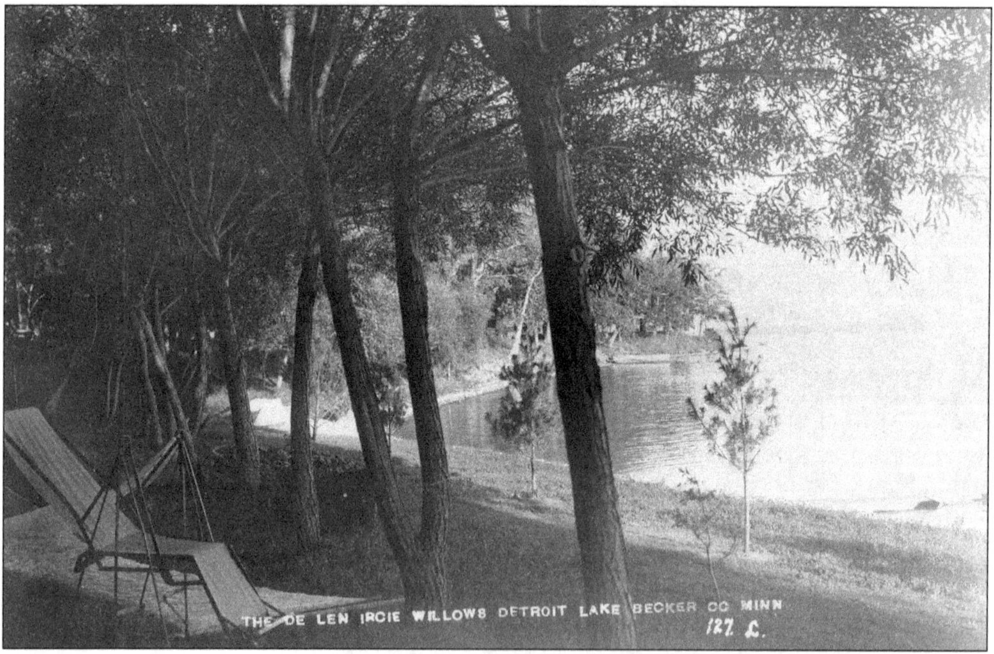

O.J. DeLandrecie, a Fargo businessman, purchased a wooded area near the edge of Detroit Lake on September 18, 1893 from John Crummett. He developed the land and constructed one of the finest summer homes in the area, and for many years, it was the show place of the lakes. DeLandrecie brought many "firsts" to the lake area, including the first motorboat and boathouses.

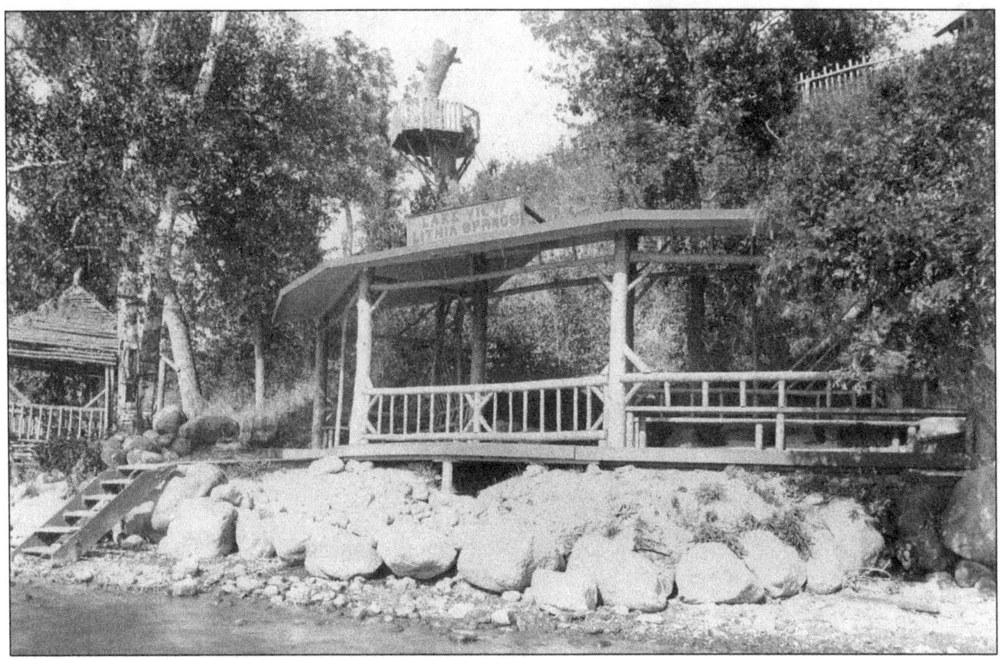

Detroit Lake, a spring-fed lake, is rare and is of the same nature of those found in Switzerland. It gave health and vigor to all those who mingled in its waters, sat upon its shores, or breathed in the air coming in over its rolling waves. During the spring, summer, and fall seasons, between 5,000 and 7,000 health-seekers came to the lake. This indicated that there was something in the area besides just talk. It was the custom of many who came to spend the summer season and to then return home in the month of August, but they made a great mistake in doing this, as the month of September has a beautiful climate and health-giving vigor. Lake View Lithia Springs is one of the places where these health-seekers came to visit in Detroit Lakes.

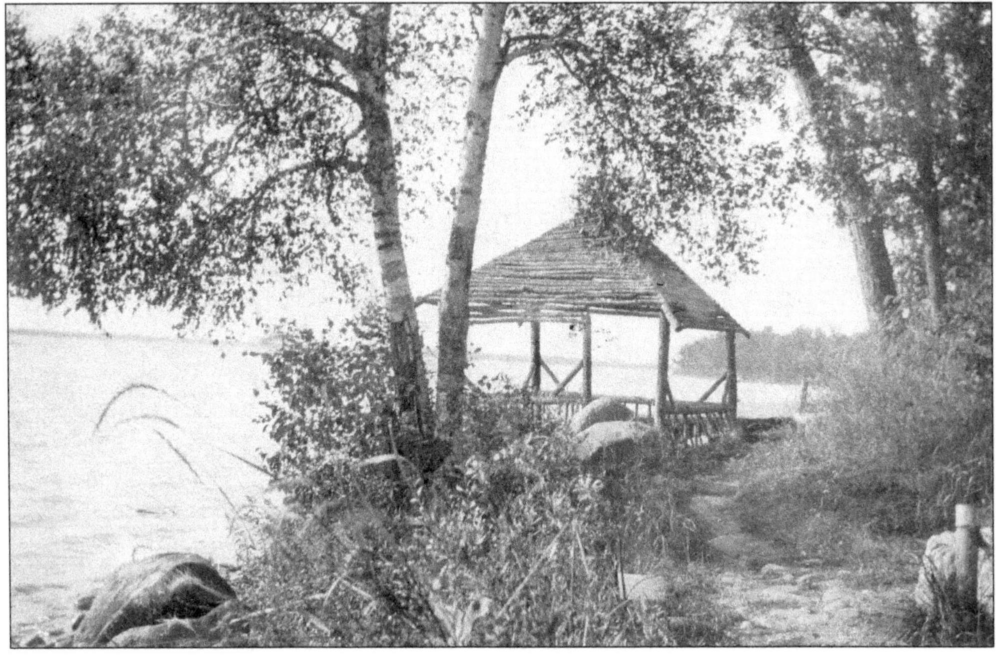

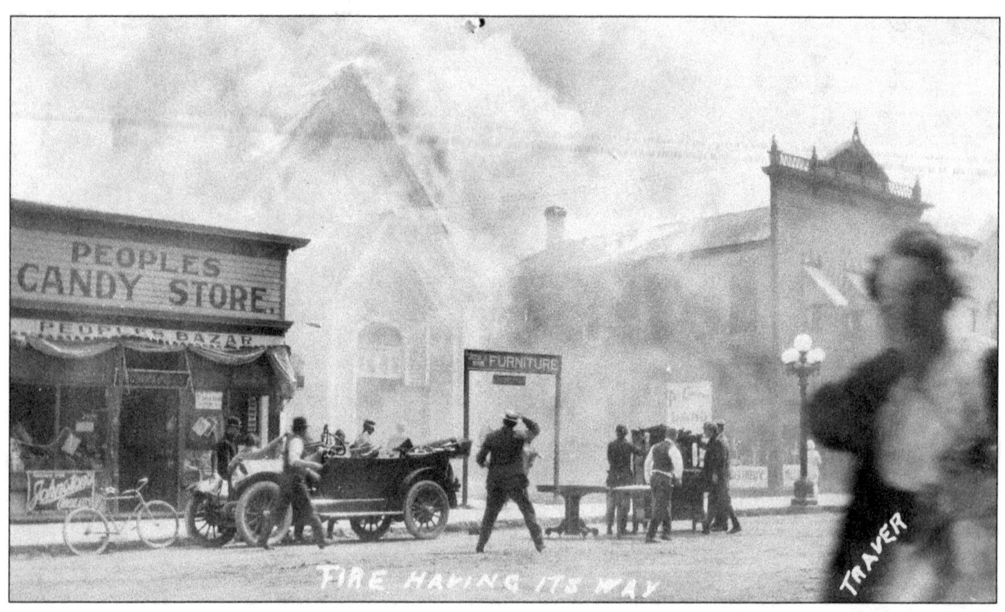

The August 13, 1914, fire that swept through Detroit was considered the most disastrous in the city's history. It ignited on the second floor of a Rahm's Livery Stable and proceeded to city hall, where it consumed Webster Blacksmith Shop, O'Kelley Blacksmith Shop, Knudsen Paint Shop, Blanding Opera House, Sheridan Hotel, J.S. Nunn's furniture and undertaking establishment, George Peoples Confectionery, Converse Millinery Store, the Security State Bank building, the residence of F.S. Courtright, and 500 cords of wood belonging to the Blaisdell Milling Company. The Detroit firefighters were assisted by the Frazee fire department, whose equipment was transported within a half hour by a Northern Pacific train, which just happened to be at Frazee when the call came. It was estimated that 26 buildings were lost for a total of $100,000 in damages.

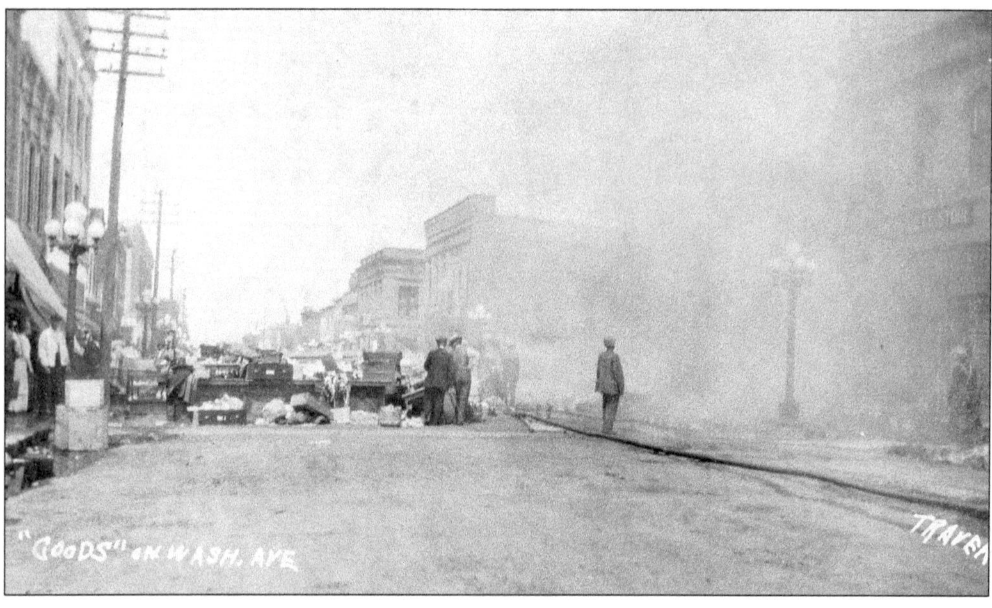

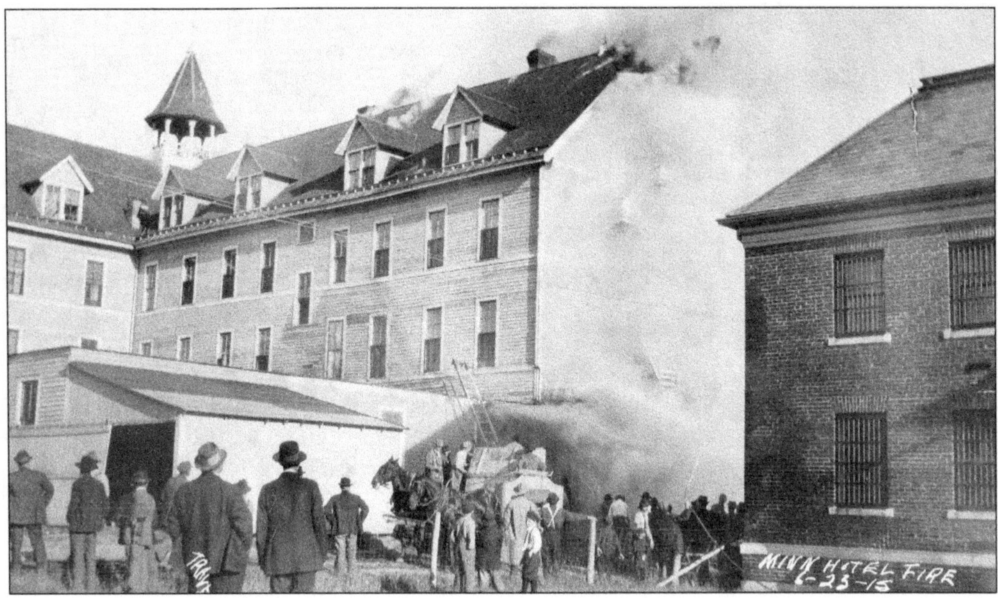

On June 26, 1915, the Hotel Minnesota was engulfed in flames. According to the *Becker County Record*, "The long-expected has happened and the Hotel Minnesota is today but a mass of charred embers and smoking ruins." Everything possible was done to stop the flames from spreading, but by the time help arrived, the flames had an excellent head start and the efforts shifted to saving the Baptist Church, the public library, and the new county jail building. The fire caught at the southwest corner, and as the wind was moderate and from slightly northwest, the suction created by the flames drew almost directly down the avenue. The fire was started by an oil stove in laundry at about 5:45 in the evening. Everyone who was in the hotel escaped, and nobody died. The 32-year reign of the Hotel Minnesota came to an end, and its loss impacted the community greatly.

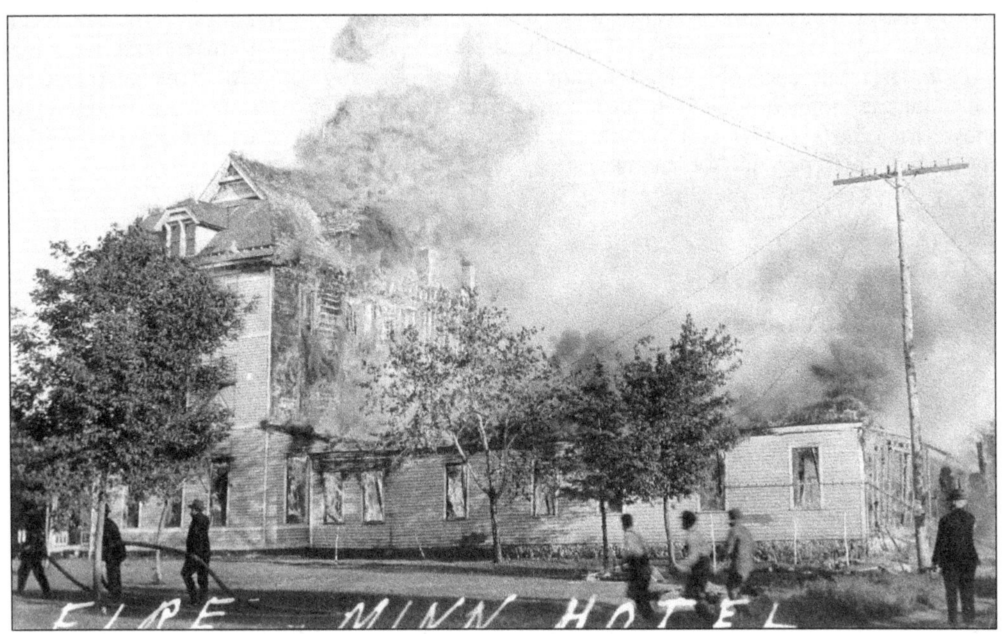

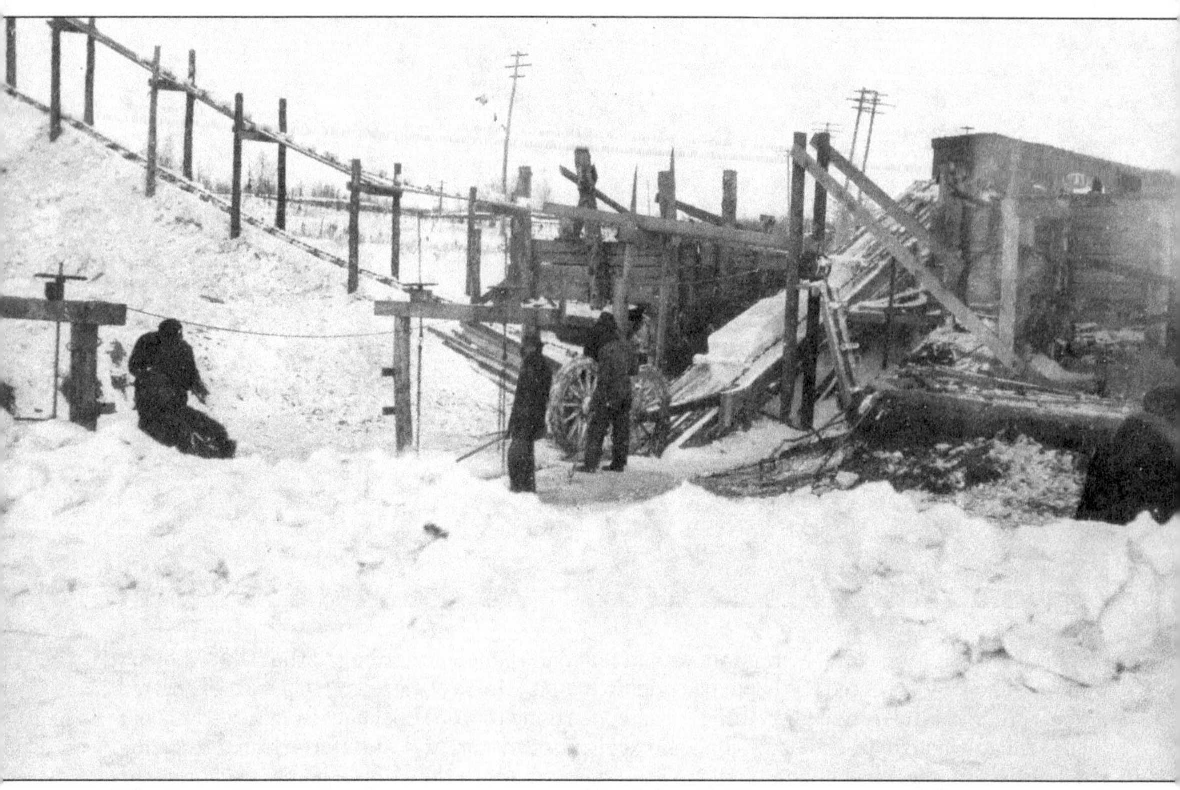

The Fargo-Detroit Ice Company, originated by John K. West, grew out of the activity and commerce of the Pelican Valley Navigation Company. It was necessary to have a sidetrack on the Northern Pacific Railway in order to ship the lumber brought up through the lakes by boats. West convinced the railroad to construct a sidetrack, pointing out that they could cut the ice for their filling stations from that location. This was done, and the company cut their own ice for two years before turning it over to West. West's associate was Joseph Ames, who took care of the Fargo end of business. After Ames's death, Mr. Lofthouse stepped into his shoes. One of the most important products of the ice company was Pokegama spring water. After the Fargo-Detroit Ice Company was incorporated in 1903, it grew from the horse-drawn sleighs being used to haul the ice from the lake, to the railroad cars, to trucks and tractors being used to remove snow from the ice field in preparation for the harvest.

Four

Struggles and Celebrations 1926–1950

In 1926, Detroit officially changed its name to Detroit Lakes because of postal mix-ups with Detroit, Michigan. This "new" city was dealing with lives lost in World War I and an identity that was struggling through the Great Depression. The county infirmary, which had been established to treat low-income patients for medical conditions, became a refuge for residents who had lost their homes. The Lake Park Children's Home, located outside Detroit Lakes, became a safe place for children of destitute families to stay until their parents got back on their feet. Prohibition closed many of the saloons that had been a staple in the city's early history, and the Women's Christian Temperance Movement gained an active membership. As a way to cope with these struggles, the plucky citizens of Detroit Lakes formed service clubs such as the Rotary, Kiwanis, and Junior Chamber of Commerce (later the Jaycees).

The Jaycees began the Northwest Water Carnival in 1935 to give the community a release from daily life, holding events that gave people a chance to gather and celebrate their city. This event was capped off with the Parade of the Northwest, which had more than 50 participants in its early years, including music groups, politicians, and city businesses and organizations. In 1941, World War II changed the environment once again when the city lost 146 Becker County boys and the food and supply rations began affecting the citizens and business owners in the city. Scrap drives, blood drives, and creative cooking became a necessity, and locally grown meat and produce were highly valued. Victory gardens sprouted up around the city and air raid drills were practiced in schools. Patriotism soared, and products "made in the USA" were marketed with great success. With the return of the soldiers in 1945 and 1946, the city, like many others in America, experienced a surge of growth.

The baby boom was underway, and new housing became imperative. An era of consumerism ensued. New cars, clothes, and leisure equipment, such as boats, were in demand. Detroit Lakes, as was the goal of its early settlers, had become a full-blown tourist town. By 1950, a total of 5,787 people called the city home.

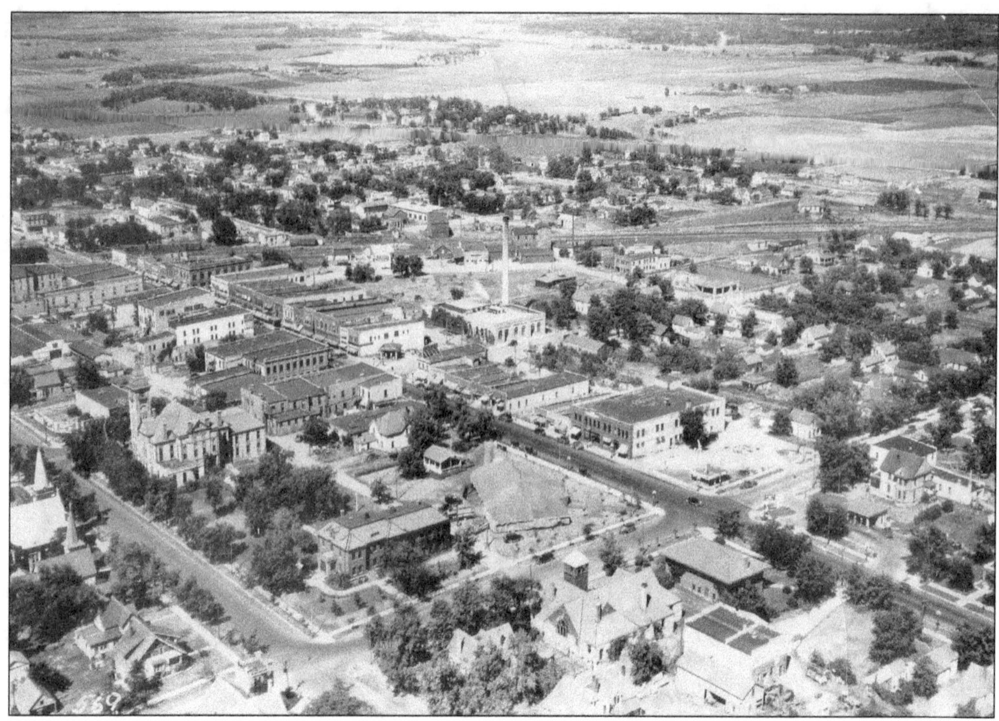

This aerial view shows Detroit Lakes around 1930. Many citizens of Detroit Lakes were extremely affected by the conflicts of the early 20th century. The Leonard Cook family of Detroit Lakes had five sons on active duty at once, as did several other families in the county. Over 2,015 Becker County men and woman served the country during this time, with 75 lives lost in World War I and 146 in World War II. The city struggled to maintain during the emotional and financial struggles that war brought.

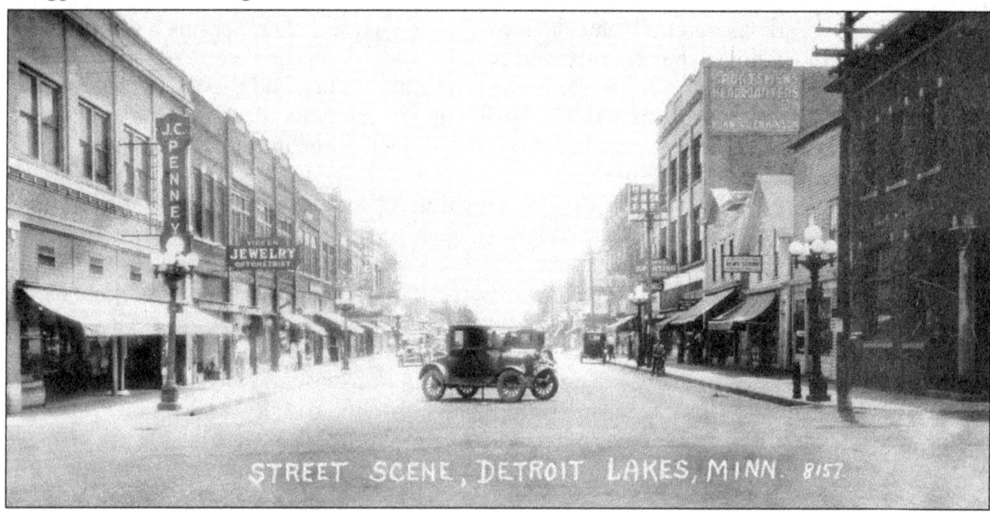

In 1926, the J.C. Penney Company built their store in Detroit Lakes where Buckmann's grocery store once stood. At first, it was a difficult process to become established in Detroit Lakes due to the fact that Blanding's and Norby's did not want a chain store encroaching on local business. After taking the case to court and getting aid from Concordia College, they were able to finance the lot.

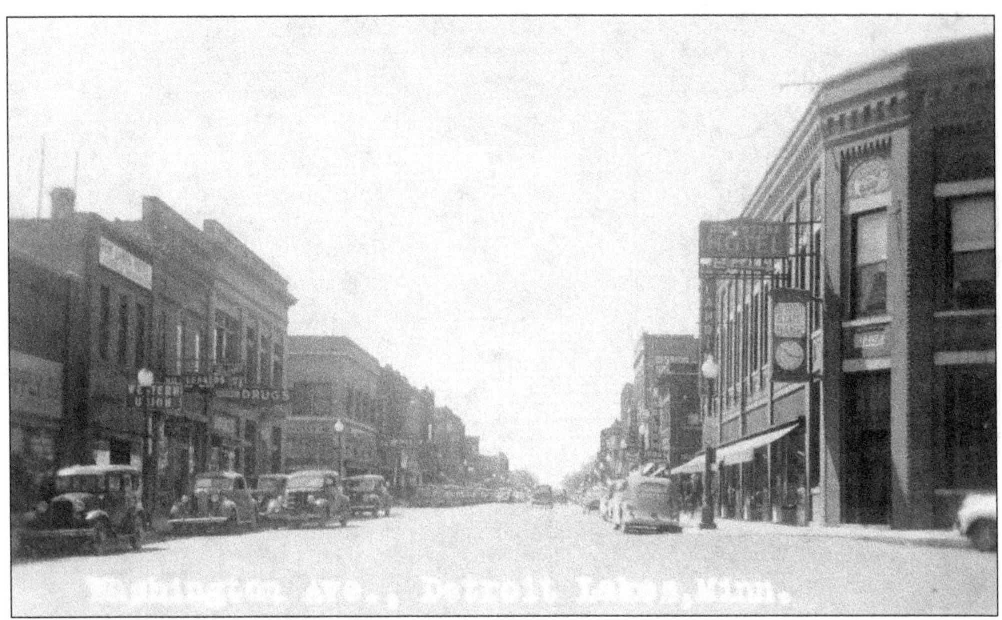

Detroit State Bank was formed in September 1919 as the fourth financial institution in the city. The bank had an initial capital stock of $25,000, which was divided into 250 shares of $100 each. It originally rented the Kuchenbecker Building at 710 Washington Avenue. In 1959, the bank put up a new building, which was ready for occupancy in 1960. It was one of the first banks to offer drive-in window service.

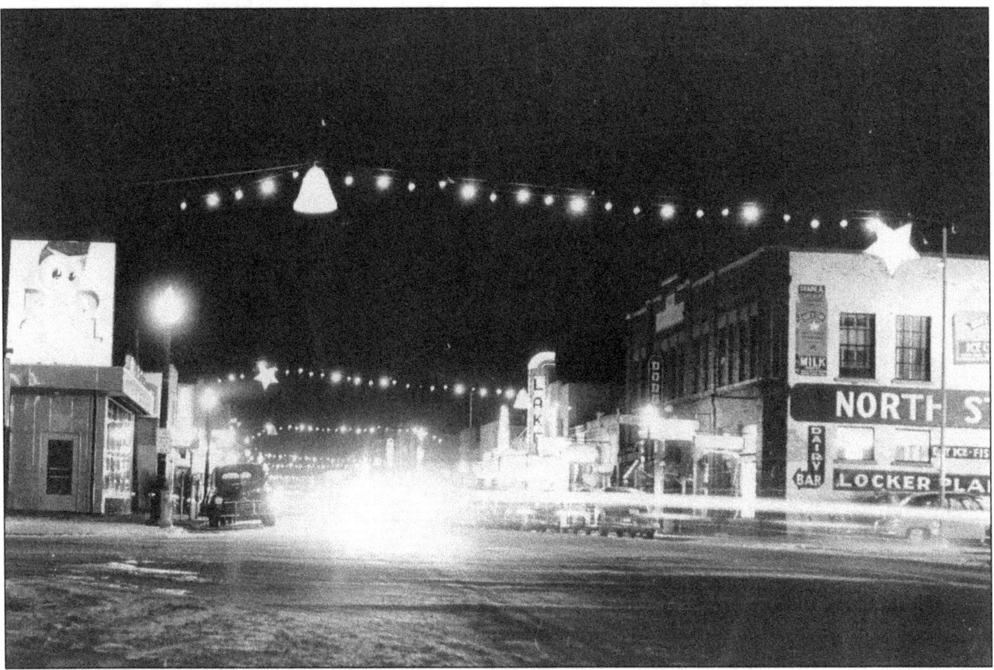

In 1937, the Red Owl opened in its new location on the corner of Washington Avenue and Frazee Street, becoming what was considered at the time a "superstore." The store was described by E.G. Maltby, the general superintendent for all Red Owl stores, as "the most modern store we have installed so far." Red Owl had been a grocery store in the area since 1922.

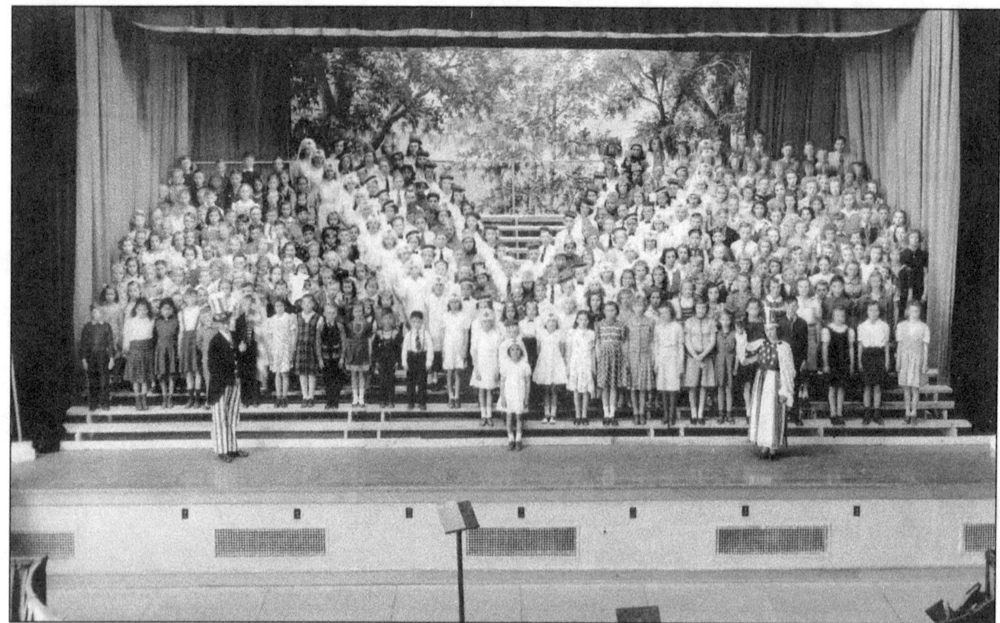

The country school's musical festival idea came from Clarissa Berquist, who developed the program and handed it out to all the area schools. Each school would practice their songs and then all children wanting to participate would meet at the Holmes School and perform under the direction of the music teacher there. The photograph above is of the 1943 musical festival.

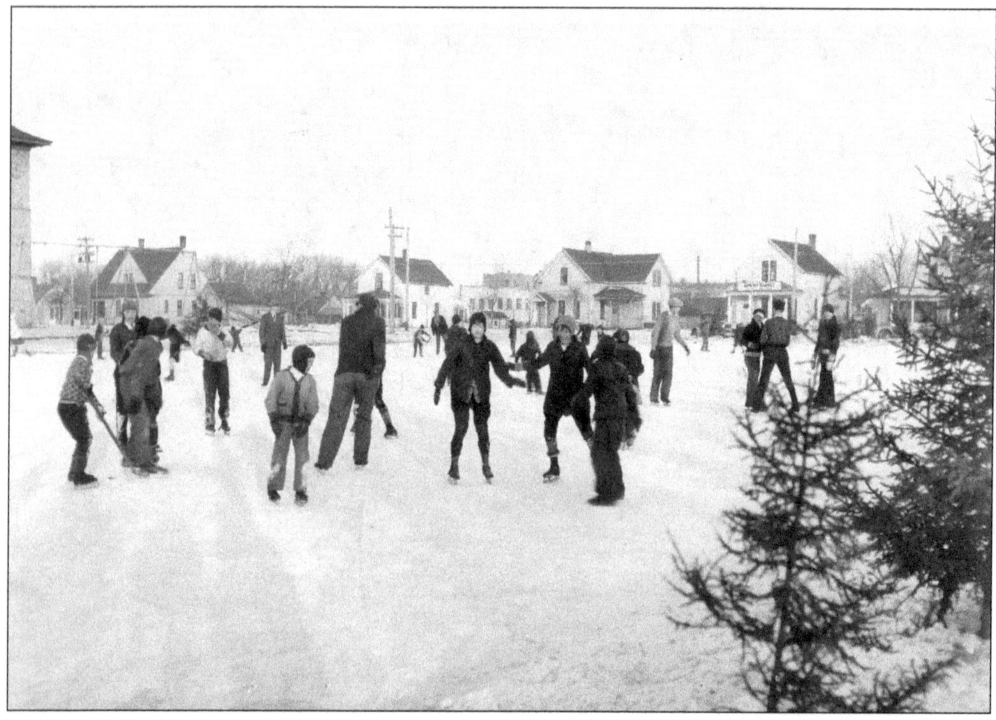

In 1928, C.C. Chase, assistant principal of the Holmes School, helped raise funds for a skating rink to be constructed south of the school building. This rink was the only one open to children at the time and was always busy.

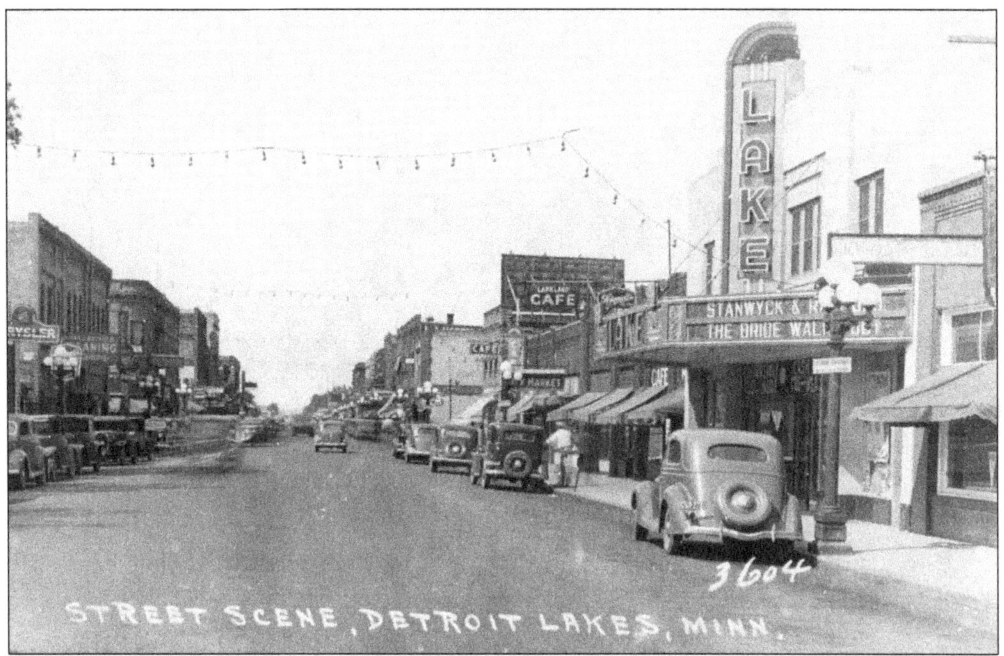

The Detroit Lakes Amusement Company, operated by Herb and Andy Anderson, purchased a lot from W.M. McCart in 1935 and announced plans to build a modern, spacious theater called Lake Theatre. It was located on Washington Avenue across from the bandstand and had a seating capacity of 750 people.

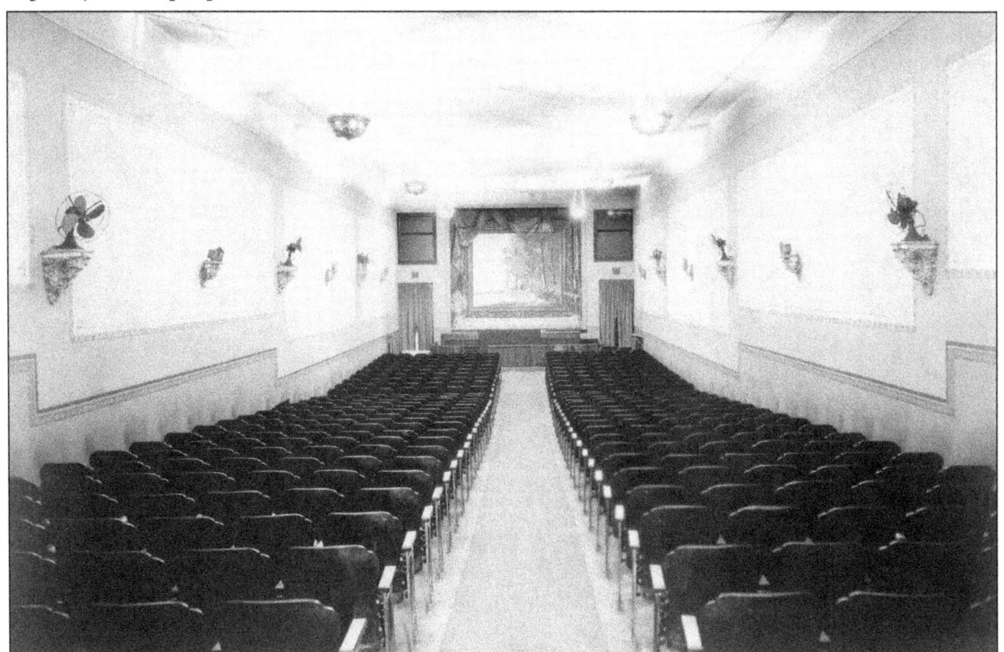

The State Theatre opened in 1921 under management of the Detroit Lakes Amusement Company. It opened with a Paramount special called *The Affairs of Anatole*, in which Wallace Reid and Gloria Swanson were among the stars. It also boasted a Fotoplayer organ, which used player-piano rolls and had every known gadget on it, from drums to a train whistle.

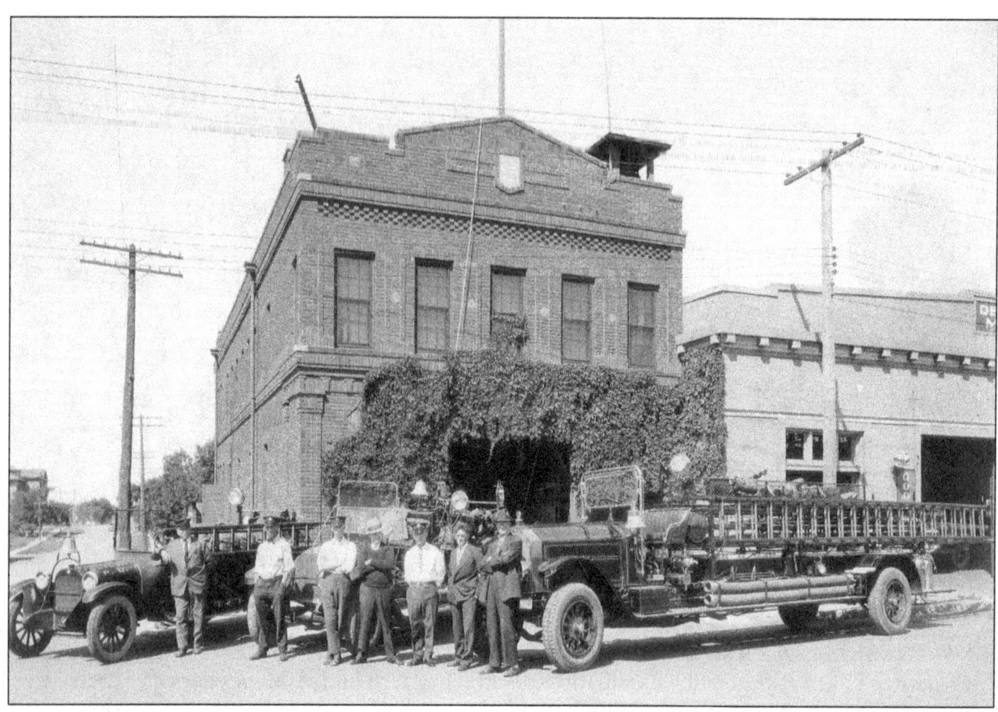

The history of the Detroit Lakes Fire Department goes back to the first settlement, when men worked together in a "bucket brigade" in attempts to save a burning building. W.A. Norcross served as the first chief. After the fire of 1914, many records were lost. William Grow Stewart emerged as a leader by reorganizing the entire fire department and turning them from an amateur organization to one that had fully-trained firefighters. The fire hall, seen here, was located at the corner of Lake Avenue and Front Street.

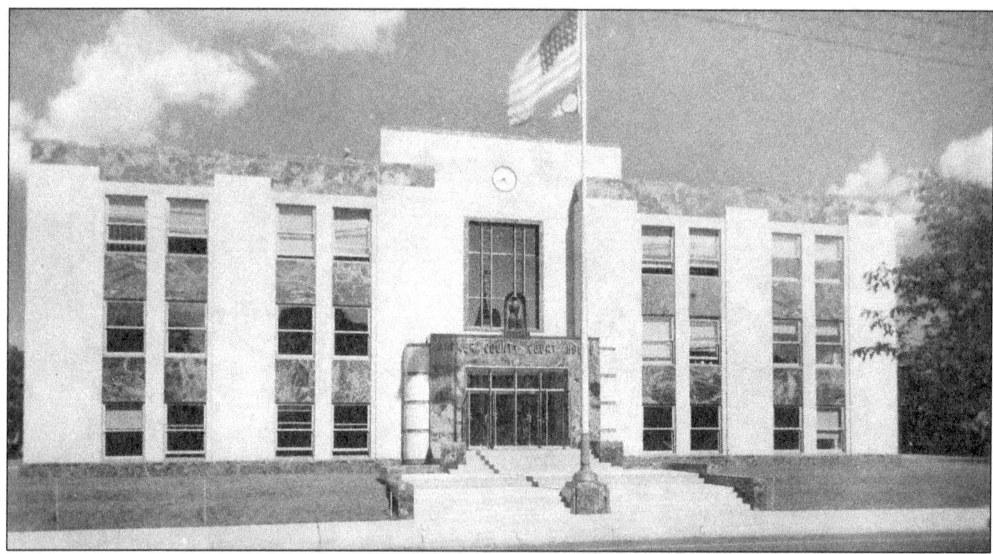

Plans for a new courthouse were authorized on April 8, 1941, and construction began on September 16, 1941. In 1943, the old courthouse was closed for a few days while the offices were moved. The courthouse consisted of three floors. The basement was home to the historical room and library, which was cared for by curator Otto Zeck.

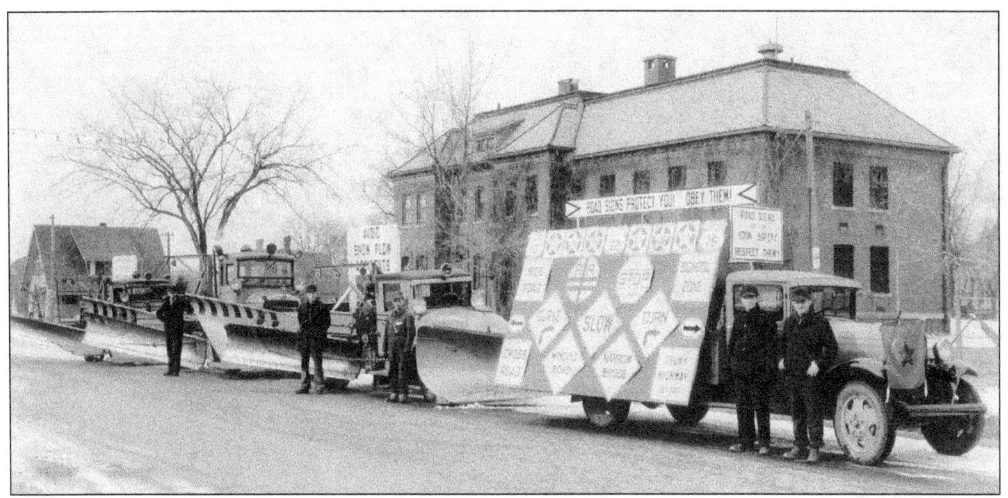

The Becker County Jail, seen in the background above, was the site of some interesting jailbreaks. Charlie Hines, of McKinney, Texas, escaped on August 21, 1930, by sawing his way out with a pair of table knives. Deputy Mox Olson nabbed him at Herman, where he was working at the fair. Another inmate also sawed his way out on September 2, 1931, but it is assumed he had an accomplice in the act.

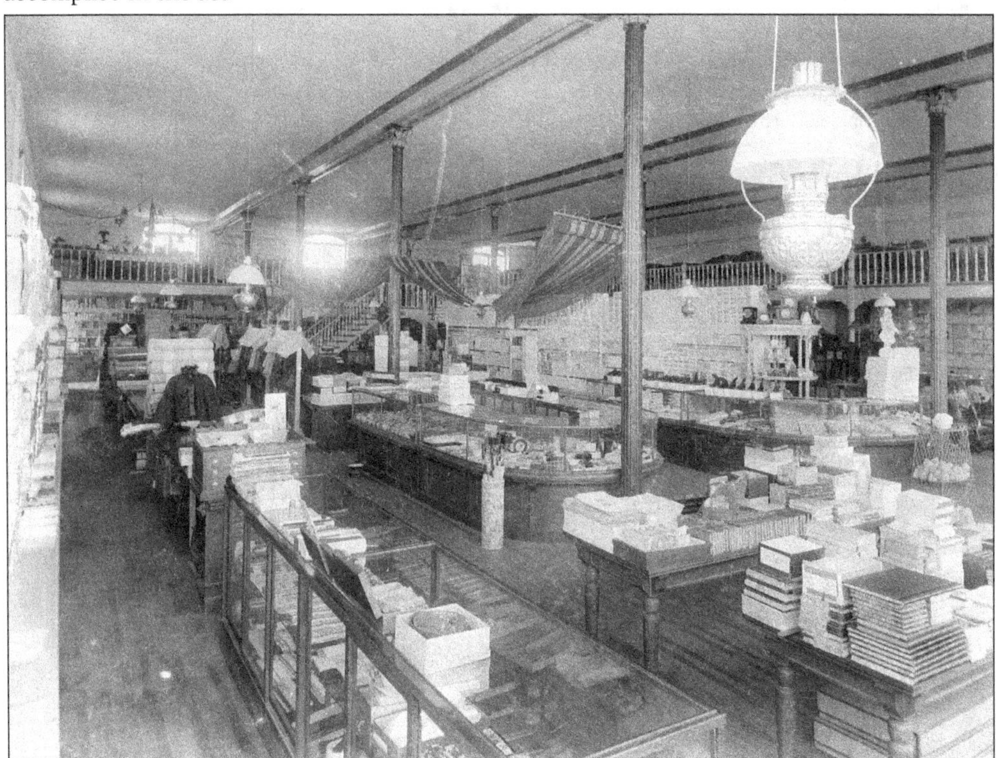

After two dissolved partnerships and the death of Arthur M. Blanding, Blanding's became an entity all on its own. H.D. Blanding and C.W. Blanding took over active management of the business in 1914, and the Blanding family acquired all outstanding stock in the company. They made many improvements throughout the years by installing a modern storefront and a cable cash carrier, along with a new fresh meats department, which opened in 1936.

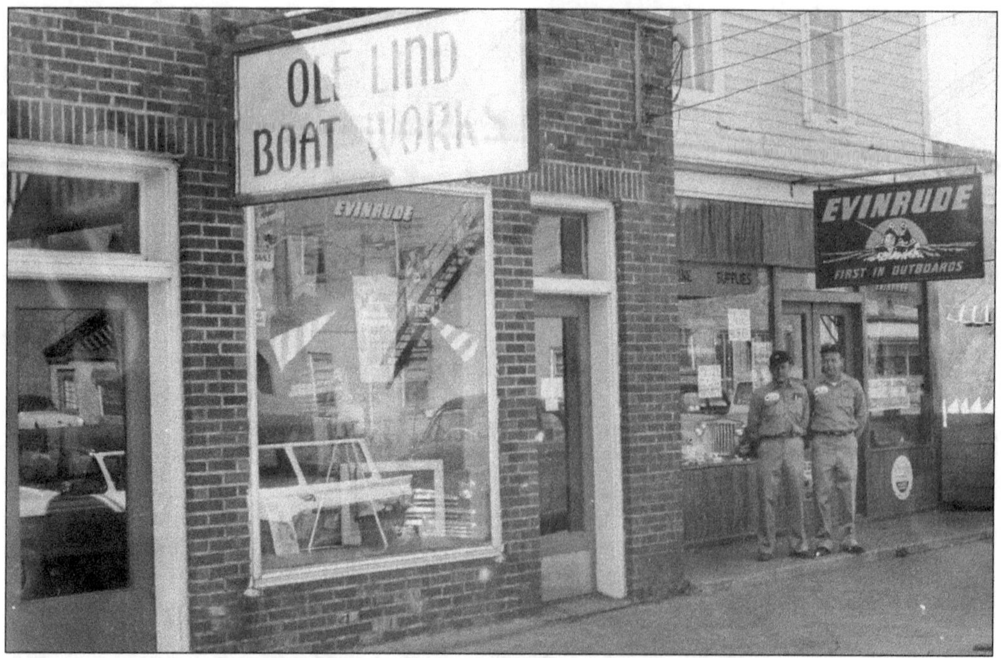

Ole Lind came to the United States in 1902, settling in the Alexandria area where he began his career as a boat builder in 1903. He moved to Detroit Lakes in 1907, where in 1908 he joined the boat firm of Albert and Ed Beckman. The Ole Lind Boatworks came into being in 1913 and built boats that, according to their slogan, "Float Like a Feather."

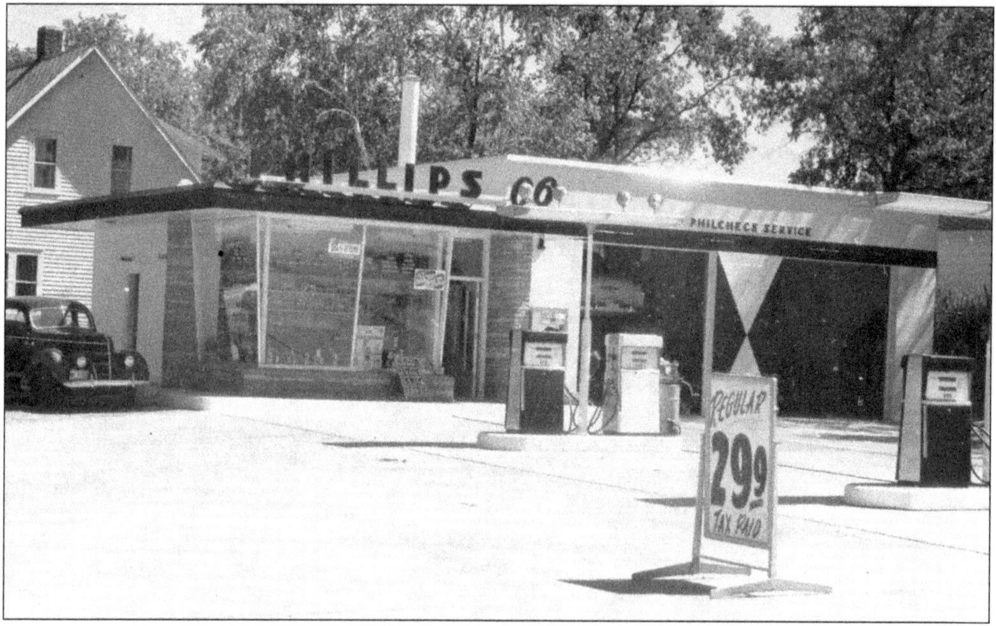

In the early days, there were more than 40 gas and service stations within the city limits of Detroit. Among them was the Phillips 66 Station, operated by the J.M. Sauer family for 22 years. Located at the southeast corner of Washington Avenue and Willow Street, it was formerly the Murphy Oil Station up until the 1950s. By the 1970s, only 13 establishments remained. The Sauers also operated the "World's Smallest Gas Station" by the Graystone Complex.

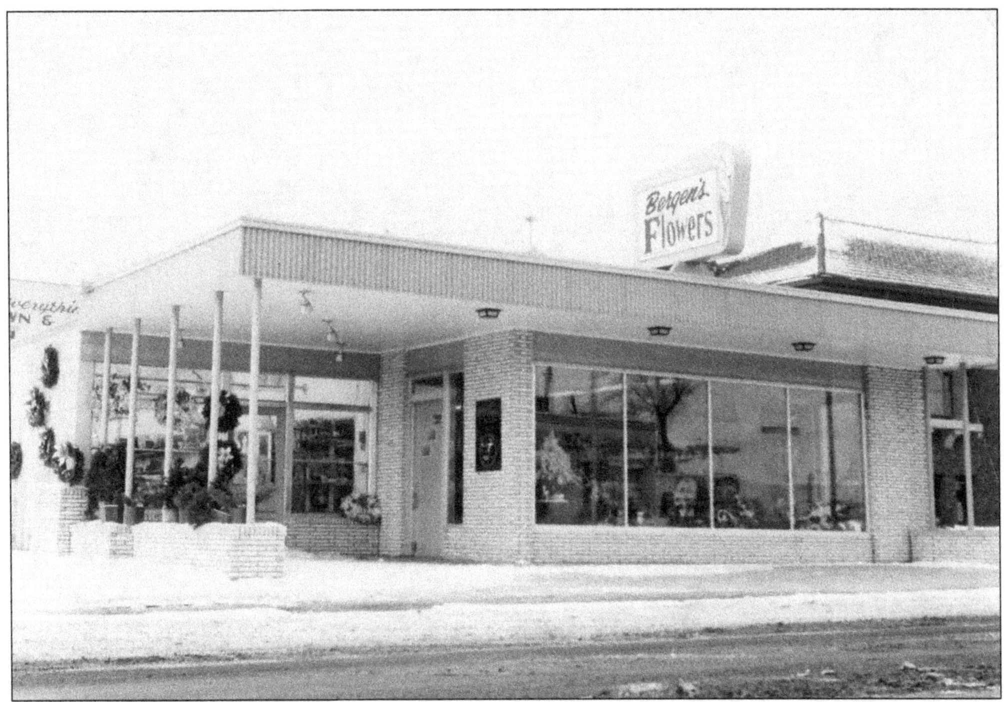

Around 1916, Joseph A. Bergen bought seven acres of land and decided to go into business with his wife, Mary. Mary and her sons, who were already raising vegetables and selling them, were making a good profit. They decided to work together and start a business, Bergen's Nursery. Their son Lawrence attended the School of Floral Arts and returned home to take over the business with his brother. They turned the focus to flowers in 1940.

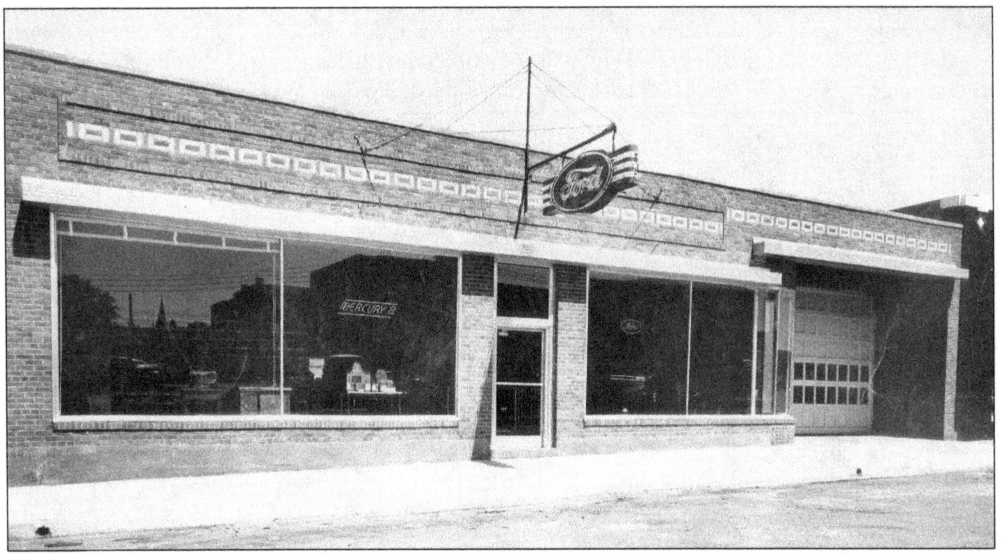

Throughout the years, the idea of automobile manufacturing has changed greatly. When Henry Ford started making cars, they used small workshops. The first car, the Model T, was designed to be simple and inexpensive, around $600 and $700. After the Model T came the Model A and Model B, the difference being that they were a little bigger and cost more. Borstad's Ford dealership, seen above, was located on State Street where Marco, Inc., is currently.

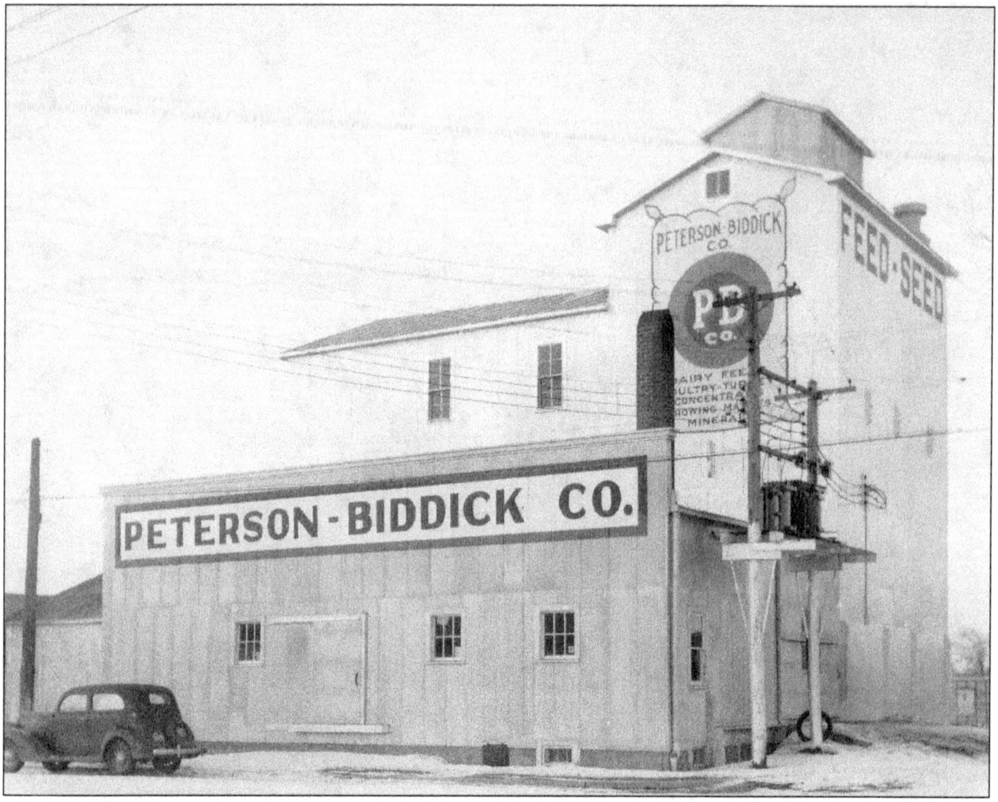

The Blaisdell Company constructed the Peterson-Biddick building in 1901. Herman Blaisdell formed a partnership with a Mr. Norris from Minneapolis, Minnesota. The building was equipped with a steam engine of 125 horsepower, which burned wood. In order to supply the engine with wood, the whole parking lot of J.C. Penney was completely filled with wood that farmers brought in exchange for flour. Moses Eckel took over after Blaisdell passed away.

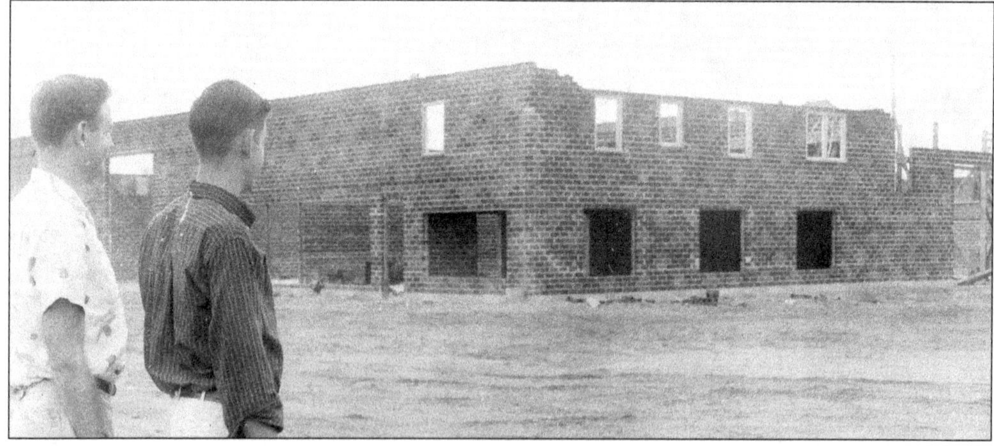

C.P. Wilcox established the Wilcox Lumber Company in 1881. He began his first career as a carpenter and contractor and was in charge of a number of the earliest buildings, both in and around Detroit Lakes. He was also in charge of nearly all public building construction on the White Earth Reservation between 1871 and 1879. After retiring, Wilcox Lumber Company was managed by W.L. Taylor. In 1945, the building burnt, and in 1970 it was sold to Peavey Lumber.

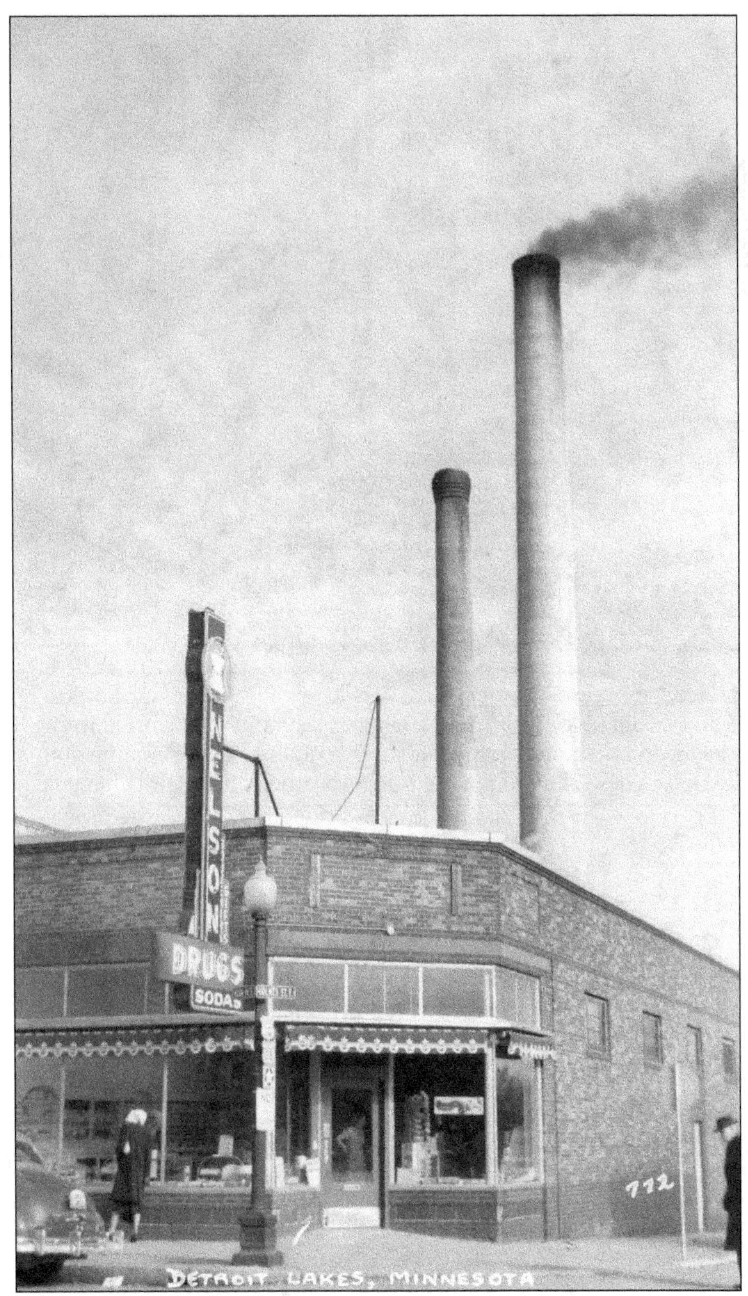

Edwin F. Nelson was born on June 7, 1899, in Minneapolis, Minnesota, and moved to Milaca with his parents when he was a child. He graduated from the University of Minnesota School of Pharmacy and served in the Army during World War I. After marrying his wife, Lorraine, he worked in Minneapolis at Staples and Brainerd before moving to Detroit Lakes, where he purchased Leach Drug Company from Bert Leach and opened his own pharmacy, Nelson Drugstore. In 1948, he relocated his business to Washington Avenue and Holmes Street. He operated the store from 1928 until his retirement on January 1, 1960, when he also sold his business to Service Drug Corporation. He was a past president of the Detroit Lakes Rotary Club and the chamber of commerce along with being a very well known civic leader. Ed passed away on December 1, 1969.

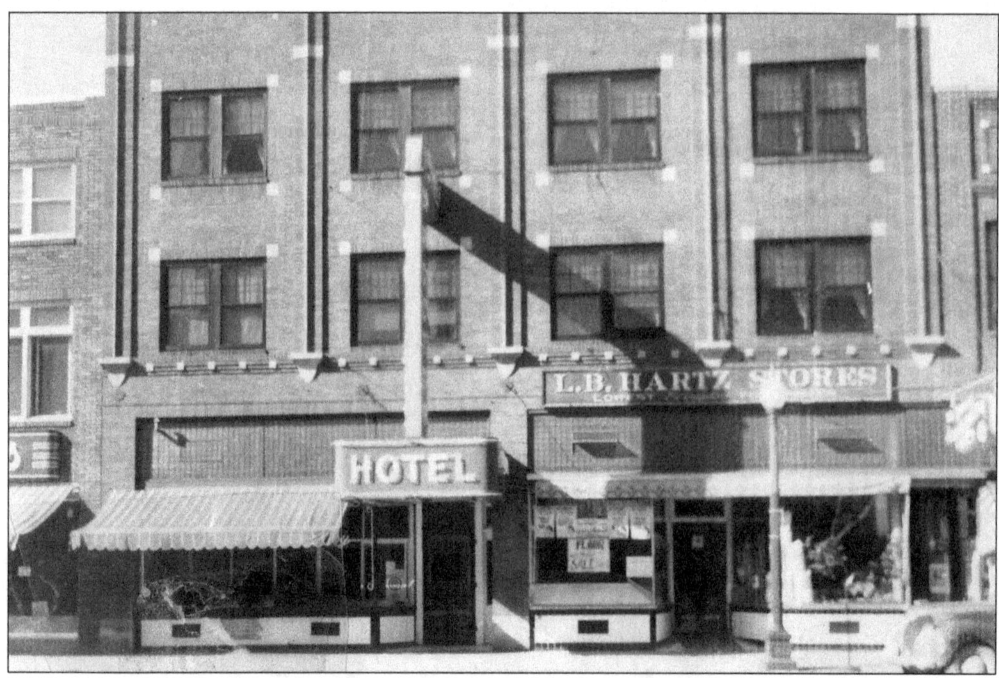

The McCarthy Hotel was one of the city's most popular eating and lodging houses. The proprietors were Clarence and George McCarthy. A fire that broke out in 1927 started in the linen room in the center of the second floor and nearly put three businesses out of commission. The hotel was completely filled with guests, but all got out safely, together with their personal effects.

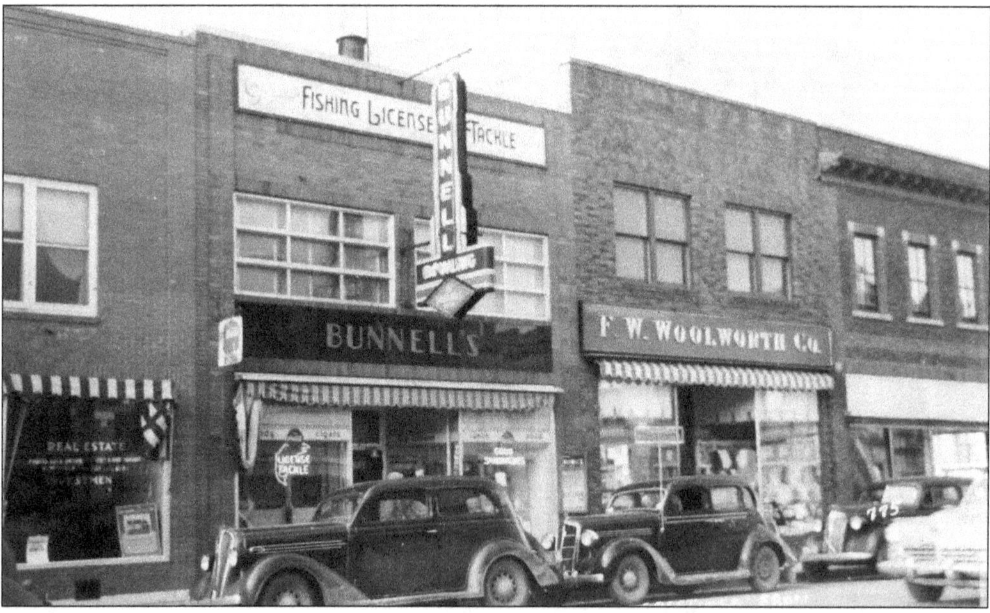

Woolworth's was built in 1929 and located at 802 Washington Avenue. It was situated between Bunnell's Recreation and the Leach Drugstore. At the time, it was the longest business house in the city. The first manager of the store was Renn H. Torbert of Sioux Falls, South Dakota. The original store was made of brick and consisted of two stories, with the upper story used as offices and apartments.

North Star Dairy announced in 1944 its plans to build a milk-drying plant in Detroit Lakes. By the following year, the dairy announced plans to build a $15,000 laboratory and warehouse. North Star was a great contributor to the relief and rehabilitation of Europe and people that were stricken by World War II.

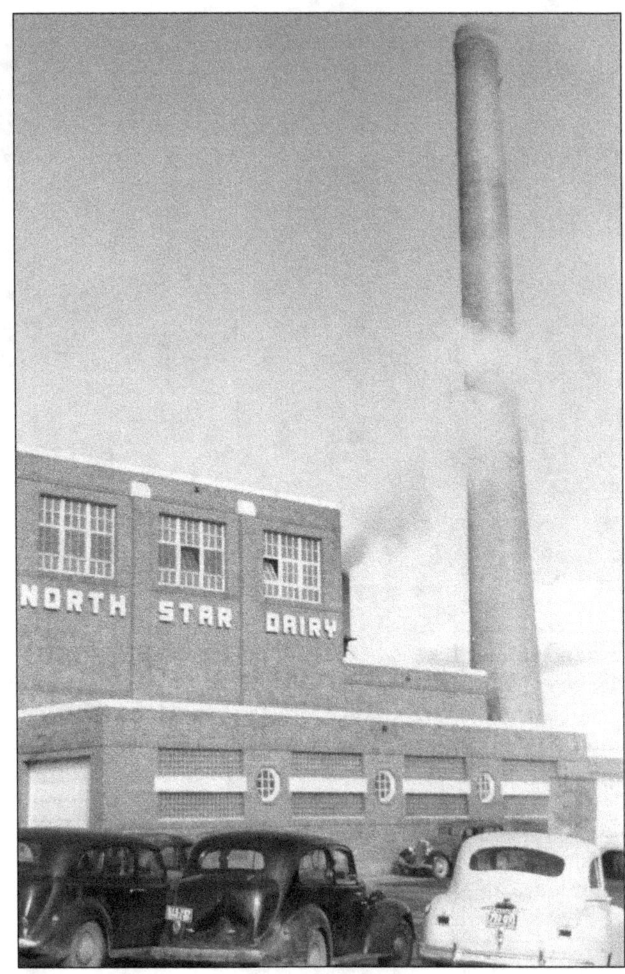

Swift and Company began in Detroit Lakes in March 1922. The small buying station purchased poultry and eggs and shipped them to markets in the east. The Swift plant was established in 1929. Originally a dairy, egg, and poultry plant, it entered the turkey business in 1954. The Detroit Lakes plant was part of the Swift Dairy and Poultry Company, which was an owned subsidiary of the Swift and Company.

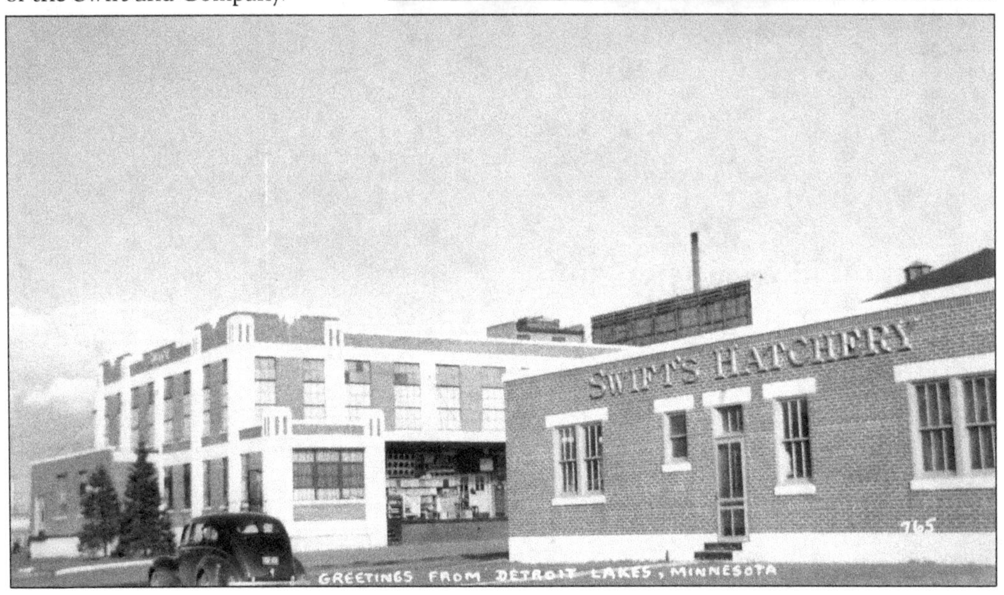

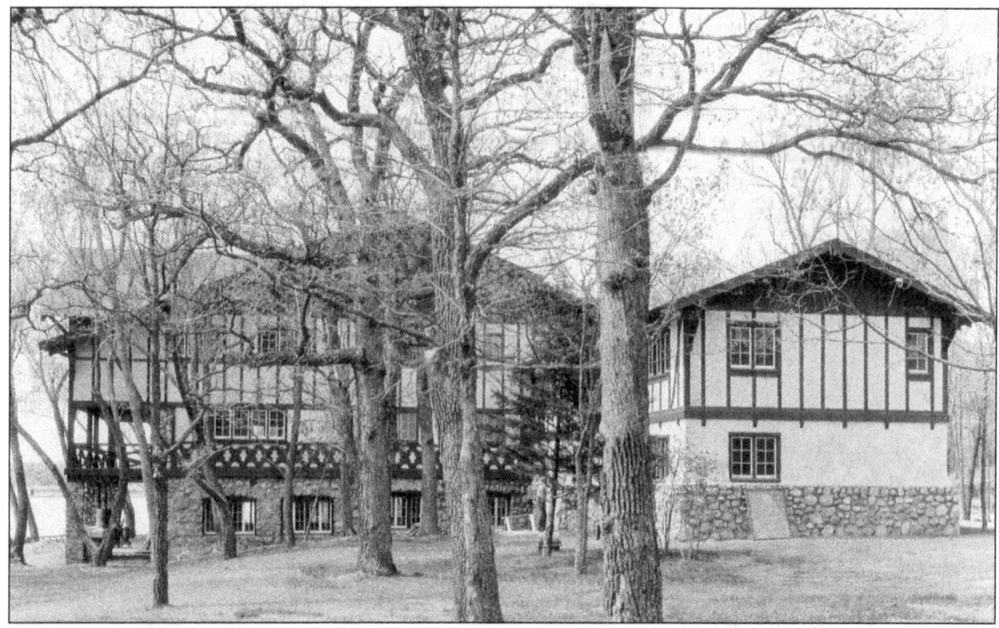

When summer homes became popular in the area, O.J. DeLendrecie purchased land east of the city park on East Boulevard of Detroit Lake, a short distance from the Pavilion. After his passing, Clarence and George McCarthy purchased the property from the DeLendrecie estate and immediately began construction on the Edgewater Beach Hotel. Finished in 1931, it was considered one of the finest structures of its kind in Northwest Minnesota. The association was taken over by the Detroit Lakes Realty Company, with F.H. Wright as president. Wright would go on to sell the property to Mr. and Mrs. Ken Kennedy, who proceeded to do an extensive remodel and also renamed the property. The Edgewater Inn installed heated pools and a golf putting green. The main lodge also got a facelift with balconies built across the front. Unfortunately, this beautiful hotel was demolished in 1978.

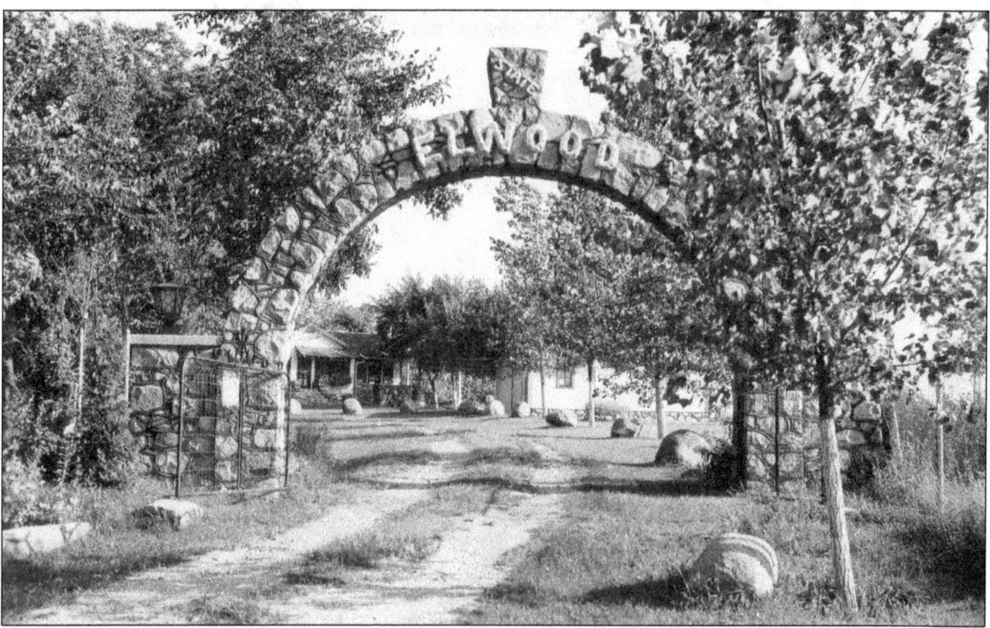

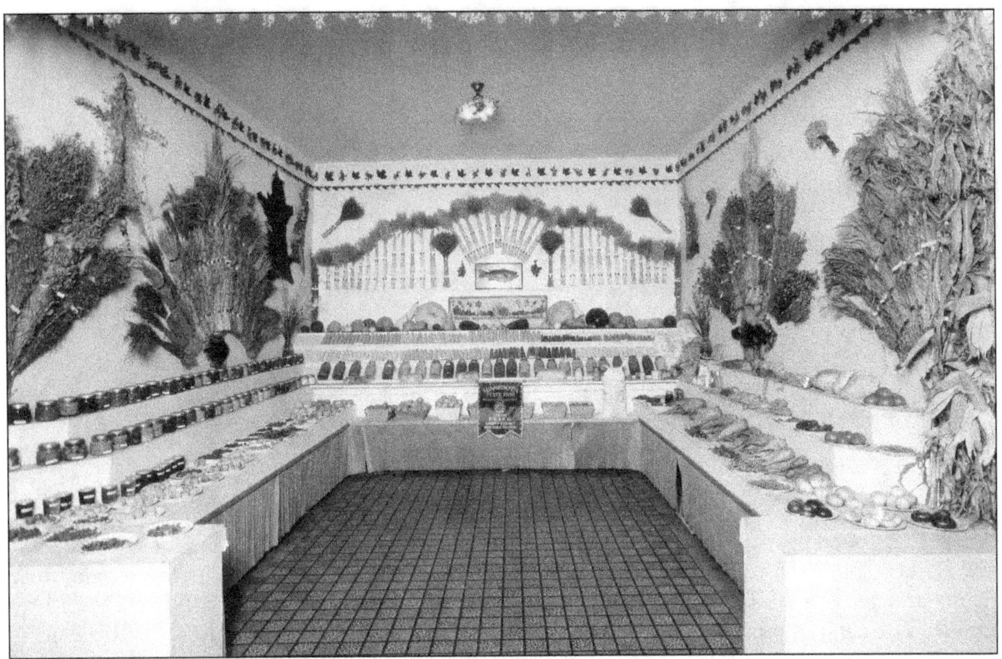

The Becker County Fair was first held September 23–25, 1891, and was organized by the Becker County Agricultural and Driving Association. Membership in the association was $1 and guaranteed free admission and project entry. The general public was charged 25¢ each day or could buy a season pass for 50¢. At the first fair, there were horse races, foot races, potato sack races, egg races, and bike races at the grandstand (seen below). These early races offered over $1,800 worth of premiums for the winners—an enormous sum in the late 19th century! Cars gradually overtook horses, and the grandstand became the center of entertainment for fairgoers. Continued improvements were made to the structure, including a new roof in 1931 to protect the crowd from the sun and rain. For the fair centennial in 1991, a new grandstand fence was built, with 800 volunteers helping in the construction. These volunteers also included 23 professionals from the building industry in Becker County, all members of the Lakes Area Builders Association. The Fair Board also provided free gate admission for this centennial year.

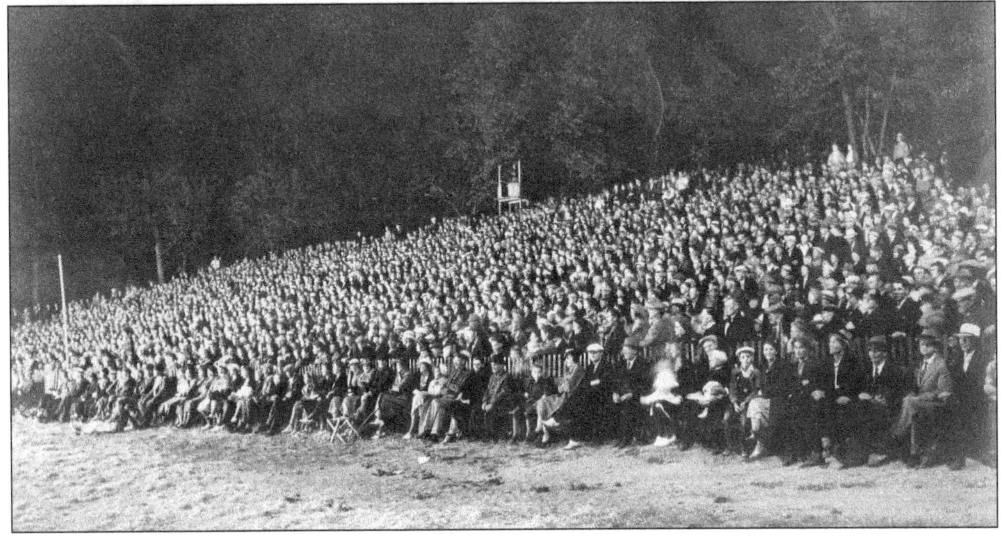

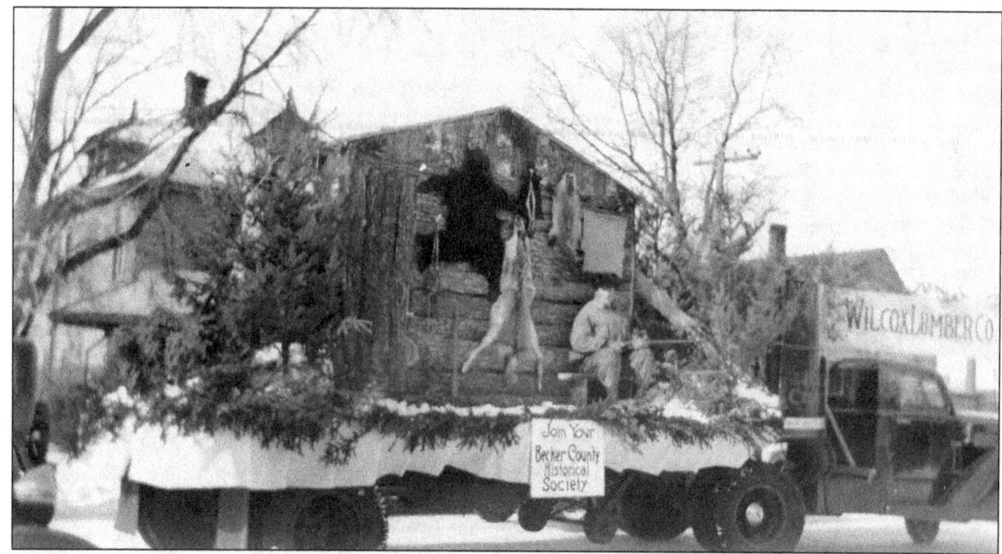

The Becker County Historical Society (BCHS) has always been an active participant in community events and activities. This float, pictured in 1936, was the BCHS entry in the Dog Derby Day Parade. The cabin represents the early settlers, many who worked as fur traders. Joe Rundlett is depicting a hunter, encouraging the crowd to join their historical society.

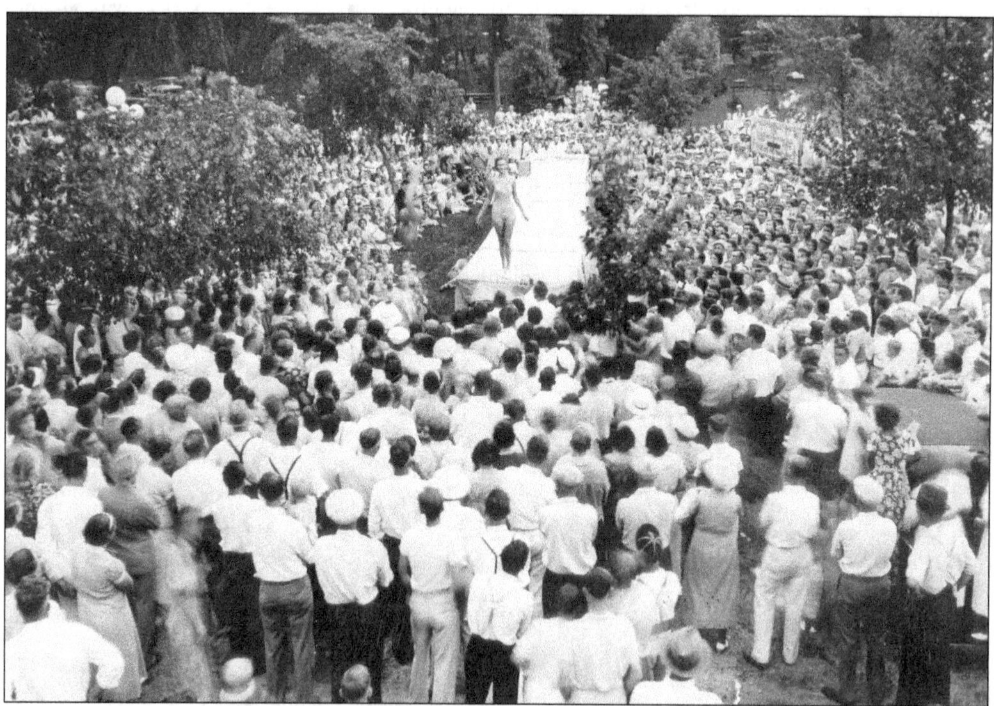

The Detroit Lakes Junior Chamber of Commerce, later called the "Jaycees," was formed in 1935. This group started the First Annual Northwest Water Carnival in June 1935 with Bert Meach serving as the admiral. 10,000 to 15,000 people attended the festivities, including the Miss Northwest pageant. Miss Francis Wright was named the winner and went on to compete in the Miss Minnesota pageant later in the year.

Five

To the Lakes 1951–1975

Between 1950 and 1975, Detroit Lakes maintained a consistent population of around 5,800 people. In 1971, the city celebrated its centennial and continued to develop its tourist appeal. A culture of family-owned drive-ins and resorts abounded, with establishments such as Ken Utecht's Red Hen, the Sandwich Hut, A&W, and Dairy Queen populating the south end of Washington Avenue. Clem's Big Dock, operated by Clem Tevogt, became a focal point of outdoor activity, offering boat rentals and a swimming beach. Sand was added to that beach and to the Pavilion, located in the Detroit Lakes City Park, where space for concerts, weddings, and community gatherings was provided. The north side of Washington Avenue offered Evans Supermarket, Hardware Hank, and the VFW.

The conflicts in Korea and Vietnam took more young men away from the city and, for the first time, the citizens could see live coverage of war on television. The immediacy of this coverage led to protest and concern from the youth population of Detroit Lakes. The feminist movement also touched the city, with an increased demand for equality in business and pay level. A march was held from the lakeside to the courthouse in support of one female realtor. As the 1970s began, Detroit Lakes took time to remember its history. The Becker County Historical Society and Museum was well-established in the basement of the county courthouse and made every effort to provide a context for the events of the city's past. By the mid-1970s, the population began to grow, so that by 1980 it stood at 7,106—a 22 percent increase in 10 years.

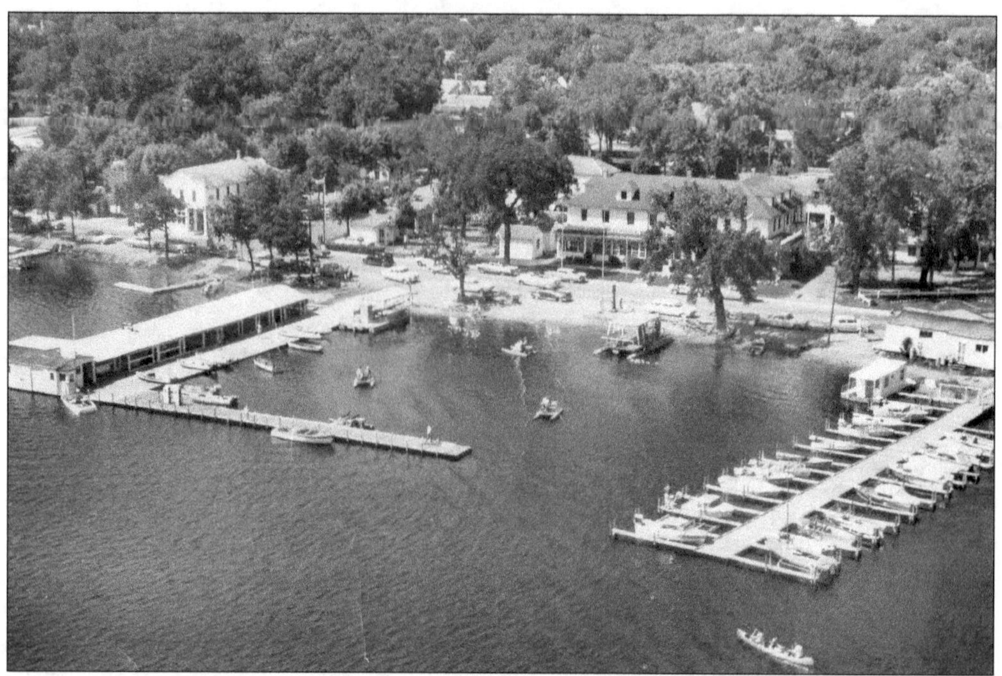

The Detroit Boat Livery was built in 1911 by Fred Weiss Jr. (whose father, Fred Weiss Sr., owned and operated the Park Hotel across the street). It consisted of one big dock next to a private swimming beach and bathhouse. Weiss rented bathing suits and offered Red Cross swimming lessons. In 1945, Clem Tevogt, who worked for Weiss, purchased the dock and renamed it Clem's Big Dock.

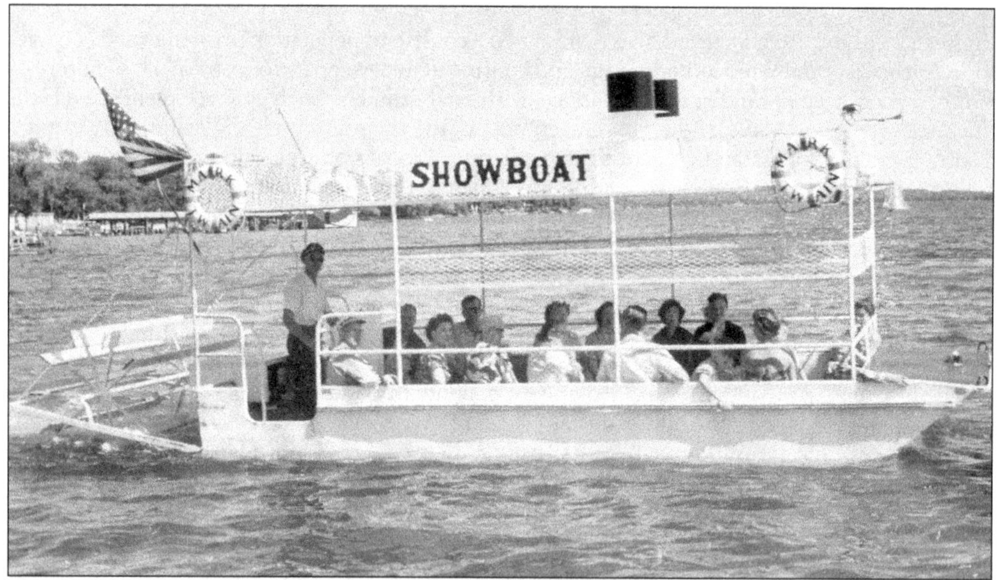

When Tevogt took over the dock, he continued to provide speedboat rides in Hackercraft speedboats as Weiss had done and popularized the "rollercoaster ride on the water." Tevogt also rented boats and sold bait, while the City of Detroit Lakes took over the public swimming area, moving it toward the Pavilion. Tevogt later bought a Higgins speedboat and a Century speedboat. He charged 50¢ for a five- or six-mile ride. In 1950, Tevogt added an excursion boat called "Miss Detroit."

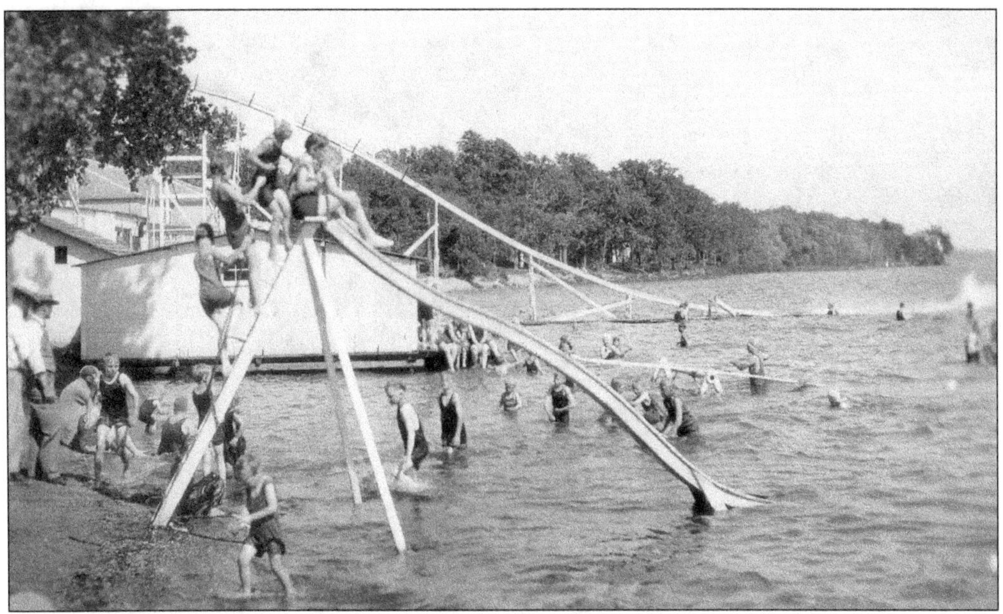

The Detroit Boat Livery offered a waterslide and diving tower, which was closed between 1928 and 1930. The waterslide later moved to the public beach outside the Pavilion during Clem Tevogt's era. At Clem's Big Dock, you could rent boats called "put-puts," which were between one and two horsepower. This dock became the stopping point for all of the tourists who visited Detroit Lakes. Tevogt lengthened and put a covering over the stall portion of the dock. He also added another dock reserved for private boats and installed a cement ramp so that people could launch their boats more easily.

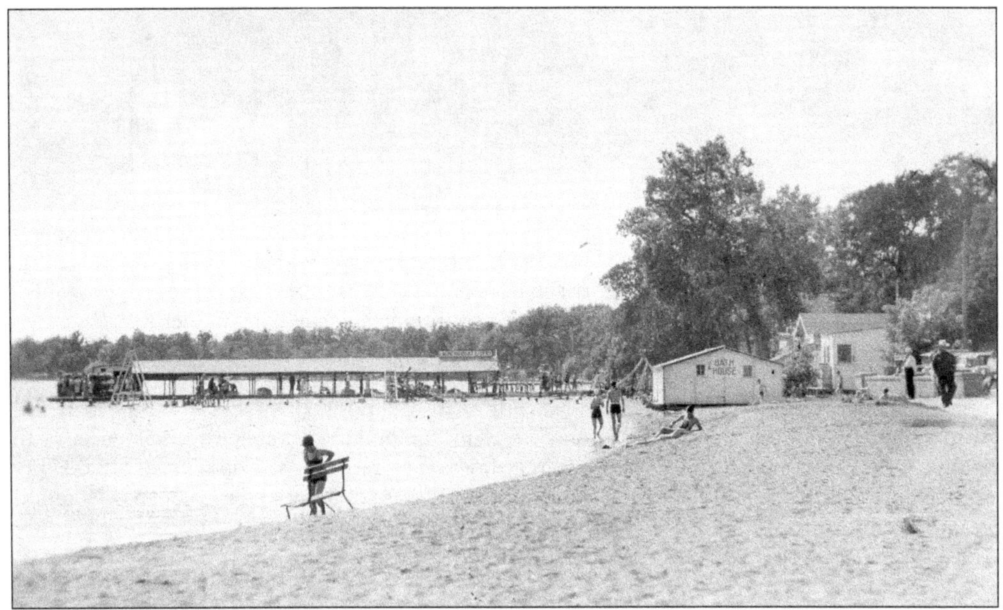

Tevogt did a great deal in helping keep the lake free of debris and weeds and generally safe for swimmers. There was something for people of all ages to do at the Big Dock, such as speedboat rides, seaplane rides, Bunyan Bike (water paddle bikes) rides, and excursion boat rides. Today, J&K Marine owns and operates the marina at the foot of Washington Avenue.

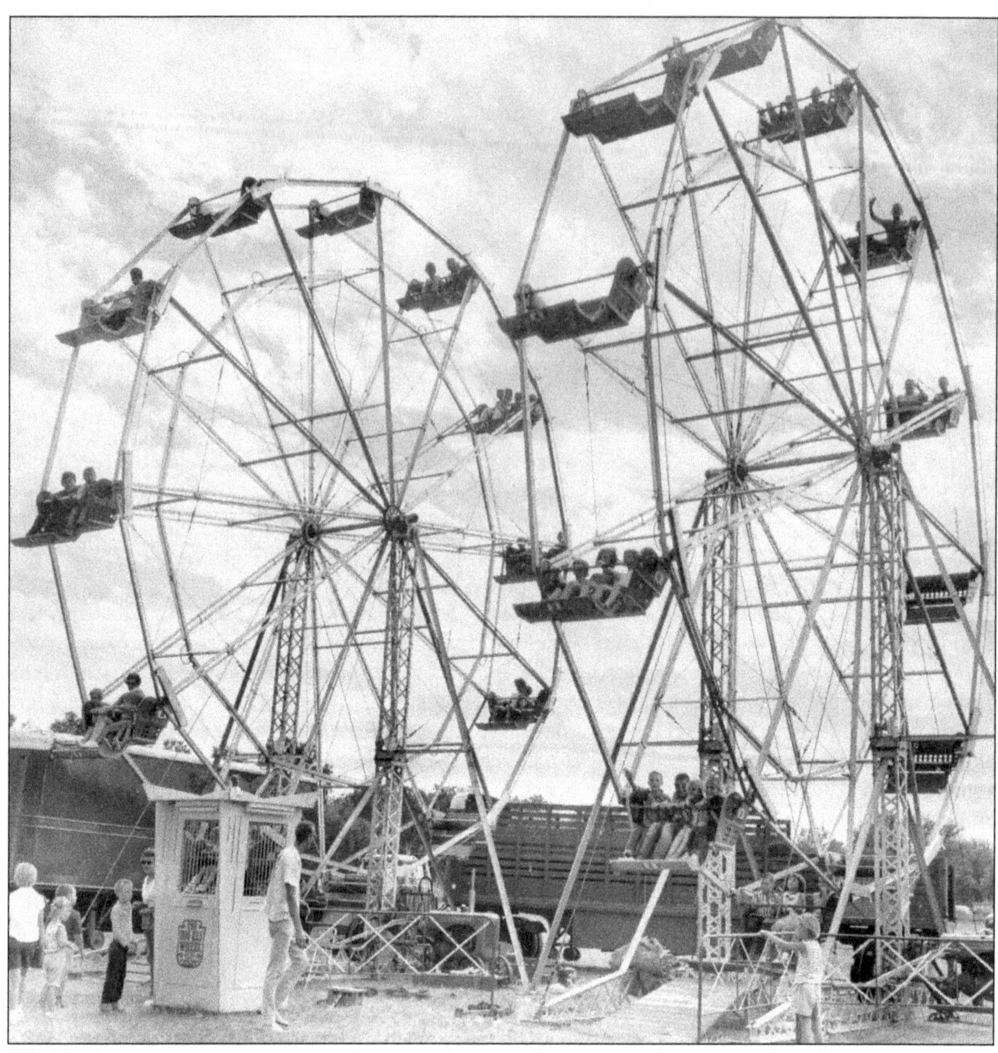

The Becker County Fair grew rapidly in the 1930s and 1940s as it became a place for entertainment and relief from the trials of life during the Depression and World War II. During the war, raffle tickets were sold for war bonds to support the boys abroad. As the 1950s and 1960s approached, the midway became a center for the youth of the county during the hot summer months when the fair dates were moved from early fall to mid-summer. A new, larger entrance and exit were added, and the fair board focused on finding new forms of entertainment for the public, including concerts and a demolition derby. In 1988, the fair nearly did not happen, because the entire fair board resigned over funding issues in March. The county commissioners called a special meeting to negotiate. By April, the fair board was back in business. The resulting fair brought in $15,000 per day and a record crowd of 50,500 people. The fair continues to this day, and includes a celebration of the county's agricultural history with a ceremony to recognize century farms each year.

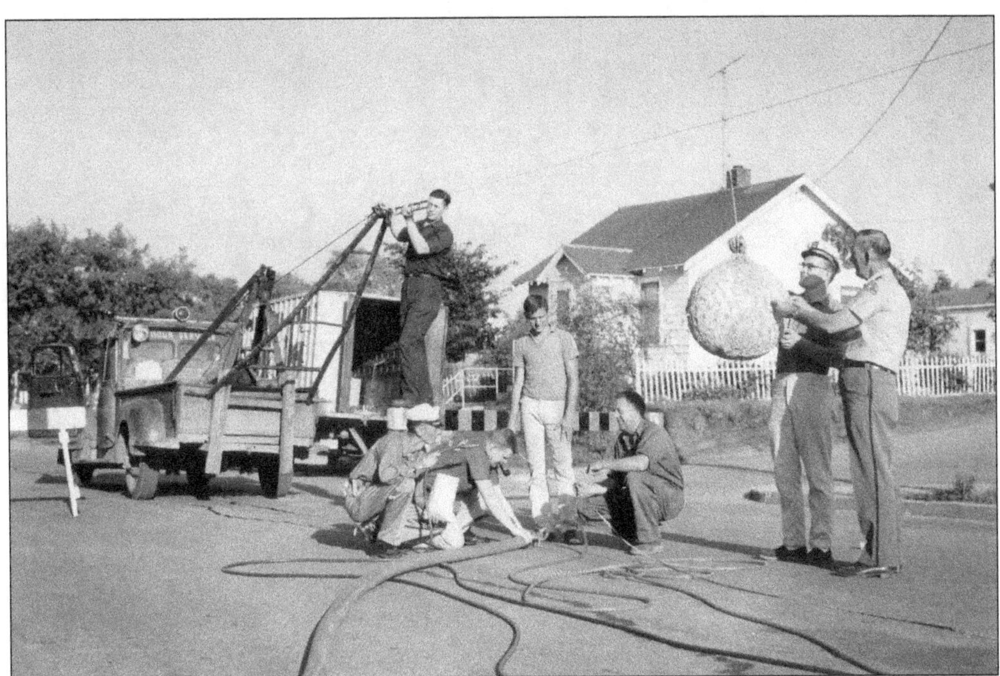

By 1971, the Jaycees had grown to 200 members and had a budget of $35,000. The Northwest Water Carnival also grew to include 10 days of activities, including water baseball, logrolling, boat races, and more. Water fights became a popular attraction, using big hoses from the fire department for the teams to compete. Pictured above from left to right are Orvald Hukee, Walley Schultz, Vernard Hanson, Buzz Tolvson, Orvil Thompson, and Pete Caron getting soaked.

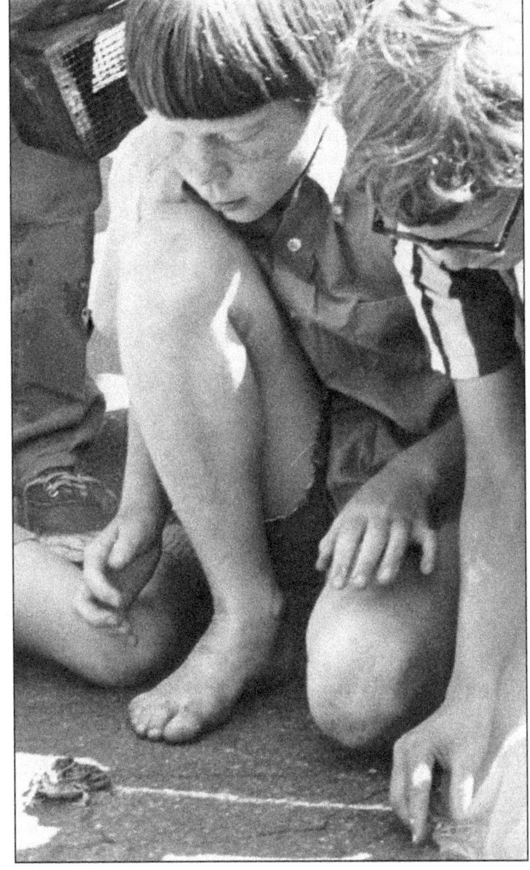

Family activities have always been a focal point of the Water Carnival. Events such as the Pet and Doll Parade, Treasure Dig, Amazing Family Race, and the Junior Miss and Mister Northwest Pageant make today's Water Carnival a family-friendly party. The Frog Races, pictured here in 1971, have evolved into the Turtle Race and Frog Jump.

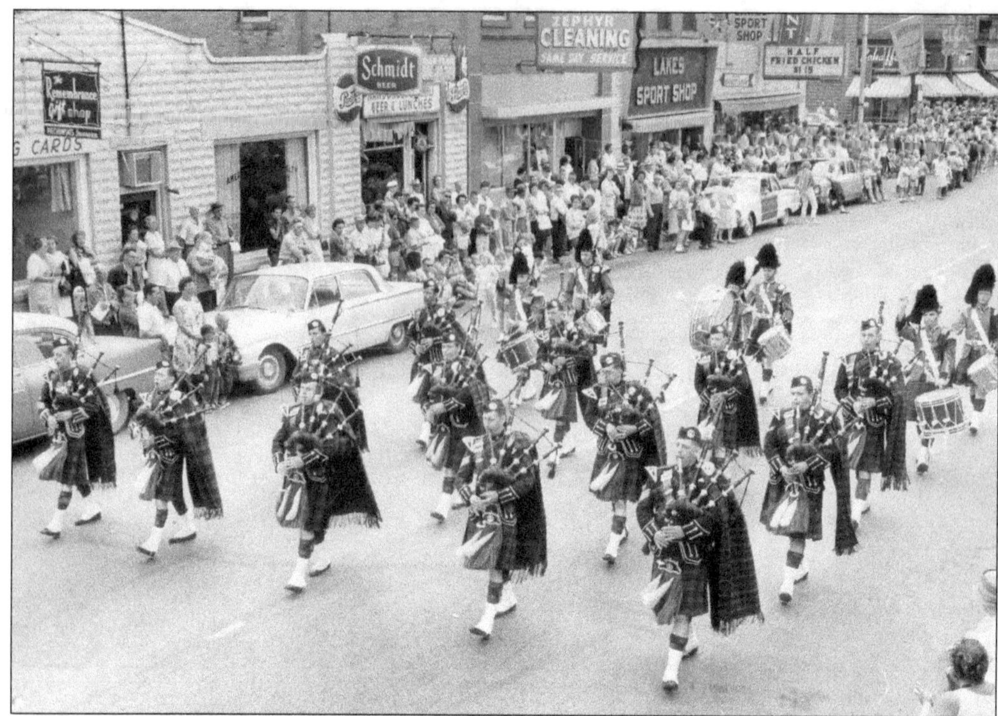

Since 1920, the Winnipeg Police Pipe Band has played around the North America, attired in Royal Stewart Tartan. Each year, they also come to Detroit Lakes to perform at the Water Carnival of the Northwest. They are a grand finish to the weekly festivities, playing at both the Bash on the Beach the final Saturday of Water Carnival, and also marching in the Parade of the Northwest.

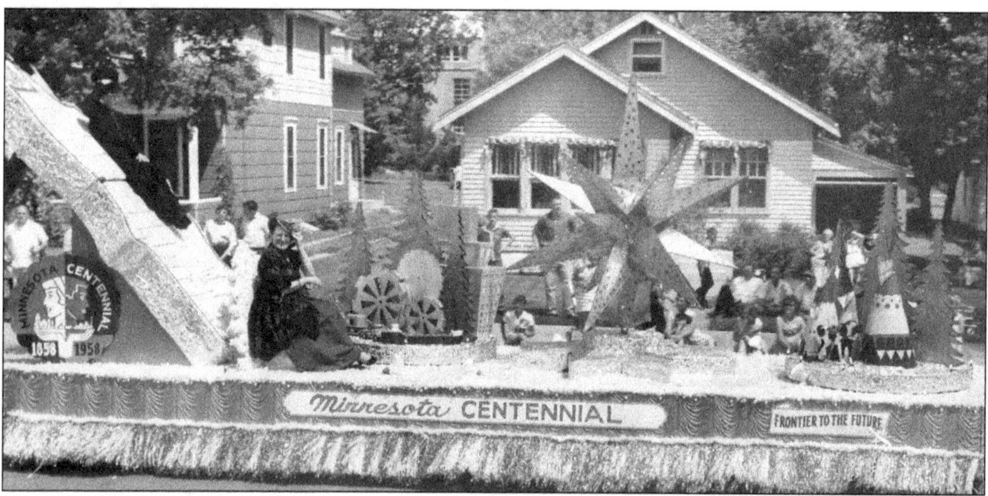

In 1958, Minnesota and Becker County both celebrated their centennial year. Floats in the Parade of the Northwest included many centennial-related entries, as seen in this photograph. Other centennial-related activities included the Centennial Train, which had 5,000 visitors in its one-day stop. There were also many community events, including a Religious Heritage Day, Young American Day, Statesman's Day, Sports Day, Ladies' Day, and a Pioneer and Homecoming Day.

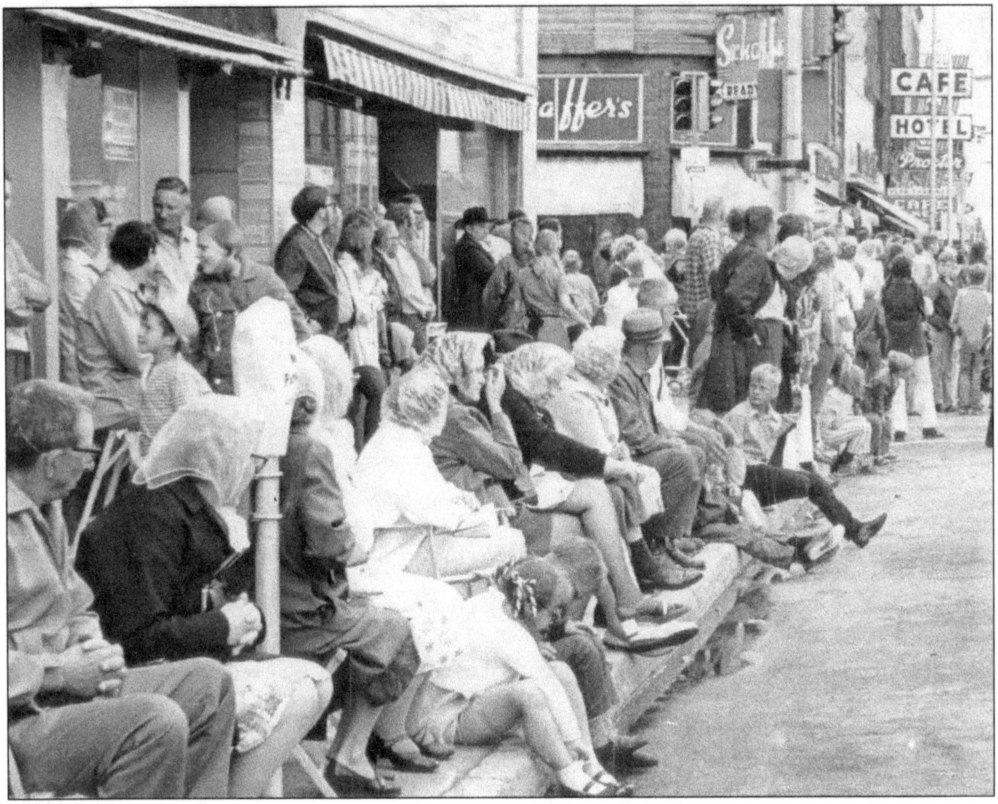

The Parade of the Northwest became a mainstay of the Northwest Water Carnival, serving as the capstone to the week's activities. In the 75th Annual Parade in 2010, More than 100 entries participated, from high school bands to congressmen to local businesses. People reserve their spots the night before along the main streets of Detroit Lakes to watch the floats pass by the following day. More than 5,000 spectators come, rain or shine, to listen to the music, gather candy, and sometimes to get a little wet. The Jaycees, who volunteer hundreds of hours to put on the event, start and end the parade in a red trolley. This trolley includes water hoses to soak the kids—and sometimes the adults—in the crowd. Members seen here, from left to right, include John Hoeglund, Jack Norby, Duane Carlson, Duane Wething, Dave Knutson, Jack Renner, Dick Johnson, two unidentified men, and Vernard Hanson. All proceeds from the Water Carnival are donated to local charities.

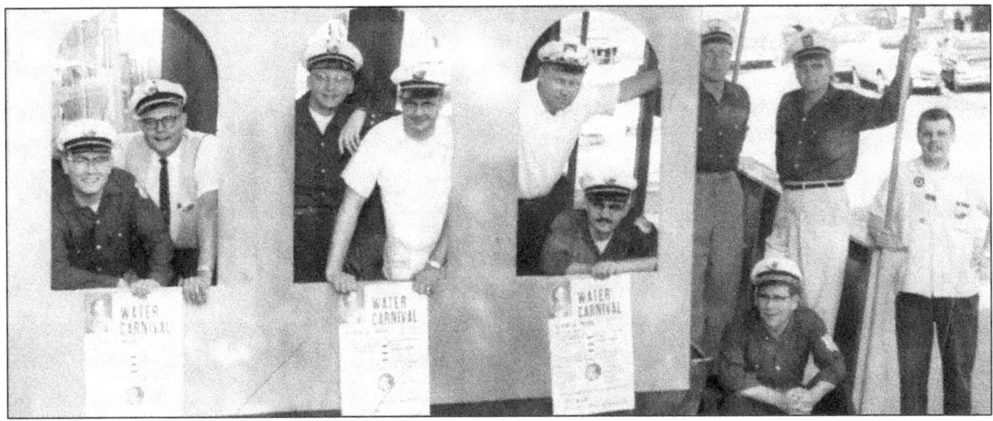

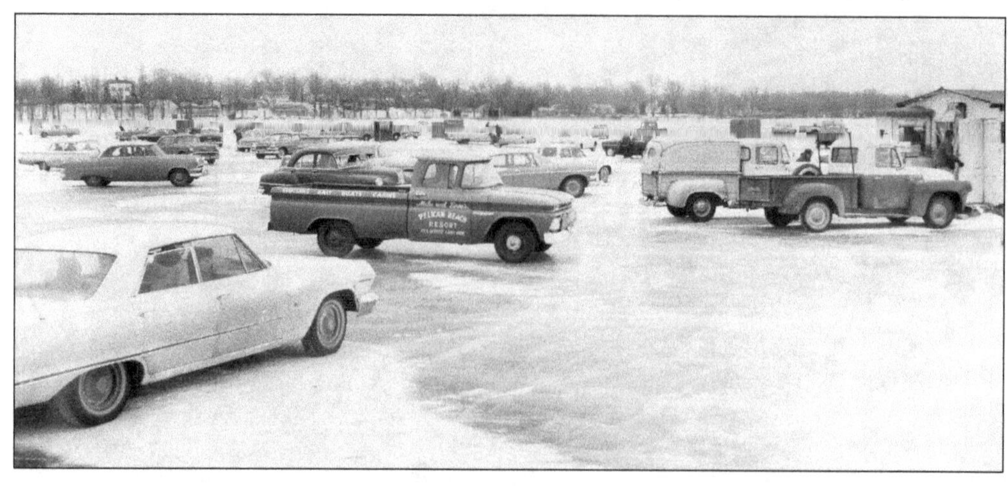

Ice fishing has always been a popular pastime in lakes country. In the early days, fishing was a way of life, providing a ready food source during the tough winter months. As time went on, the draw became more recreational and ice house "villages" grew up on each of the hundreds of lakes in Becker County. Little and Big Detroit Lake become a thriving community from late fall to early spring, and hundreds of people come to participate in the fun, as seen in these photographs from 1963. Some local community clubs have turned it into a fundraiser, hosting fishing derbies to raise money for local charities. The Knights of Columbus reported a record turnout for their 1978 derby, with 1,200 fishermen participating, 200 fish caught, and 444 cars on the ice. Today this tradition continues with the Poles and Holes fishing tournament, sponsored by the Breakfast Rotary club and held in conjunction with Polar Fest, a 10-day celebration of winter held each February.

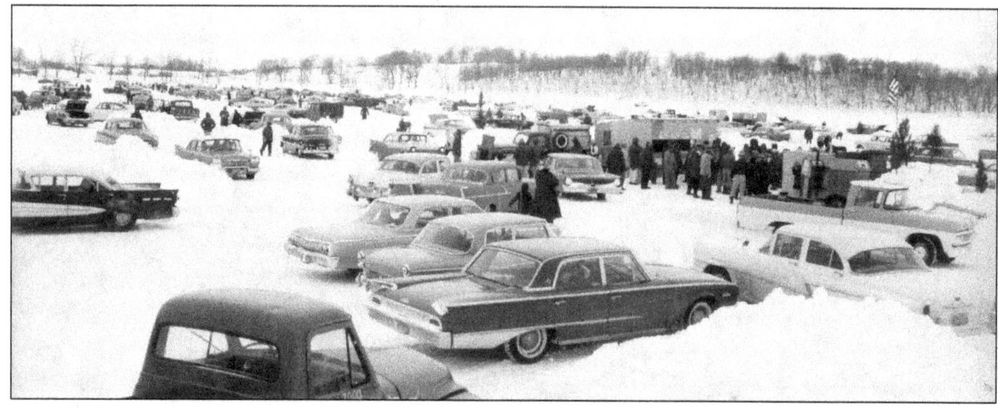

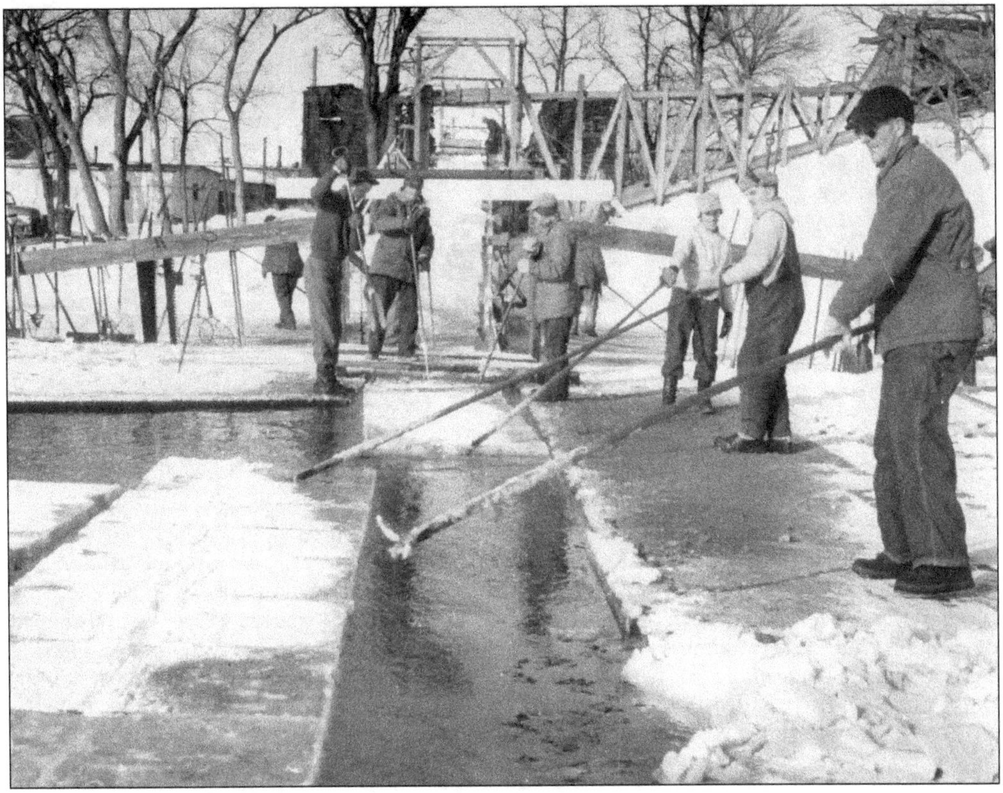

The Fargo-Detroit Ice Company operated in Detroit Lakes for nearly 80 years, from 1887 until 1970. This company supplied ice for locations as far away as Texas, Washington, and Florida. More than 200,000 tons of ice were harvested annually and stored in sawdust-lined storage buildings. In the photographs shown here, ice floes are being removed from Little Detroit Lake, and the remnants produced after the ice was cut into blocks are being pushed into the "cripple pile" to be used for crushed ice at a later time. This business employed a large number of local residents and offered delivery to homes, businesses, and resorts in the area. With electrified refrigeration, the demand for block ice lessened, and eventually the Fargo-Detroit Ice Company closed in 1970. The Holiday Inn was later built on the same piece of land and included the Ice House Bar, in remembrance of the history in that location.

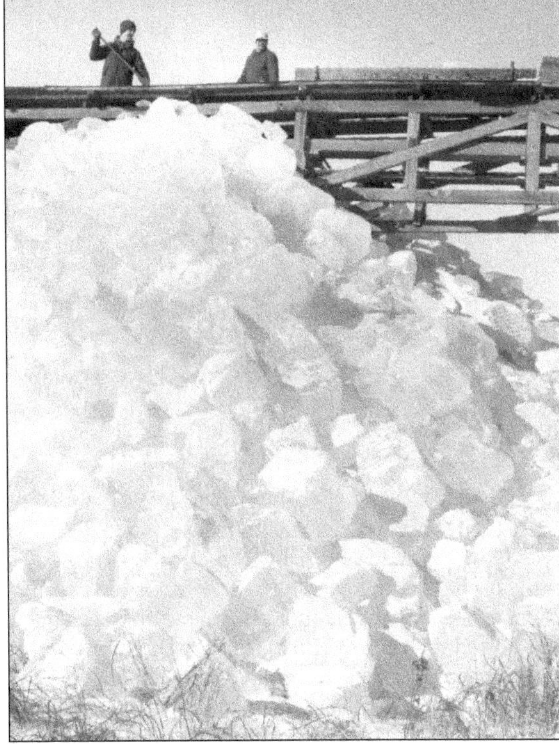

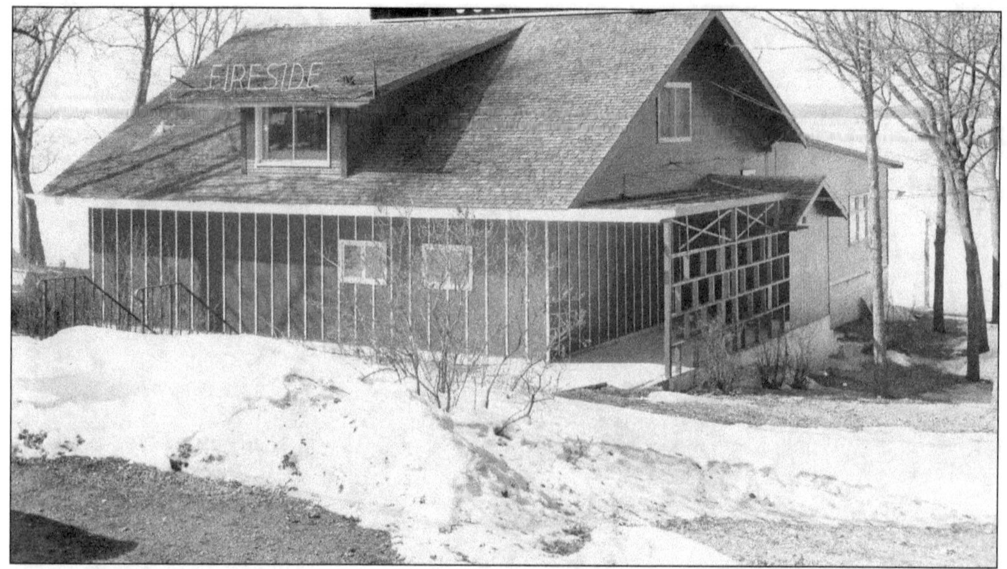

The Fireside Supper Club opened in 1951 at 1462 East Shore Drive along Big Detroit Lake. The building was a private home for a time, and between 1948 and 1951 was known as the Lu Ray and Blue Moon Club. The restaurant is uniquely situated only 10 feet from the water's edge. Fireside has had many owners, including Wilfred and Fern Emard, Clinton Stacy, Gene and Alys Graff, Don Osterberg, Larry Mills, and Jerry Danner.

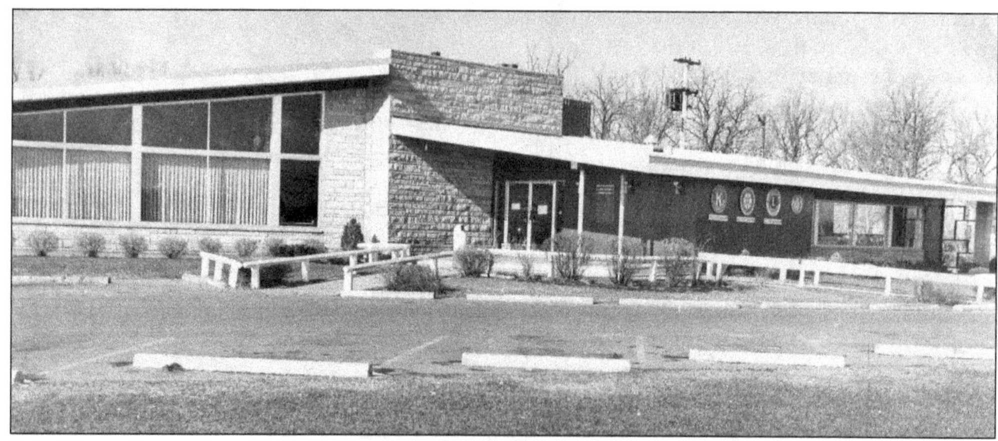

Erie 34 was located on Highway 34 just outside of Detroit Lakes. It started as a supper club and lounge, which burned down in the 1950s and was later replaced by the Broken Wheel Restaurant. Owned by Clayton Blacknik, the follow-up to Erie 34, Erie Jr., opened in 1960 on Highway 10 East and hosted such community groups as the Lions and Kiwanis. In May of 1979, the restaurant was sold by current owners Kenneth and Delia Seaburg to a group of business investors from Bismark and Mandan, North Dakota. It was renamed Rafferty's café in 1981, but closed only nine months later due to poor economic conditions in Detroit Lakes.

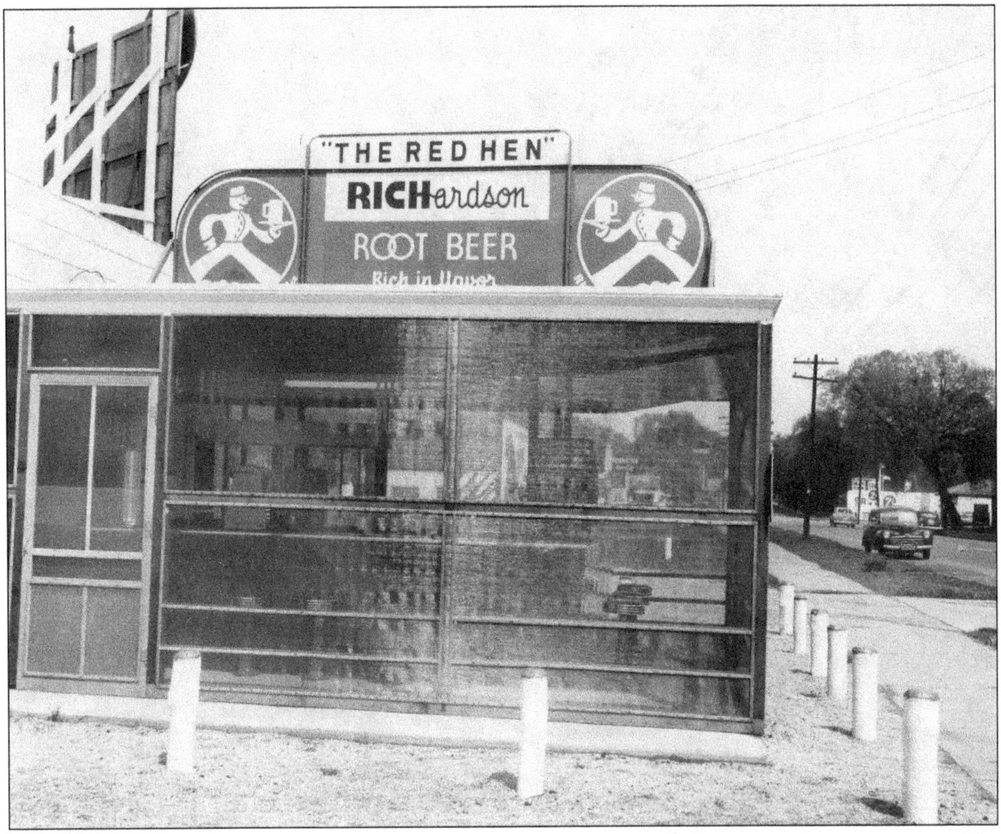

The south end of Washington Avenue quickly became the youth hangout in the 1960s. The public beach, drive-ins, ballpark, and city park were located in this block. A row of businesses, including Washington Grocery, Walther's Outboard Services, Rite Food Market, Dairy Queen, and the A&W Root Beer Drive-In catered to the summer crowd. The Red Hen, pictured above in 1964, was located at 1218 Washington Avenue. Owned and operated by Ken Utecht, this business was a perfect combination of drive-in appeal with a dining area in the back for larger dinner parties. The Sandwich Hut, seen below, was located at 1214 Washington Avenue and was the epitome of a 1960s drive-in, with convenient car-side service.

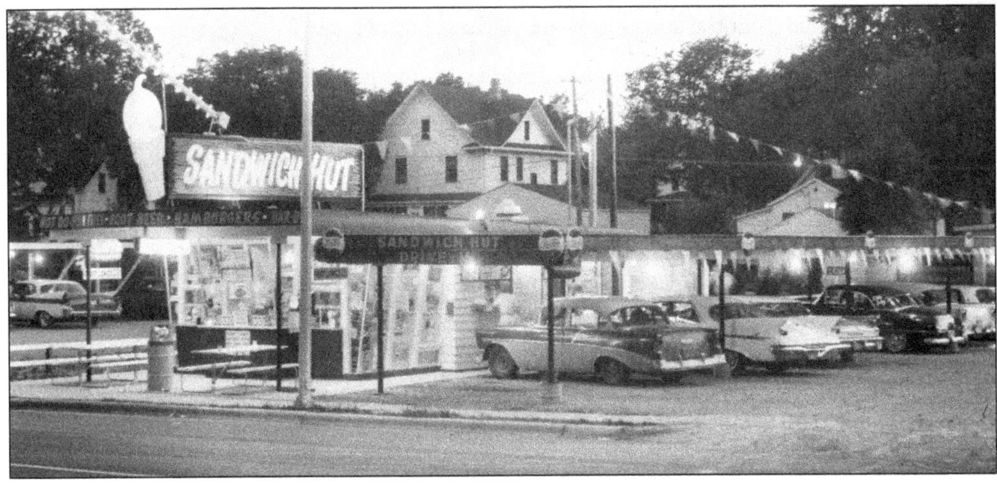

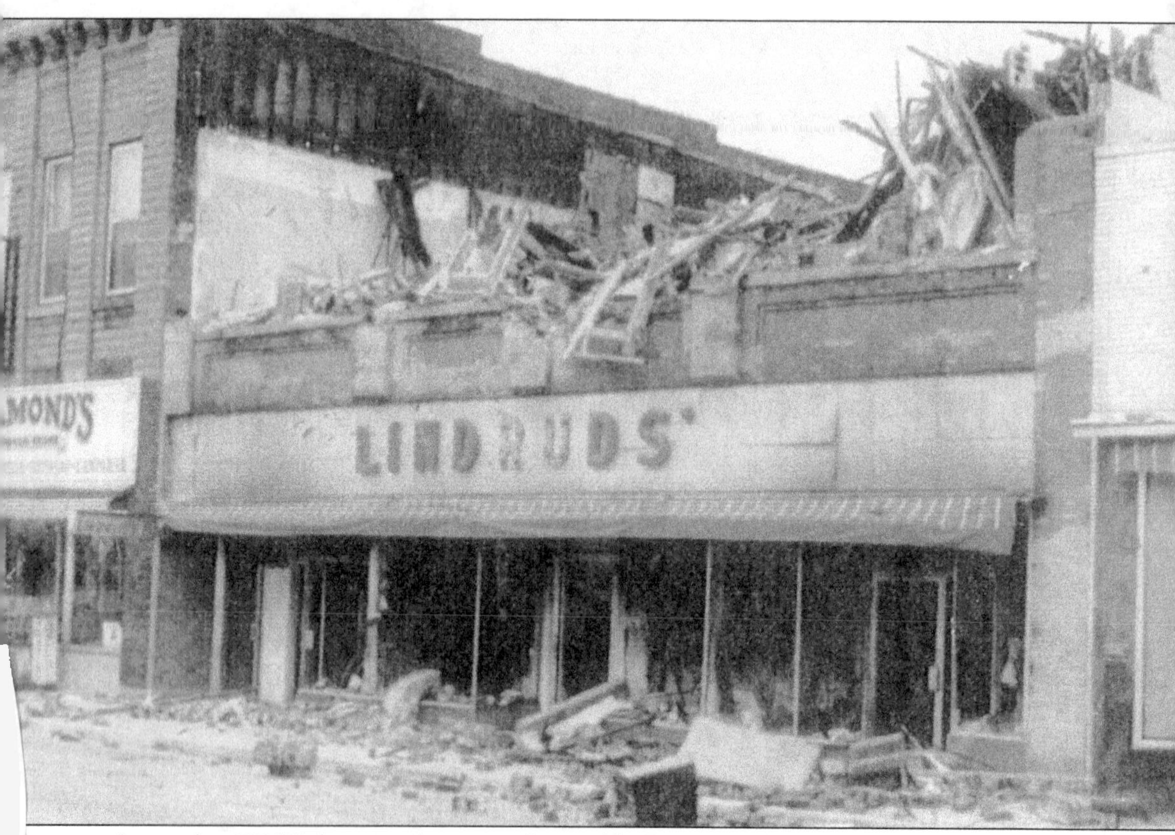

Located at 828 Washington Avenue and owned by Bernie Lindrud, Lindruds' Variety Store was a staple of downtown Detroit Lakes for many years. On June 14, 1984, the store was destroyed in a fire that was called, at the time, the largest fire in the history of the city. Arson and burglary were later tied to the fire, which began in the basement of Lindruds'. Fire departments from Detroit Lakes, Lake Park, Perham, Carsonville, Audubon, and Frazee answered the call at 5:13 in the morning, and the blaze was said to be under control by 7:45. Four firefighters were injured, including Mike LeDoux and Mark Hagen of Detroit Lakes, Bob McTaggart of Frazee, and Clarence Anderson of Audubon. Lindruds' was a complete loss, as were many other businesses, including the Eagles Club, Irvine Law Office, Diamond's, Lady's Unique, and Woolworth's. There were also six people evacuated from the apartments above these businesses.

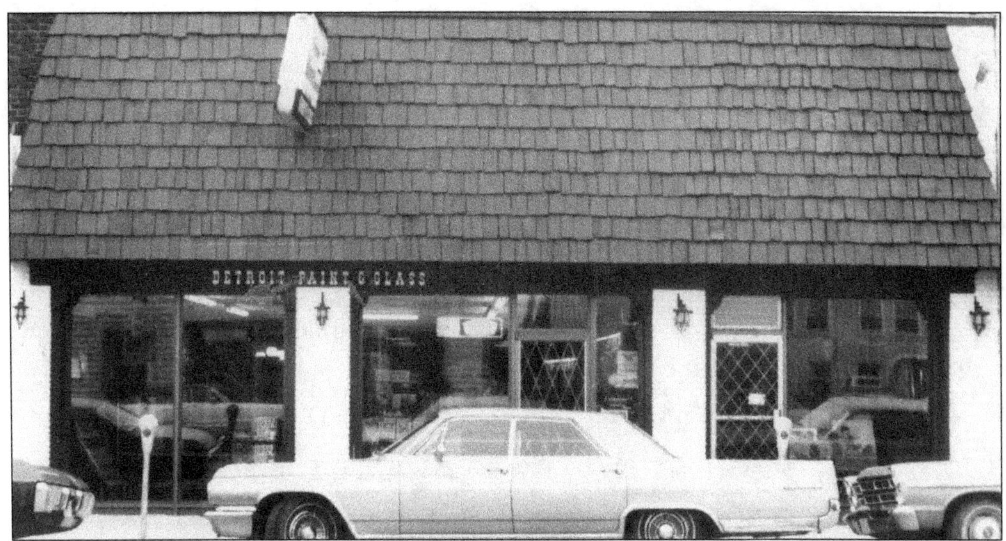

In the 1950s, Wes Johnson opened a new business at 915 Washington Avenue called Detroit Paint and Glass. An "all-in-one" home shop, Detroit Paint and Glass featured Benjamin Moore Paint, picture windows, window glass, custom-made desktops, tabletops, mirrors, and a complete floor-covering department. In the late 1960s, Steve Bakken purchased the store and hired a young widow named Phyllis Acklen. Phyllis became the interior designer for Detroit Paint and Glass and later married Bakken. The Bakkens expanded the business to include more complete design services and tripled their wallpaper selection, floor coverings, and accessories. They employed five full-time employees including two glass specialists, a paint specialist, a bookkeeper, and one person to help customers. In 1987, Matt and Chris Brenk purchased the business.

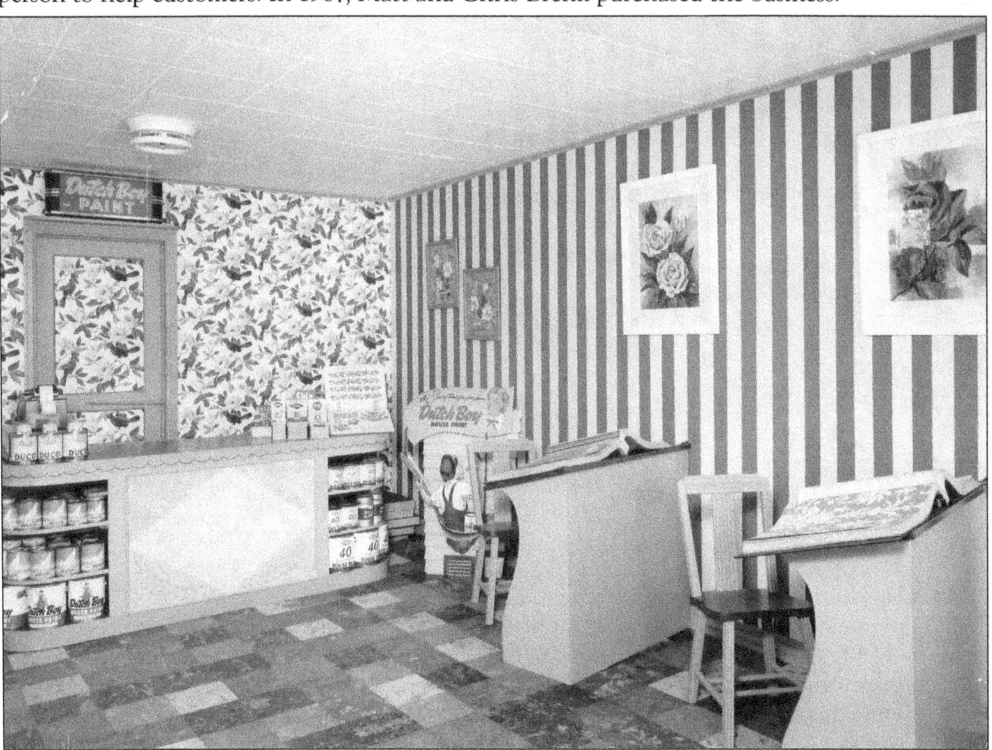

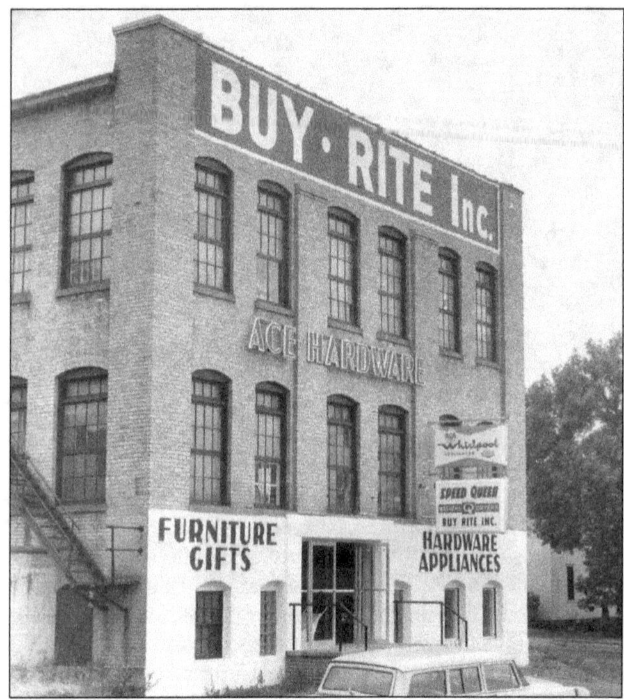

Buy-Rite, Inc., was established as a new Detroit Lakes business firm in January 1962. This company began business in the former Boggs Manufacturing Company building at 518 Summit Avenue (occupied previously by the Swift Company's egg department). The new firm handled furniture, jewelry, appliances, floor coverings, and sporting goods. In 1964, Leo Eilertson and R. Knutson were listed as the owners of the facility.

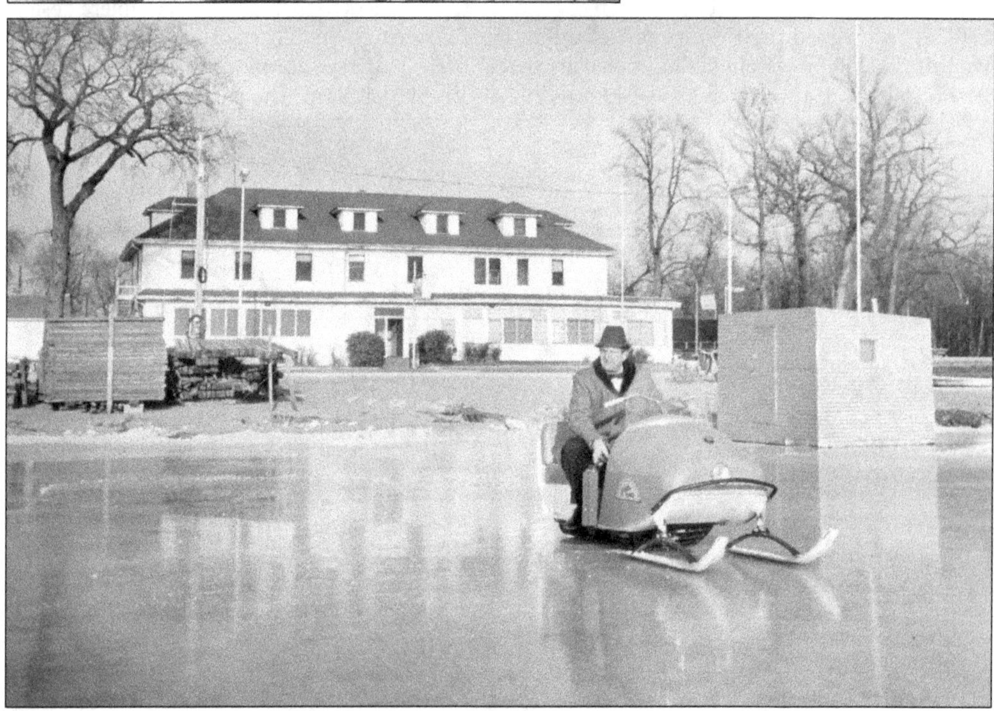

The Park Hotel was located on the shores of Detroit Lake, which was said to be "one of the most beautiful of the 412 lakes within a radius of 25 miles of the city." The hotel advertised rooms equipped with "hot and cold running water with convenient bathrooms on all floors," and the dining room was said to be "large and commodious." In 1961, the building was sold to Elks Lodge No. 2261. In this 1971 photograph, Willard Stienke is seated on the snowmobile.

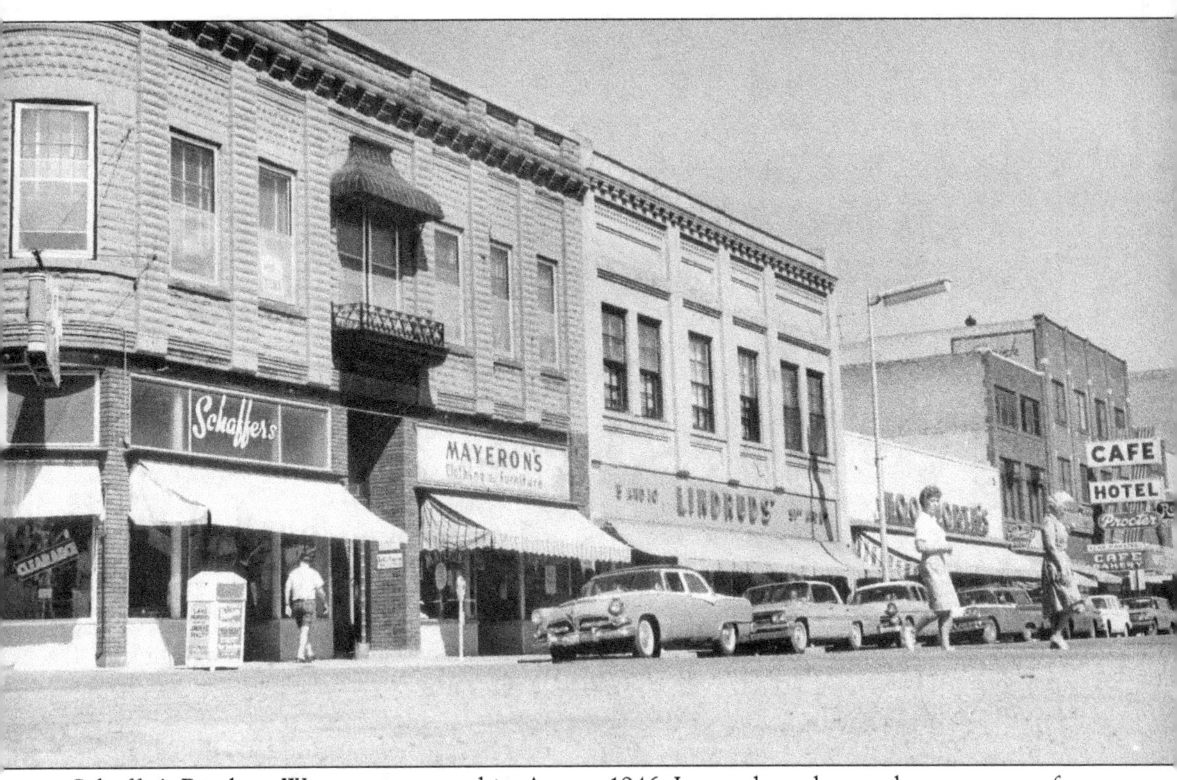

Schaffer's Ready-to-Wear store opened in August 1946. Located on the northwest corner of Washington Avenue and Holmes Street in the building formerly occupied by Carlisle Hardware, the store gifted a rose to each female visitor attending its grand opening. The store offered ready-to-wear clothing for women and girls and was managed by Frank H. and Lewis D. Schaffer. Featuring "fluorescent lighting throughout, contrasting shades of soft pastels, orchid and pale blue," Schaffer's was marketed as a "place where you can feel at home and a place where you will be welcome always." Also seen here is Mayeron's Clothing, which was owned and operated by Mr. and Mrs. Art Mayeron, who purchased the building at 832 Washington Avenue in 1959. In February 1974, Jerry Muench and his family purchased the building. Muench owned and operated Muench's Family Resort and was one of the organizers of the Northwestern Minnesota Resort Association. He is said to have come up with the idea to name Detroit Lakes the "Sunfish Capital of the World."

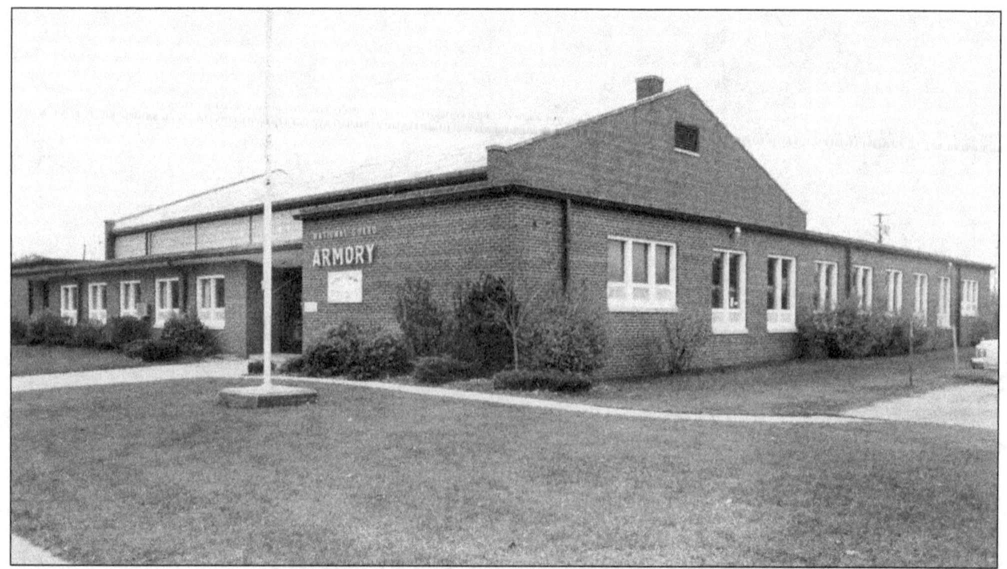

An armory is defined as any building legally owned by a state for military administration, training, supply, or storage of one or more units of the armed forces of the state. The Detroit Lakes Armory was completed in March 1955. Home to the 47th Infantry Division, 136th Infantry Regiment of the National Guard, the armory was constructed on Rossman Avenue, just north of the Becker County Fairgrounds.

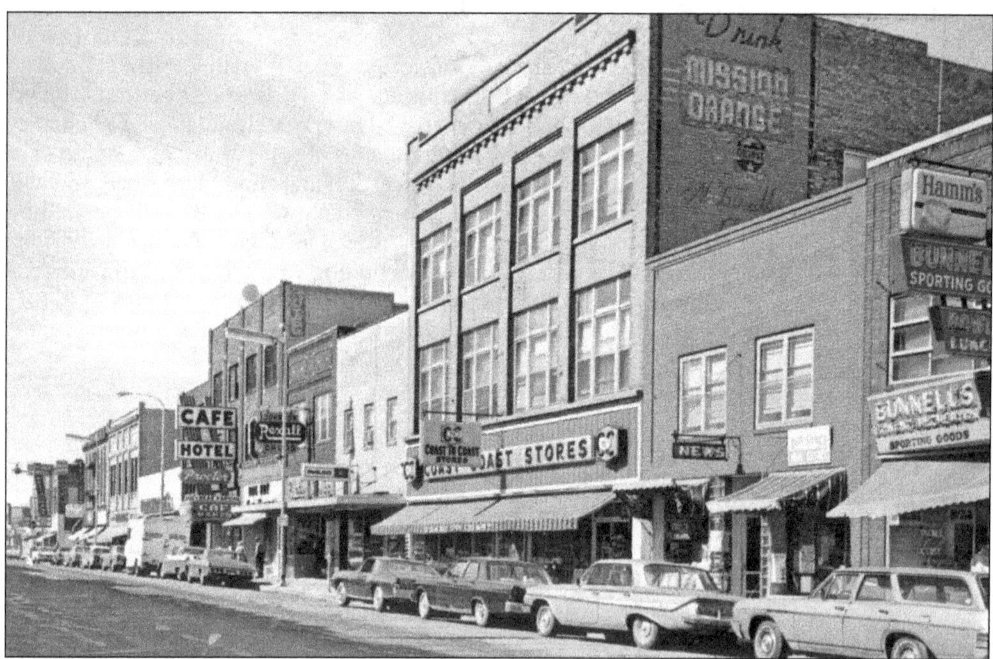

In 1910, L.M. "Mert" Bunnell opened a pool hall on the east side of Washington Avenue in a rickety wooden building. By 1935, Bunnell's Recreation settled in its permanent location at 804 Washington Avenue. It was at Bunnell's where bowling was first introduced to Detroit Lakes in the 1920s. Bunnell's was set to close in April 1970 but was maintained until November 1980, when a kitchen fire consumed the building.

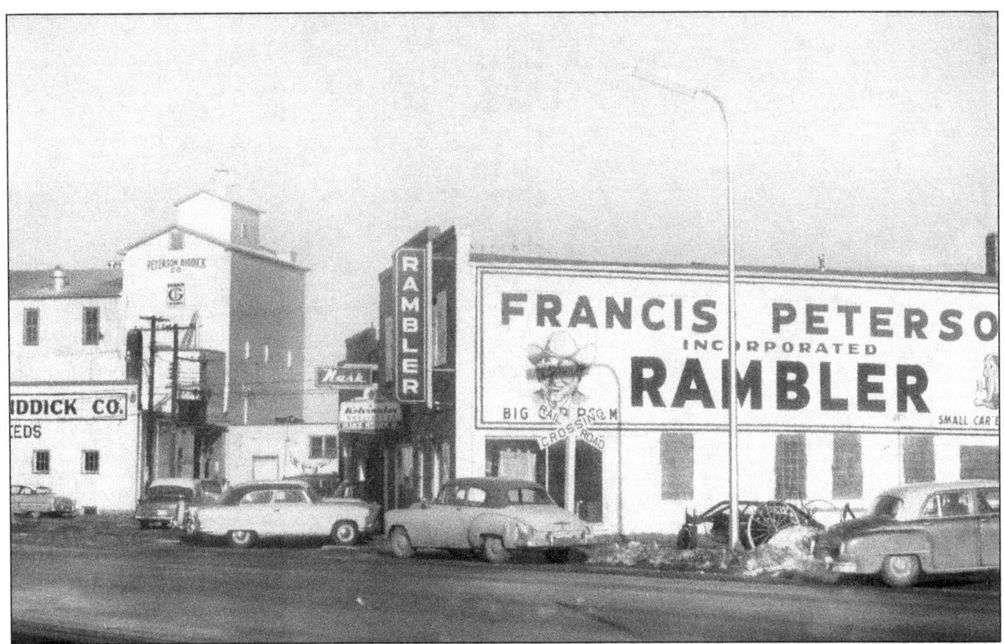

The Francis Peterson Rambler Dealership (above) was located at 819 Lincoln Avenue. They advertised the "smartest cars for town and travel," including the Rambler, Ambassador, and Metropolitan. Owned and operated by Alton Peterson, they remained in business until 1962. Morse Motors (below) was located at 714 Lake Avenue and erected by Charles E. Morse in 1917. In 1926, it was taken over by S.C. "Duke" Halvorson, who changed its name to the Detroit Lakes Motor Company. Beginning in 1931, the business was originally at two different locations on Washington Avenue before purchasing the former Morse Motors building in 1945, renaming it Kandt Motors. Milford Kandt owned the business for 42 years, starting as a part-time salesman in 1934 and working for his father. They began as a Chrysler-Plymouth dealership, but when they moved to Lake Avenue, they became associated with General Motors and began to sell Pontiacs.

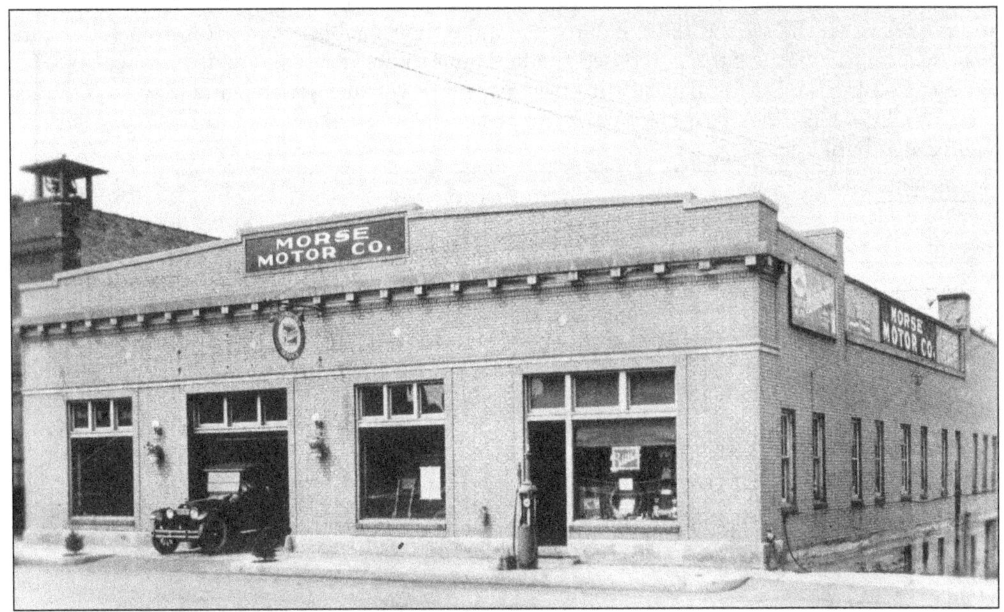

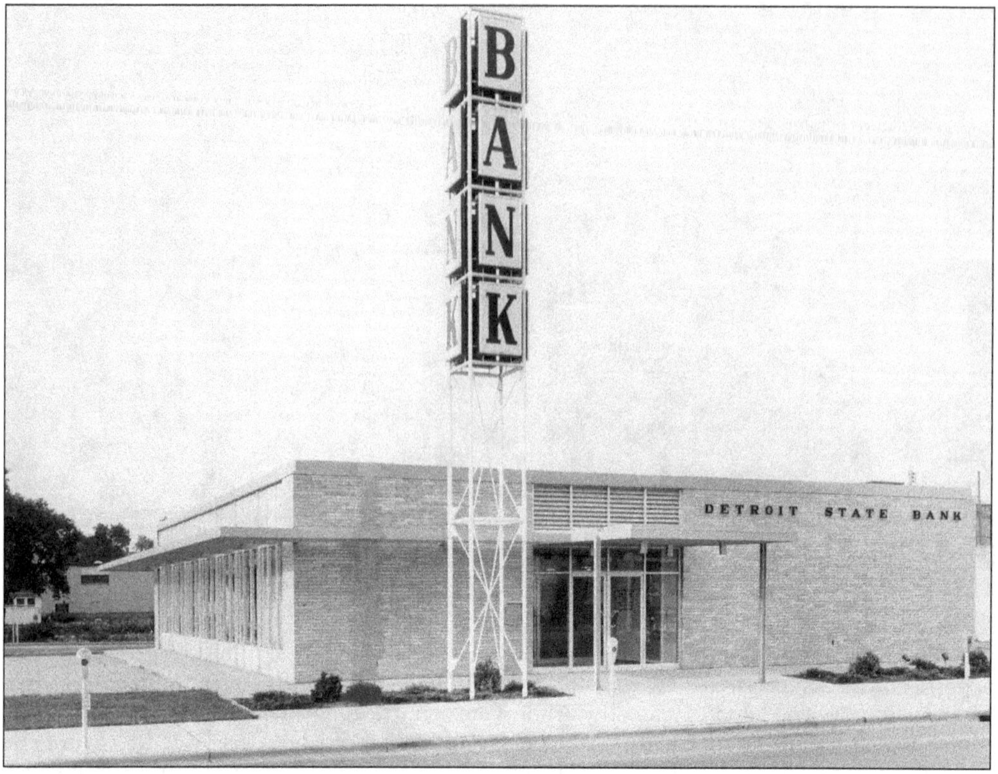

Many of the financial institutions in the Detroit Lakes area had a long history, serving the community for over 50 years. Detroit State Bank opened in 1919 on the corner of Washington and Pioneer Street, with an initial deposit of $62,040.53. During the Great Depression, it was at one time the only financial institution open for withdrawals. By 1960, the bank had constructed a new building at 115 Holmes Street, pictured above. The First National Bank remodeled their building at 717 Washington Avenue in 1961 with new exterior facing, brick on the first floor, and porcelain on the second floor. Floor space more than doubled from 2,200 to 5,400 square feet. In spring 1966, the bank purchased the buildings to the north and added a drive-up teller window, causing the Detroit Lakes Police Department, Ray Hale's Jewelry, and Mattson's Barber Shop to relocate. In 1994, First National Bank became Norwest Bank, and in 2000 they became Wells Fargo Bank.

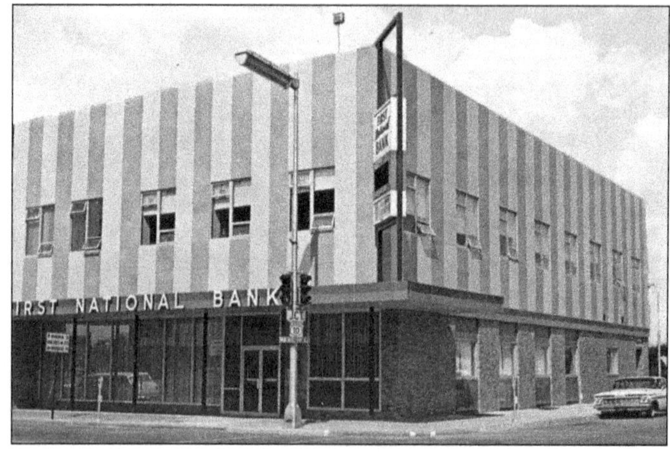

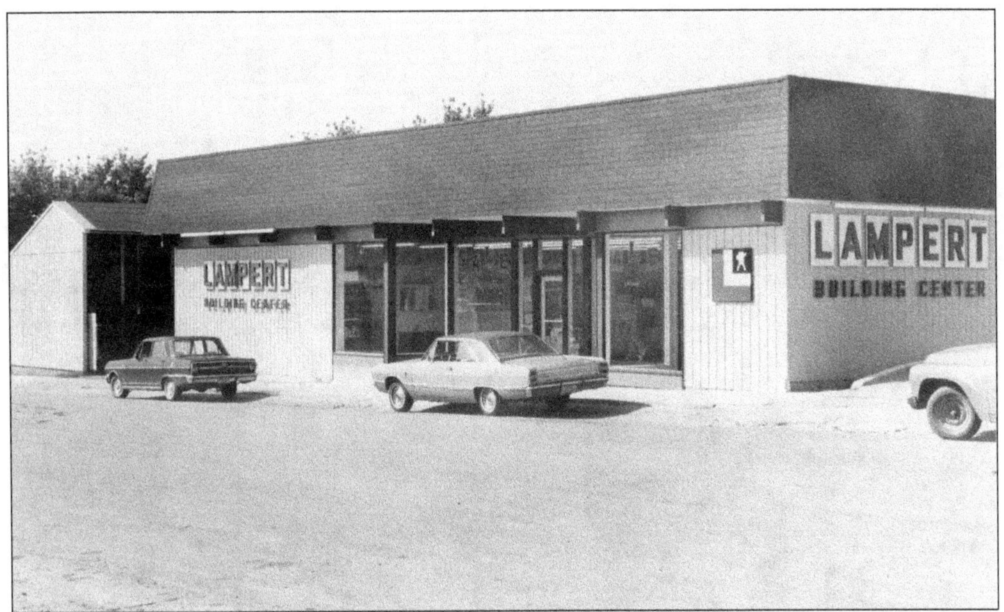

Lampert Building Center was located north of the Northern Pacific tracks at 114 Grant Street, now Mark's Electric. It was known as the Hanson-Hage Lumber Yard until 1943, when it was purchased by the Lampert's chain. The Lampert Lumber Company began when two brothers started a retail lumberyard at Wadena in the 1880s. In 1968, the building in Detroit Lakes was completely remodeled to include 2,500 square feet of sales rooms and offices. At this time, there were more than 60 branches of Lampert's in Minnesota, North Dakota, South Dakota, and Nebraska.

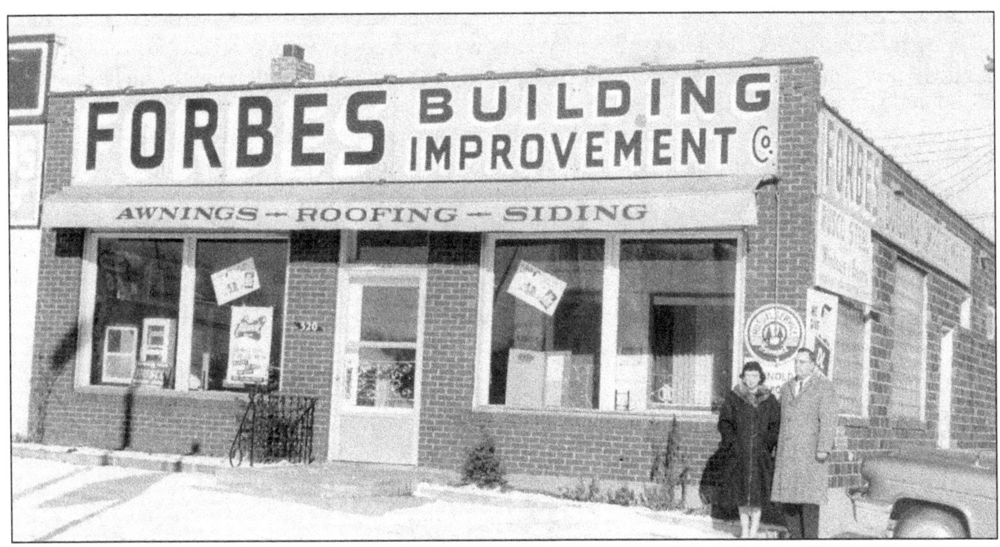

Forbes Building Improvements was owned by Sheldon and Dorothy Forbes and moved numerous times over its tenure in Detroit Lakes. In 1957, Forbes was located at 620 Davis Avenue, and by 1960 the business had moved to 320 Frazee Street. They moved again in 1973 to 714 Randolph Road, which was the last location for Forbes.

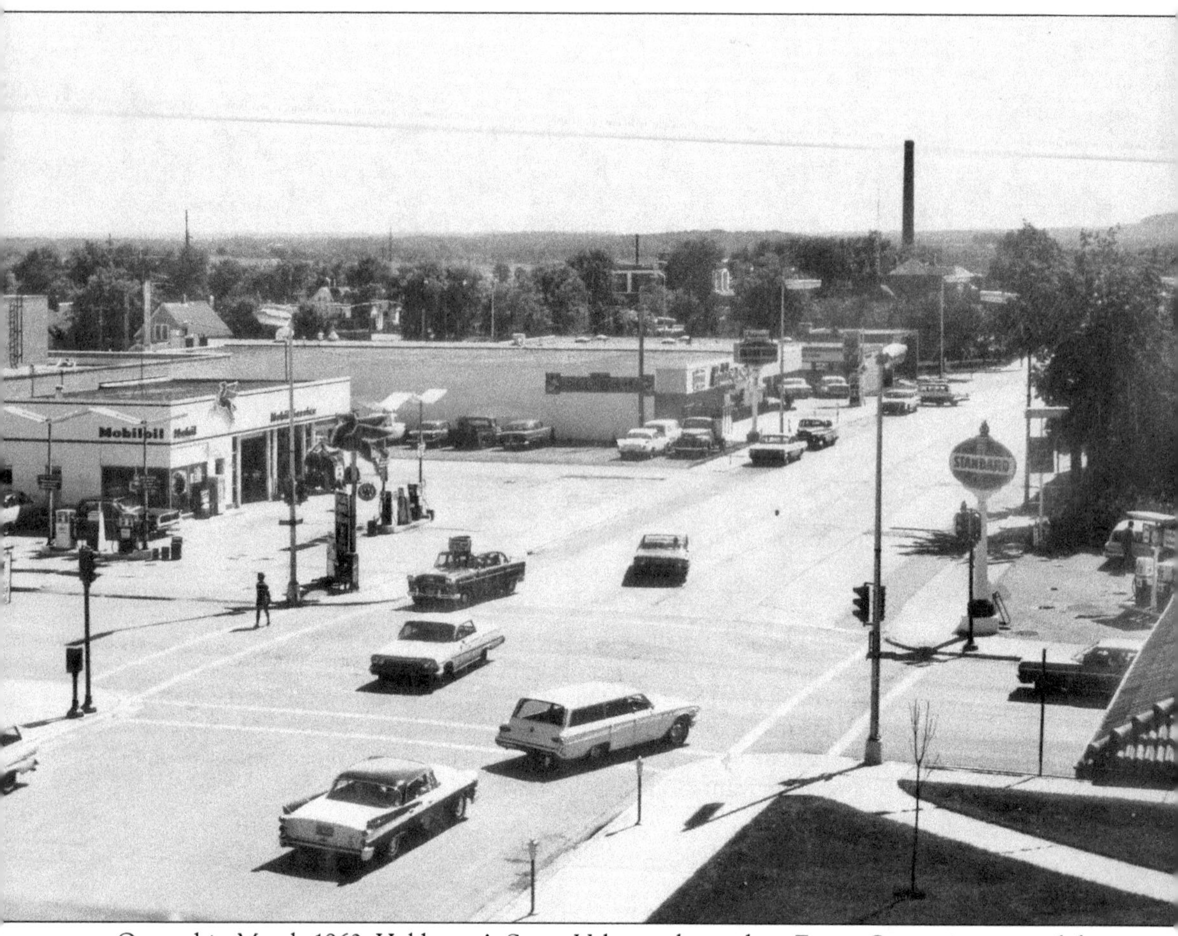

Opened in March 1960, Haldorson's Super Valu was located on Frazee Street, just east of the public library. Seen here in 1968 from the belfry of the Baptist Church, along with the Fingalson's Mobil and the Standard station, the store employed 15 people. Said to contain all the "modern facilities" available, Haldorson's featured in-store music, automatic checkouts, a complete housewares department, air-conditioning, a reach-in dairy case that "eliminated bending and squinting," refrigerated fruit and vegetable cases, and a large self-service meat department. James (Jim) Haldorson was the owner and had been in the meat and grocery business in Detroit Lakes since 1938, with the exception of three years when he served with the US Navy during World War II. The Super Valu retail chain had over 600 locations in 1960, serving over a million customers in eight Midwest states.

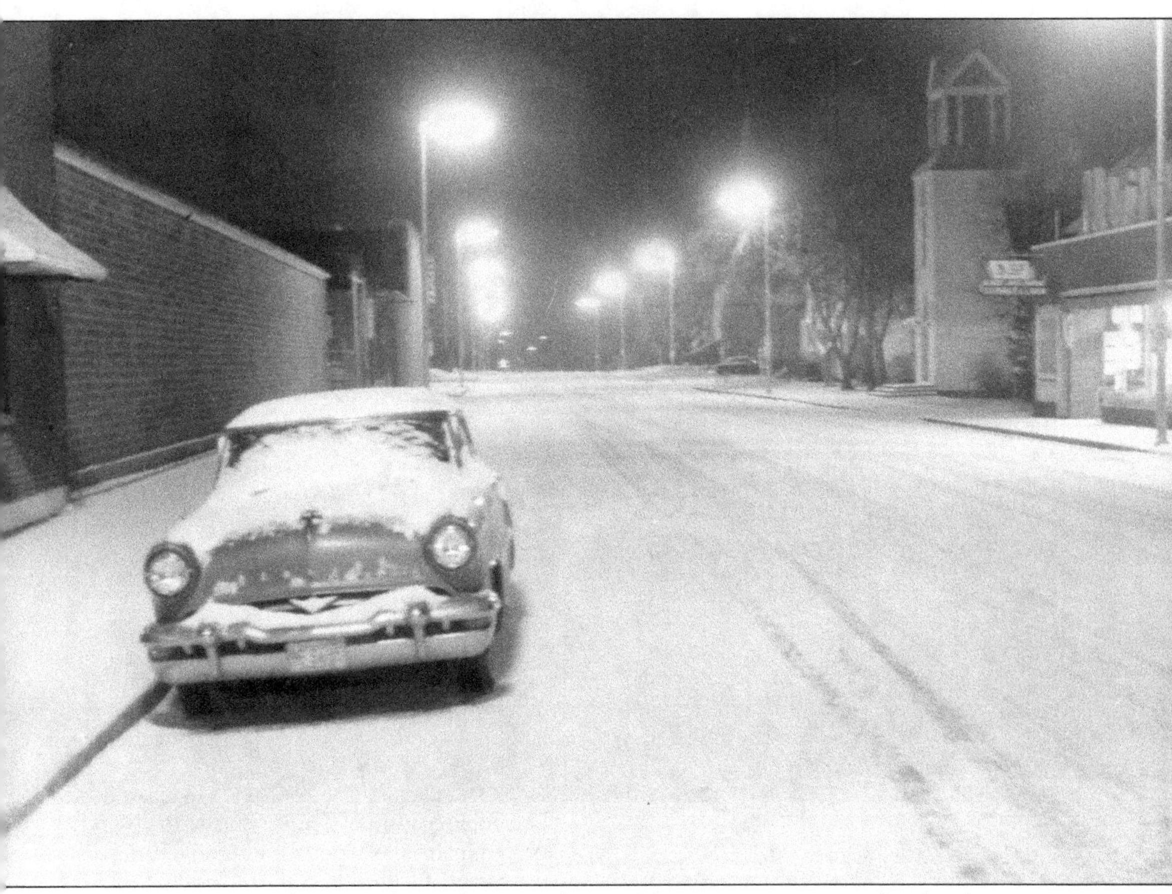

From Saturday, March 17 until Monday, March 19, 1951, a winter storm said to be the worst since the blizzard of 1941 came through Detroit Lakes. More than 500 travelers were stranded in town when 14 inches of snow fell over three days. Hundreds of these folks were on the road returning from the Minnesota State High School Basketball Tournament, including the teams from Felton, Ada, Bismark, Mahnomen, Warren, Fisher, and Oslo. People opened their homes to these stranded motorists after a call was sent out on WDAY from the Graystone Hotel, which was overtaken by requests for sleeping space. Winds up to 35 miles per hour, and temperatures ranging from one degree below zero to nearly 30 below, created havoc on the roads. The highways did not reopen until Tuesday, and the total snow for the winter of 1950 and 1951 was 87 inches, a new record for the Detroit Lakes area.

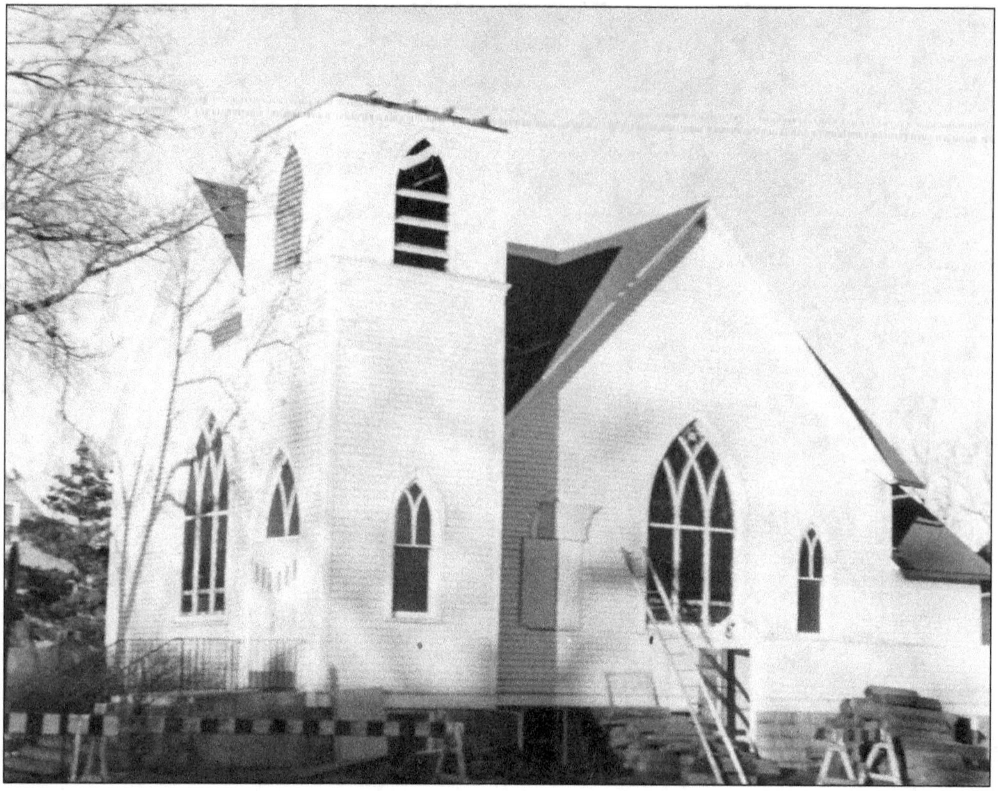

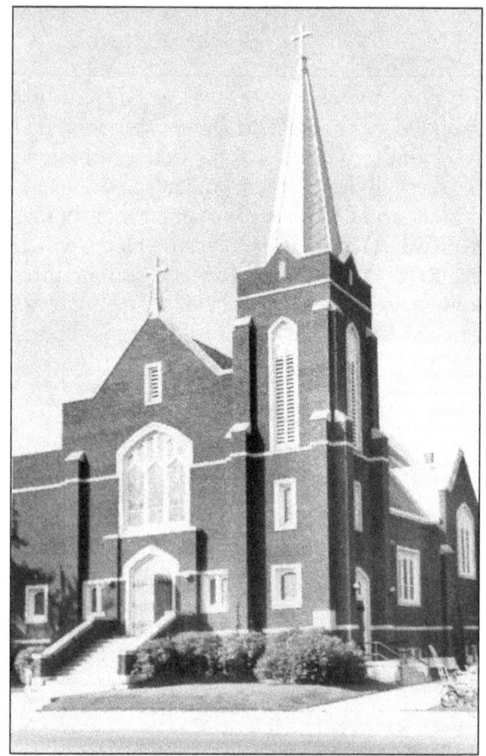

The congregation of Trinity Lutheran Church formed in 1871 as Upsala Lutheran Church, just north of Detroit. By 1897, Upsala, Lund Lutheran, and Swedlanda (Augustana) were sharing ministers. In that year, a centrally located unified parish in Detroit Lakes called Trinity Lutheran formed with members from each of the original congregations. Originally located at the corner of Washington Avenue and Grant Street in a building vacated by the Baptist congregation, Trinity moved in 1961 to its present location at 1401 Madison Avenue.

First Lutheran Church was formed by the merging of three churches in 1917 and became known as the Norwegian Lutheran Church of Detroit. In 1927, the name was changed to First Lutheran Church. In 1961, with the merger of three synods, it became part of the American Lutheran Church. The property at 912 Lake Avenue was purchased as a site for the new church in February 1921. In 1923, the new building was dedicated to seat 500 people. The Parish Education Building was added in 1954, and an extensive remodeling project improved the space in 1978.

Holy Rosary Catholic Church underwent a renovation in 1966, with ground breaking at the new site on August 15. Portions of the old structure, pictured on the right, were reused as a community hall for the Holy Rosary parish. In April 1967, the altar site and cornerstone of the new building were blessed, and in December of the same year, Bishop Lawrence Glenn of Crookston came to bless the three bells to be used in the church, including the original bell from the old tower. The bells, named Ana (dedicated in 1903 in memory of Anna Smith), Joseph, and Mary (donated by Nick and Myrtle Kappel in memory of Mary Coyle) were used to call people to worship. The new building had a capacity of 1,000 parishioners and a reconfigured main entrance to the church from Washington Avenue to Lake Avenue. The blessing and dedication were held May 19, 1968.

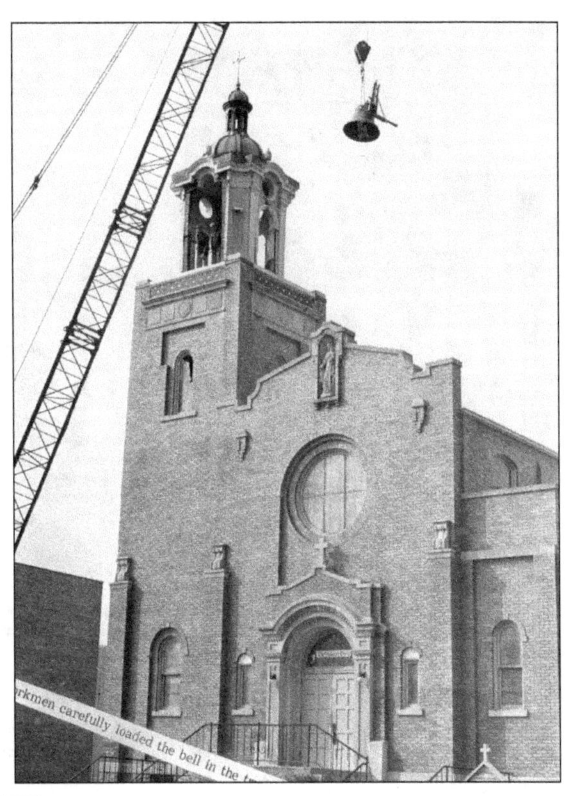

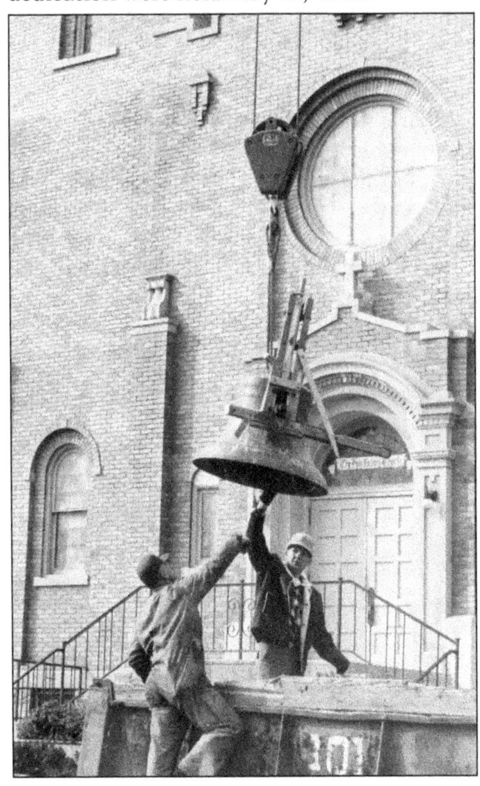

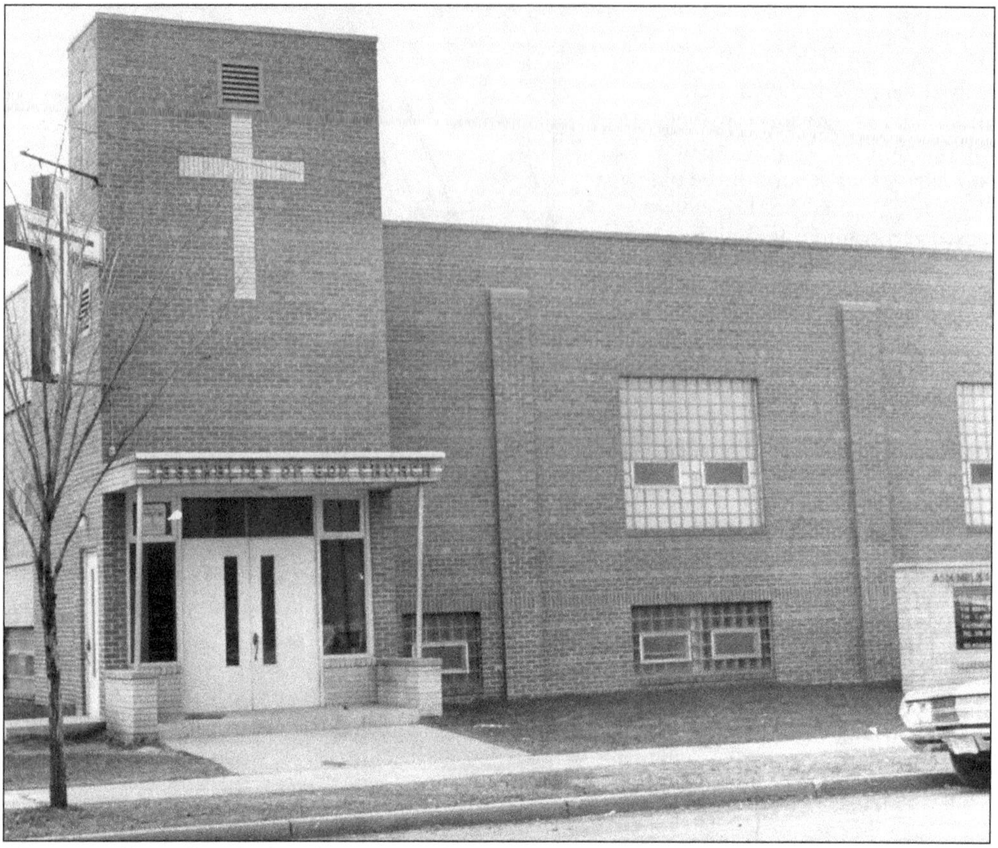

The Assemblies of God Church was started as a series of cottage prayer meetings in 1918. These home-based gatherings were moved to a permanent building in 1928 on north Rossman Avenue, now the Mount Olive Lutheran Church. In 1948, the congregation outgrew their building and purchased the lot at the corner of Summit Avenue and Front Street, with the cornerstone for the new structure being laid on November 25, 1948. On December 12, 1956, a furnace explosion in minus-five-degree weather caused the total loss of the building and contents of the Assemblies of God Church. Church services were temporarily held in the Lincoln School basement and later in the Nazarene Church basement while construction of a new church was underway. A larger building was erected on the same site and the cornerstone was laid in 1958.

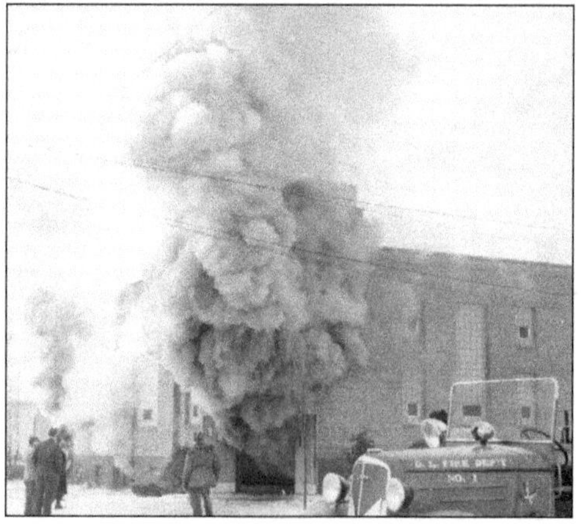

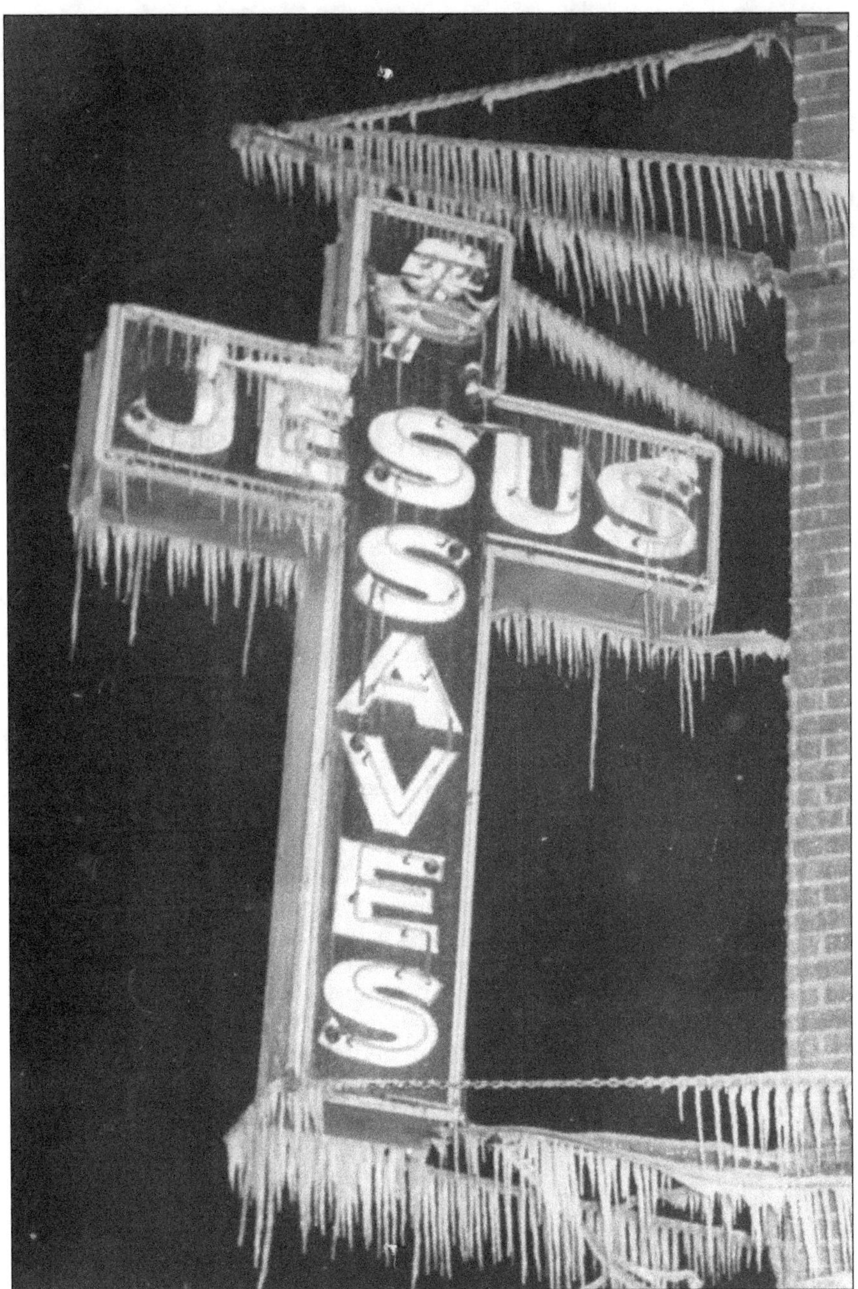

The Becker County Historical Society purchased the Assemblies of God Church building in 1988 and, with slight modification, moved it from its original site in the basement of the Becker County Courthouse to this new museum site. The focus on making the collection and archives more accessible to the public was accomplished in this building by creating a research library, writing grants to get copies of newspapers on microfilm beginning in 1872, building exhibits that showcased artifacts from all parts of the county, and welcoming new types of educational programming. This building, still in use today, has served both its congregation and its museum patrons well and continues to grow and evolve along with the history of Becker County and the city of Detroit Lakes.

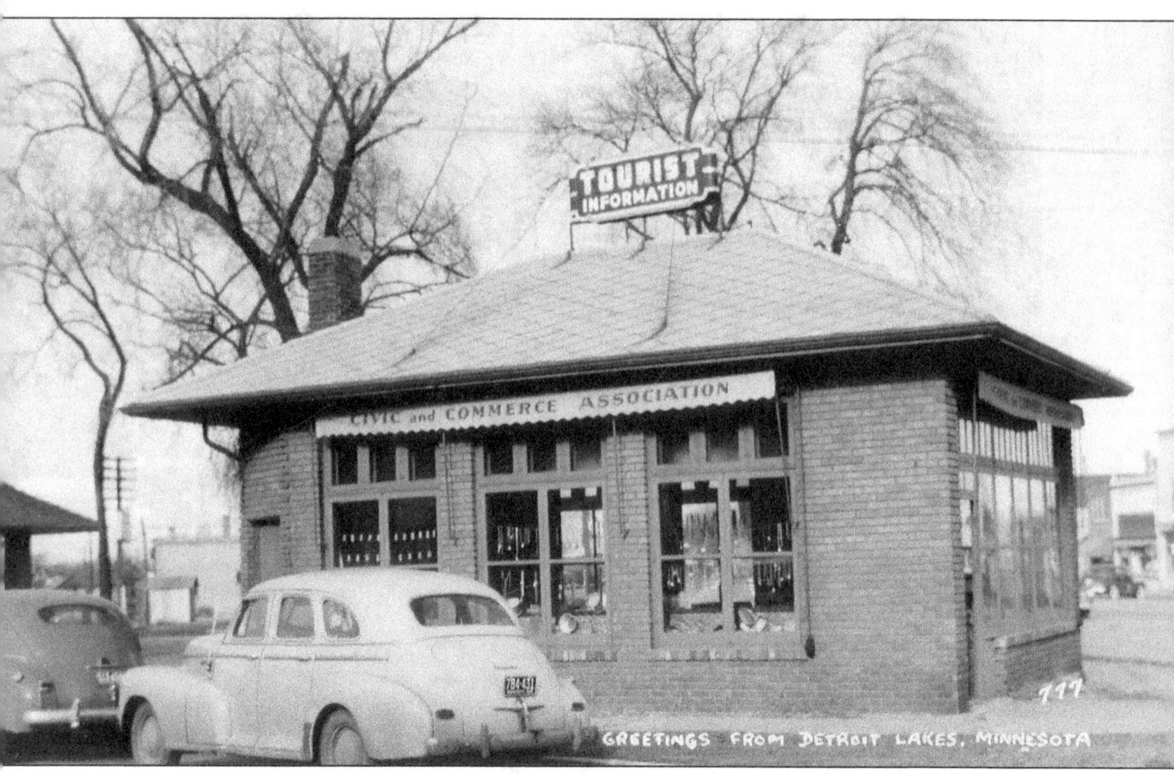

Formed as the Commercial Club in 1921 and renamed the Businessmen's Club and the Detroit Lakes Civic and Commerce Association, the Detroit Lakes Regional Chamber of Commerce has a long history of promoting local business and tourism in the region. Meeting in a variety of locations for some time, the chamber moved to 700 Washington Avenue in November 1936 after a visit to the office of Dan Nelson, secretary, on Pioneer Street, which was a triangular space three by four by five feet, with one chair and a table only about 8 by 18 inches. The new building, formerly the Detroit Floral Company, served the chamber until October 2005, when construction began at the current location at 700 Summit Avenue. Like the businesses it supports, the chamber of commerce has gone through many changes. One suggested plan in 1955 was to construct a new building, built to resemble a giant northern pike that would be 200 by 36 feet. The proposed structure, designed by Ernest Koncikson of Erskine, would house the chamber offices, a game fish aquarium, a wildlife museum, public restrooms, and a reception room. Since no printed results of this meeting exist and the building was not constructed, it can be assumed that it was not met with approval.

Six

KEEPING HISTORY ALIVE
1976–PRESENT

In the 1980s, economic challenges struck Detroit Lakes. Approximately 500 people left the city in search of work, and this left local businesses struggling to survive. Many well-established retailers, such as the Blanding Department Store, closed during this time. The Washington Square Mall, situated on the west side of the 700 block of Washington Avenue, changed the style of downtown commerce. Coast-to-Coast Hardware, now Beug's Ace Hardware, moved across the street so that the buildings attached to the mall could be opened from both sides. The industrial park off of Randolph Road grew, bringing new economic opportunity to the city, such as Lakeshirts, established in 1984. As a new base of industry grew, so did the population. By 2000, the city boasted 7,348 residents, a 10 percent increase from 10 years prior. Today, Detroit Lakes sits at 8,569 people.

In 2008, the focus of the city shifted when Minnesota Highway 10, which had formerly gone through the downtown corridor of Washington Avenue, was rerouted to bypass the city. This led to the loss of the earliest street, Pioneer, which had been the hub of the city for more than 100 years. As the citizens adjusted to this new layout, business developments moved west to the outskirts of the city to make space for large chain retailers. City officials have recently responded by working on the development of the central corridor, with improvements being made to Washington Avenue to make it more pedestrian friendly and improve the curb appeal. A new development along Highway 10 is underway that will provide opportunity for more downtown business. The Pavilion has been remodeled and is once again a center point for community activity. The Becker County Fair continues to endure, having just celebrated its 120th year. Tourism thrives. WE Fest, a country music festival established on the east side of Minnesota State Highway 59, is booming, bringing in approximately 10,000 to 15,000 visitors each summer.

As it moves into a new decade, Detroit Lakes and its citizens are optimistic for the future. Its history is alive and its future is limitless. The small settlement once called "Swamp Town" has become a vibrant, bustling city that its pioneers would be proud to call home.

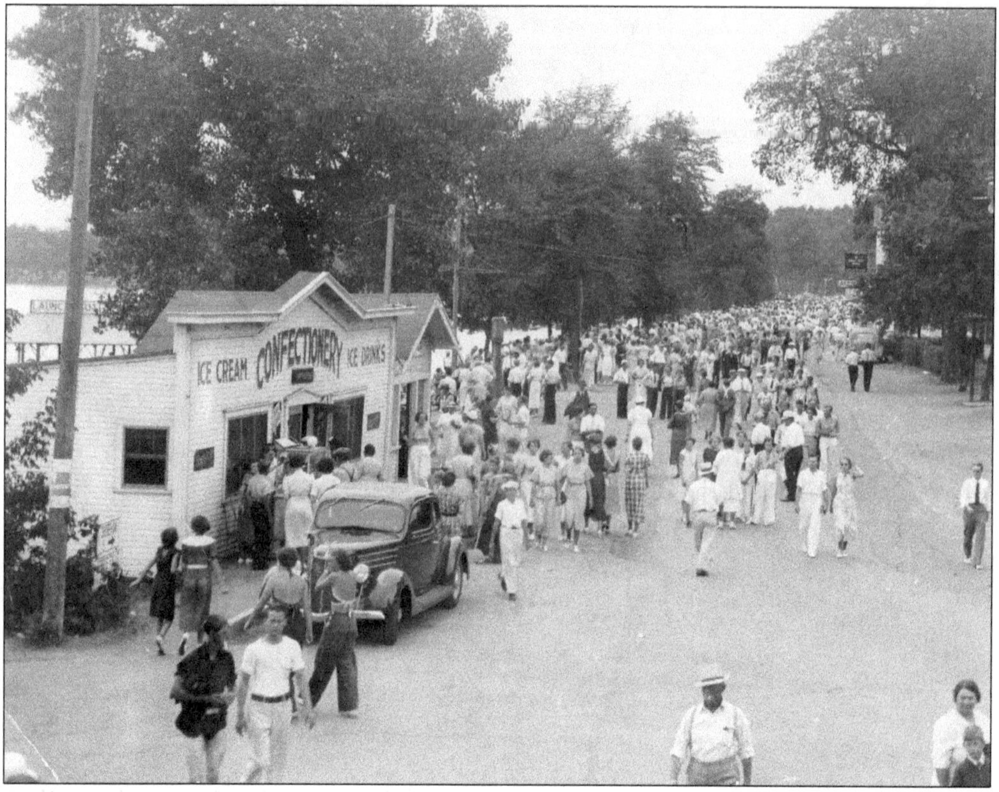

As the city of Detroit Lakes has moved forward, it has also retained some of the old traditions and celebrations. Seen here in 1936, the south end of Washington Avenue is still the hotspot for lake activities. The folks in the photograph above are celebrating the Northwest Water Carnival, which in 2011 marked its 76th year. The confectionery building has since been razed, and J&K Marine stands in its place (below). Today, kayaks, canoes, paddleboats, wave runners, and boats can be rented from J&K and provide a chance for visitors to get out and onto the water. The public swimming beach sits adjacent to the dock and has provided hours of entertainment for the public for generations.

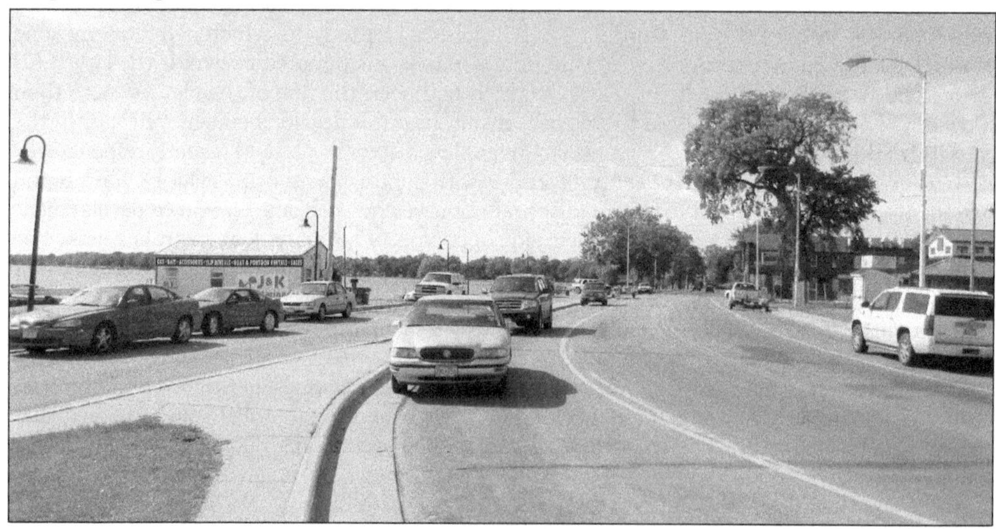

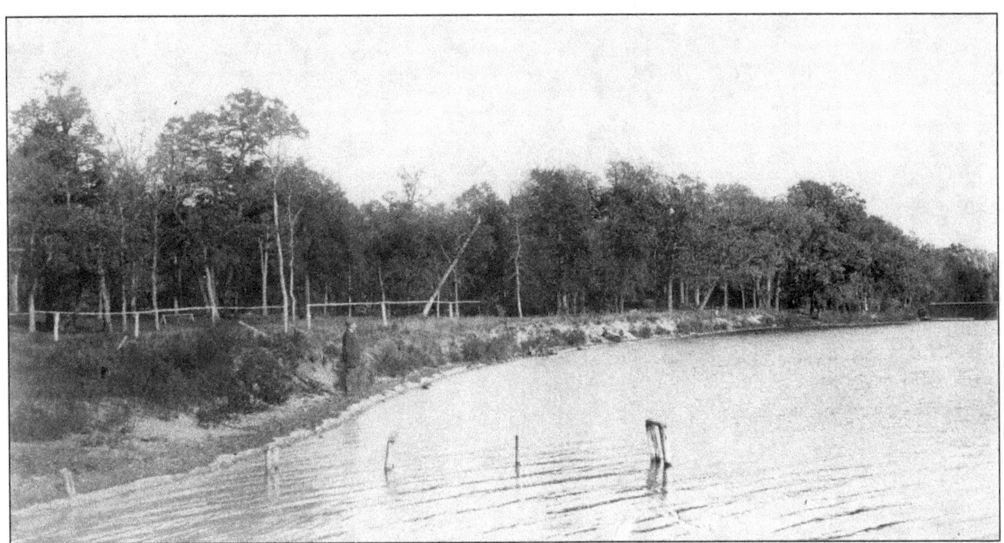

The Detroit Lakes Pavilion, built in 1915, has long served as a gathering space for the city of Detroit Lakes. Music and dances were the most popular activities at the building, but the original lease signed by a group of six young men (H.A. Baker, R.B. Rathbun, C.A. Baker, J.L. Pryor, A.A. Baker, and Fred Sanders) required that the building also provide park concessions, refreshment stands, and amusement attractions, but not ballgames. The renters, who paid $500 per year, were required to enclose the pavilion verandas with glass windows and provide space for public meetings, which were free except on the Fourth of July. They also were required to give one week free during the month of September, used for the Becker County Agricultural Society. Today, the Pavilion, which has been recently remodeled by the Detroit Lakes Area Builders Association, is still a busy space for weddings, the Water Carnival, and Park Fest.

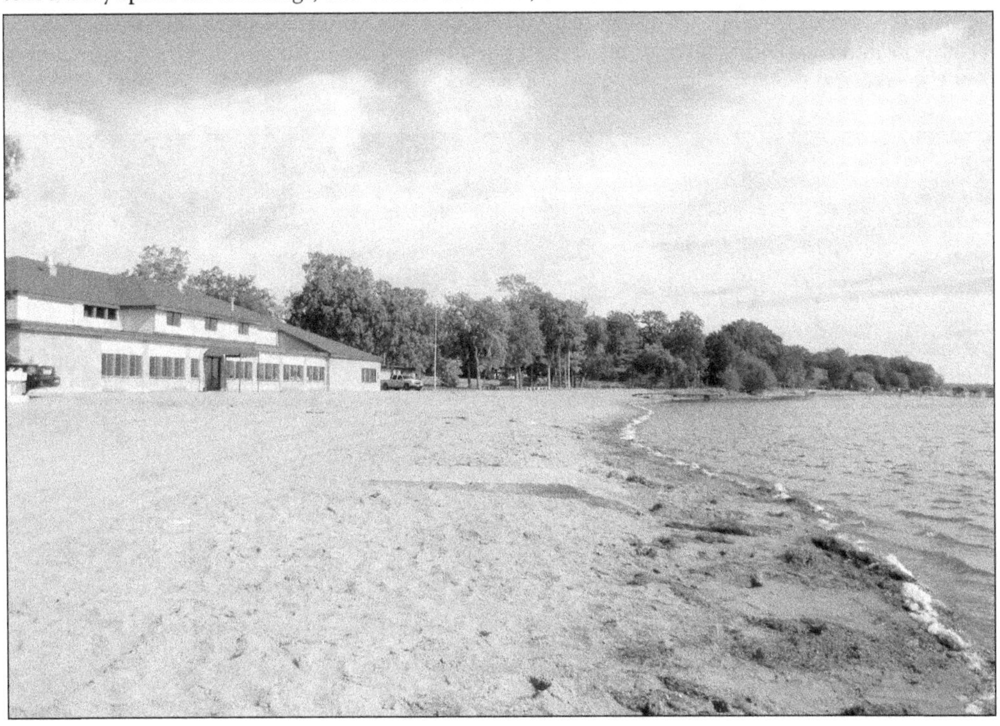

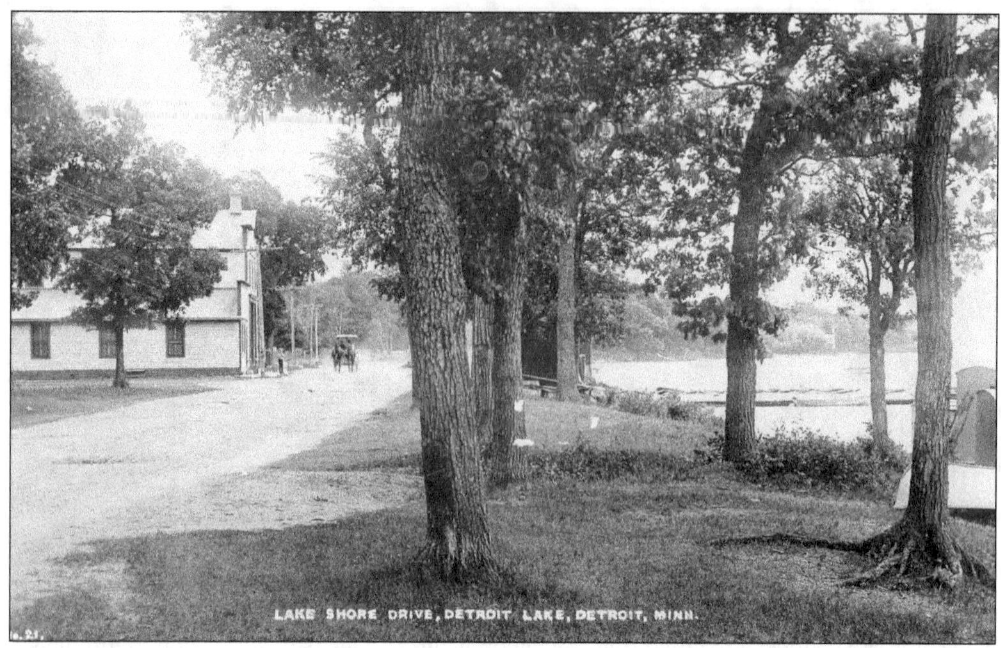

Lake Shore Drive developed from a small, rutted wagon trail to a well-maintained street by the 1920s. Early in its history, this street served the fur traders and American Indian residents that came to the lakeshore for fishing and water. As time went on, Washington and Summit Avenues were extended to the lakeshore and the city began to expand its residential neighborhoods from Frazee Street south. Lakeside Tavern, the white building seen in the early photograph above, is the oldest continuously operating business in Detroit Lakes, established in 1891 and still going strong today. Lake Shore Drive bustles today with both homes and businesses, providing a scenic drive for visitors and a gathering area for residents during events, such as the Fourth of July fireworks over the lake and the Polar Plunge during Polar Fest.

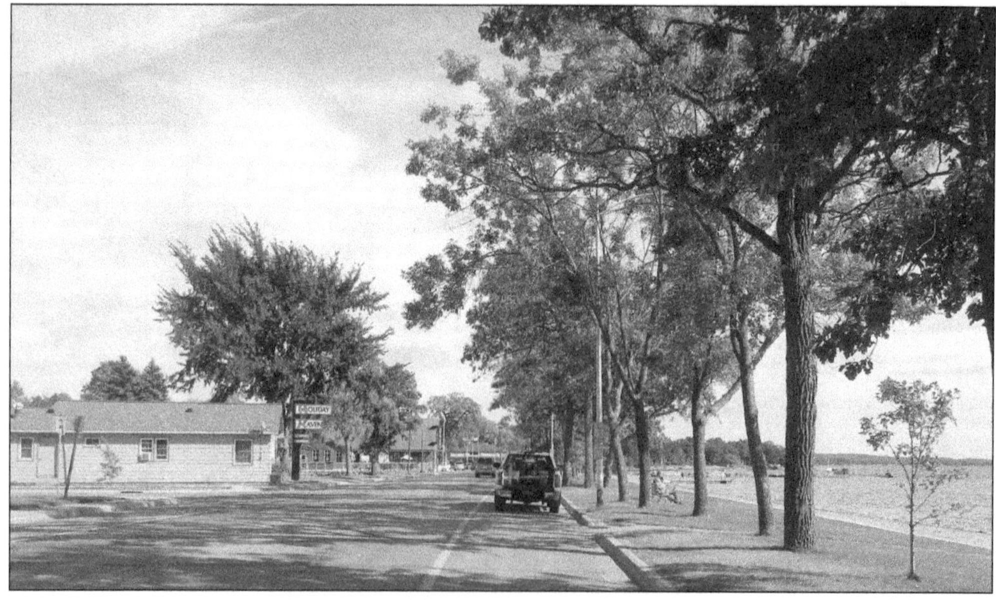

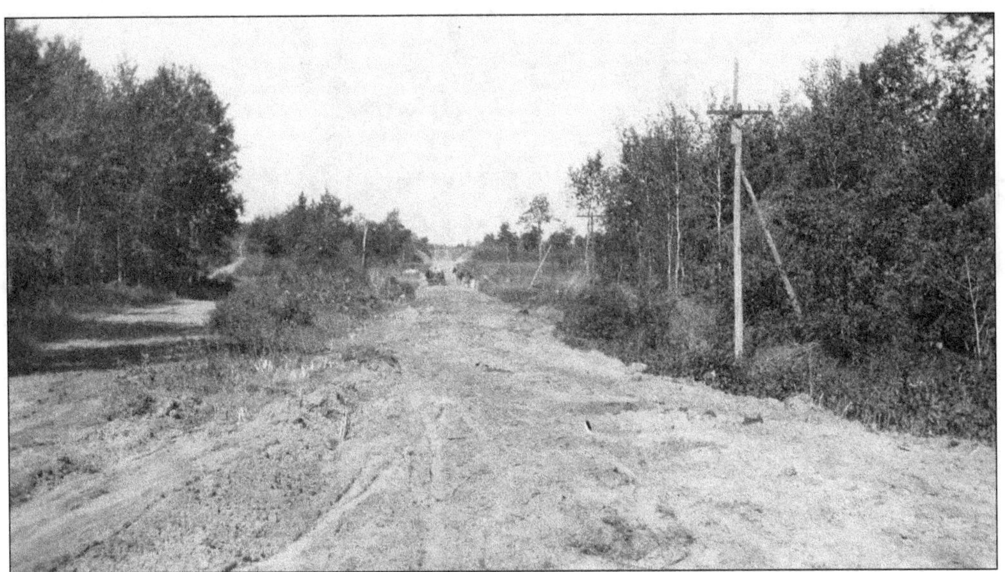

Summit Avenue is a street in Detroit Lakes that is literally a trip through history. Some of the oldest homes in the city sit on this stretch of road, which extends from the lakeshore to the new Minnesota State Highway 10 bypass. Originally created (above, under construction) for access to the lake and as a site for the Chautauqua educational gatherings, Summit remains the center of culture today. On the north end are the Detroit Lakes Cultural and Community Center, home to the Historic Holmes Theater and situated in a building that was the Holmes School, built in 1895. Its neighbor is the Becker County Museum, home to the Becker County Historical Society and Heart O'Lakes Genealogical Society. On the south end, seen below, one finds the cultural icon of Zorbaz, a pizzeria that developed during the 1960s and has now grown to include live music and more than 10 locations nationwide.

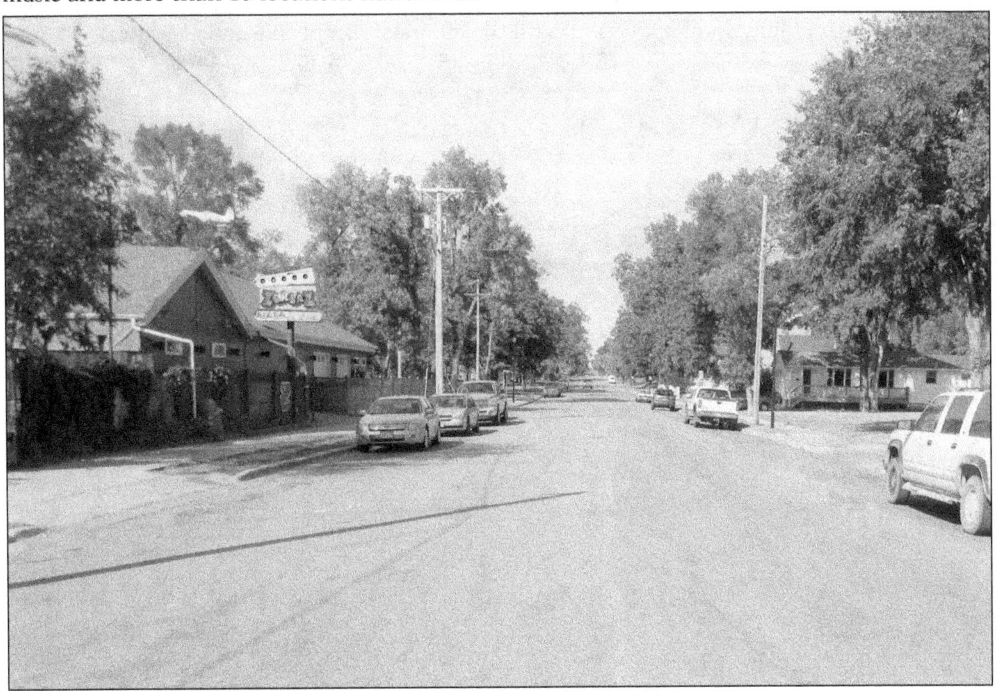

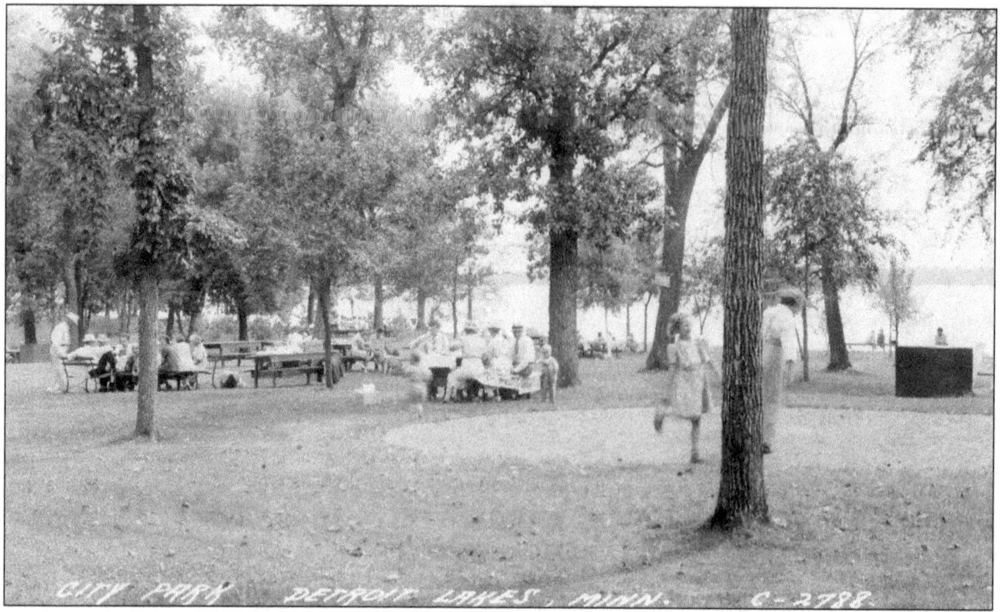

The Detroit Lakes City Park developed in the early 20th century as a natural retreat for the residents of the area. Purchased piece by piece and developed along with the Pavilion, the city park was host to a variety of activities. A band shell was built along with picnic shelters and charcoal grills. Music and festivals filled the space over the summer months. As time went by, the band shell was torn down and the park became instead a hangout spot for the children of the city, with a waterslide and log ride next to the swimming beach. When the Pavilion was recently remodeled, the band shell was also rebuilt, and Tuesdays in the Park brought live outdoor music back to the public. Vendor events, such as Art in the Park and the Detroit Lakes Area Farmers Market, take place in the Detroit Lakes City Park and Peoples Park down the street. The Water Carnival, Fourth of July, and Park Fest also fill the grounds with people and activities.

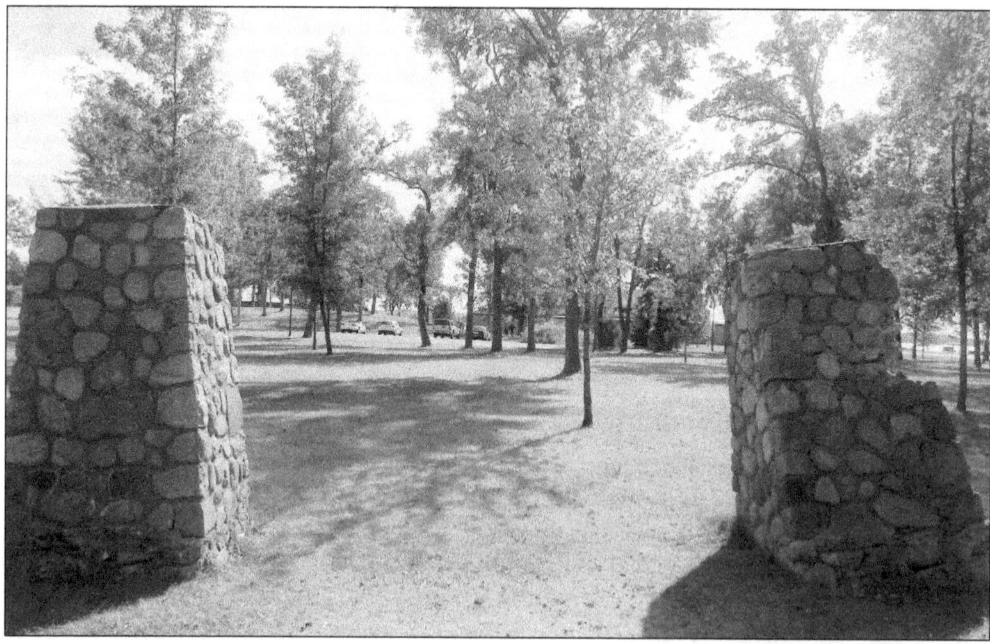

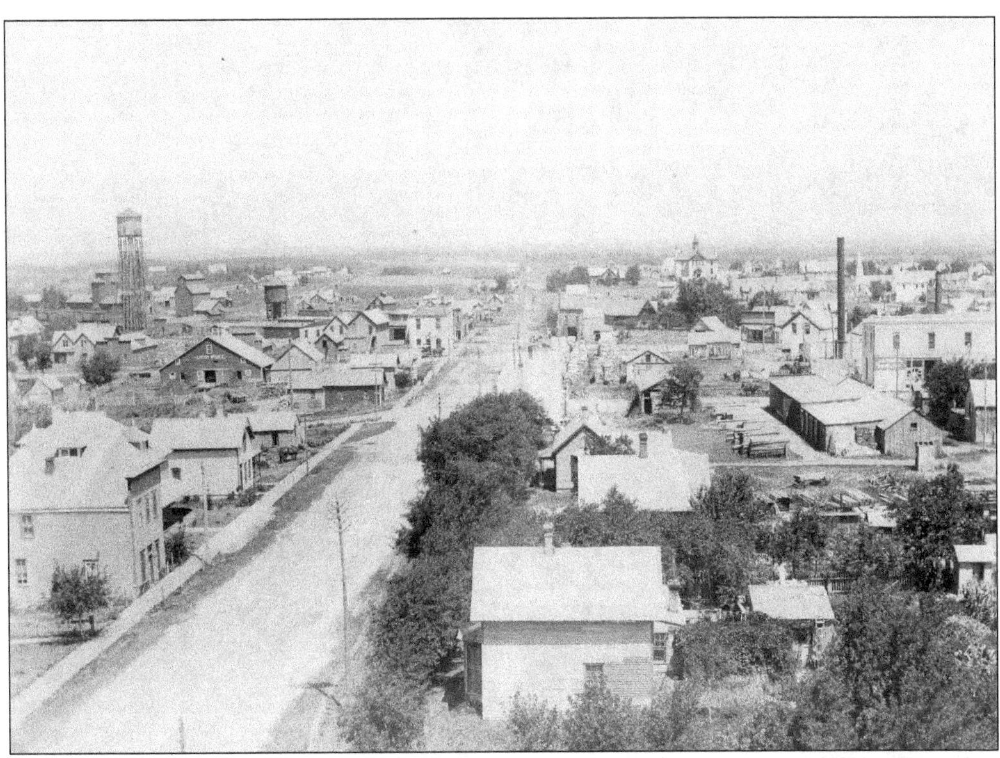

Lake Avenue, running parallel between Washington and Summit Avenues, has served as the civic center of Detroit Lakes since 1884. Seen in the above photograph from the tower of the original courthouse in 1903, the street was originally home to the city hall, fire department, courthouse, and county jail. The courthouse, first opened in 1885, was the tallest building in the city and provided an excellent bird's-eye view. In 1942, a new courthouse was constructed in the Art Deco style. In 1945, the old building was condemned and torn down. Within the last five years, Becker County has remodeled the courthouse and added offices and courtrooms. The Department of Motor Vehicles moved to this location, and the Becker County Museum moved out of the basement and into a building on Summit Avenue.

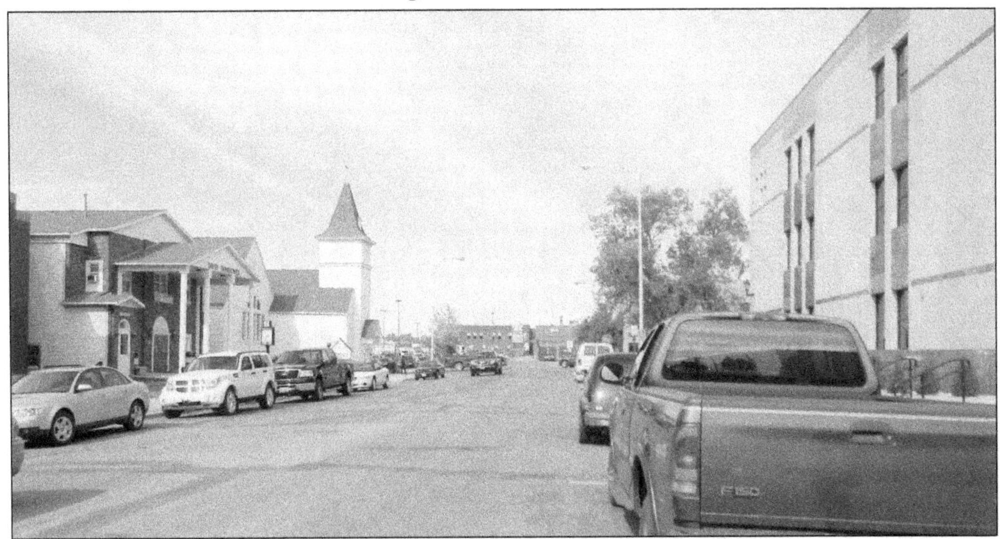

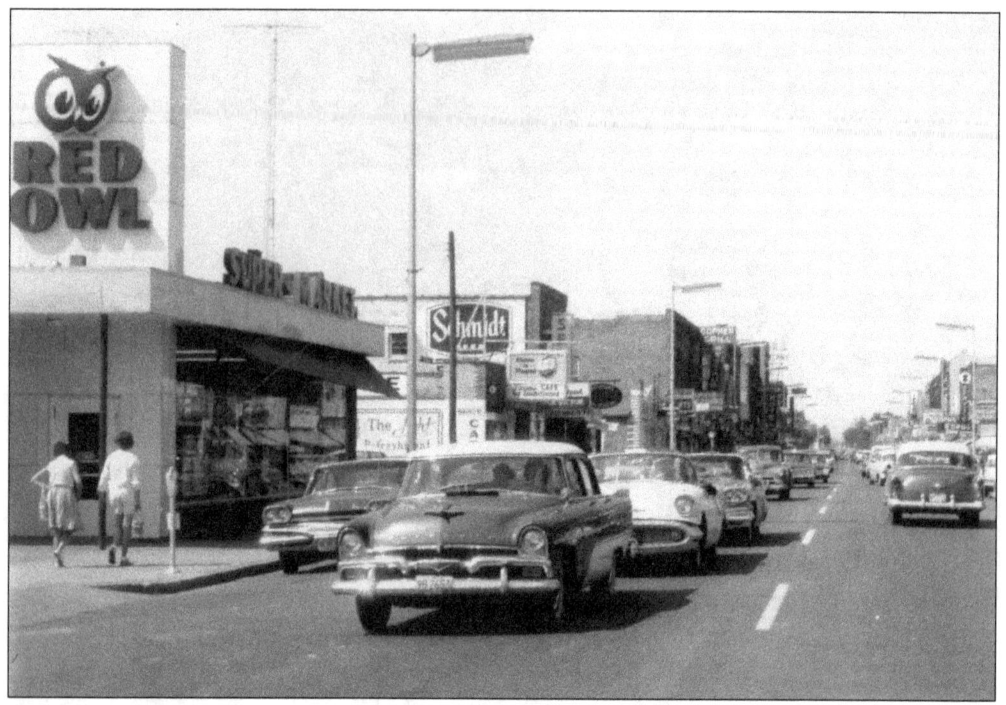

The corner of Frazee Street and Washington Avenue has been a fixture in Detroit Lakes history. In the early years, it stood at the edge of town with the "wilds of Detroit" still existing to the south. In the 1880s, the Hotel Minnesota, a grand two story wooden structure with more than 100 rooms, became a landmark of the city. In 1915, this structure burned to the ground and the Graystone Hotel, on Washington and Pioneer Street, grew up to replace it. Various businesses later sat in this spot including the Red Owl, which opened in its new location here in 1937. Today, Lakes Sport Shop fills the space and provides service to the region for all its outdoor and active lifestyle needs.

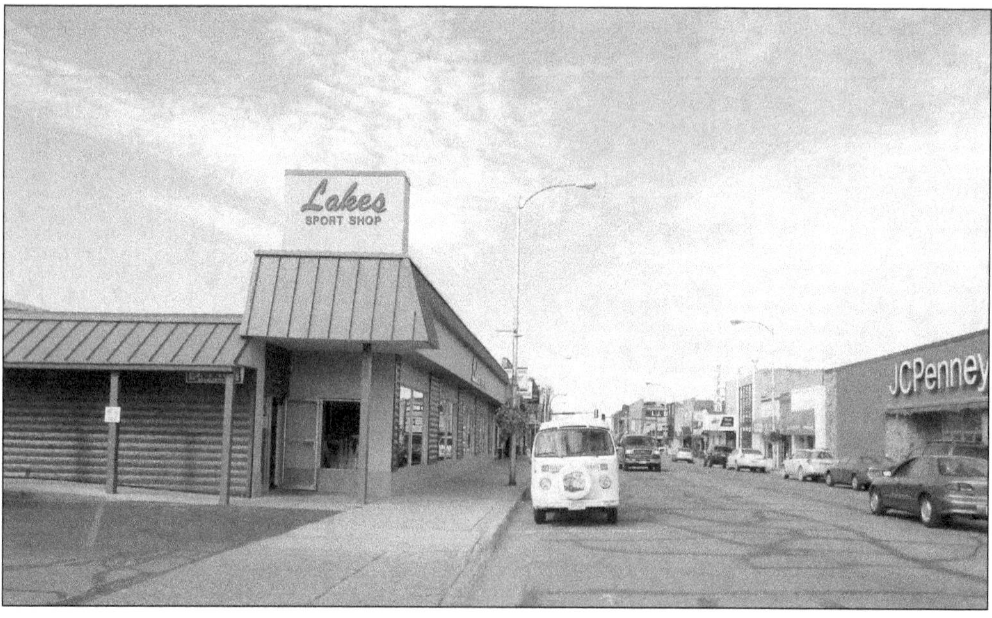

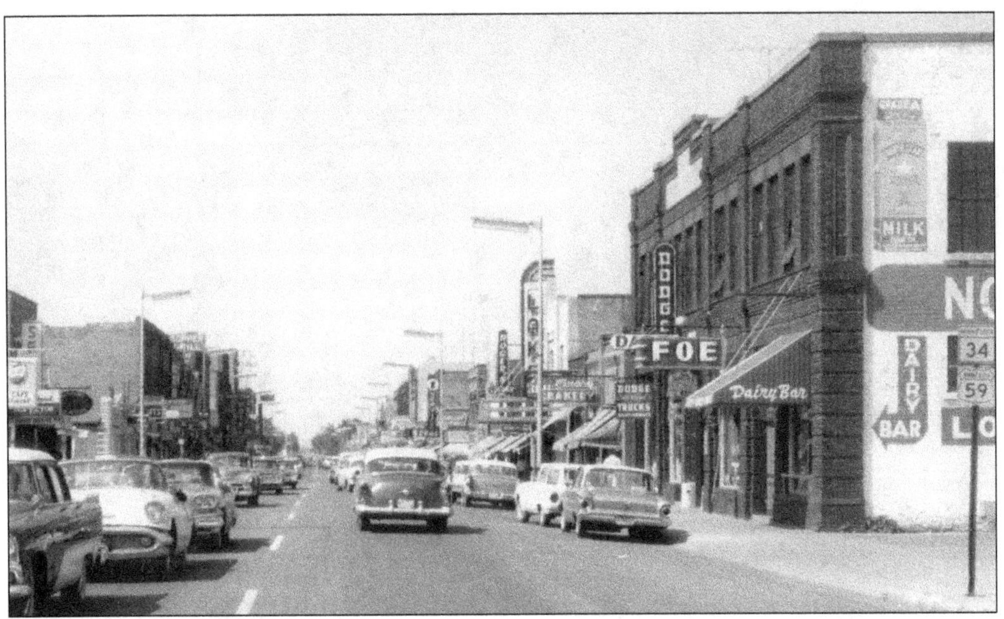

The 900 block of Washington Avenue remains a central business district today. In the photographs seen here, you can see changes that have occurred over the years, with the FOE (Eagles Club) now replaced by J.C. Penney, which originally sat at the north end of the 800 block. The Lakes Theater building, now vacant, was most recently the 917 Club. The Gopher Grill now serves the public as the Main Street Café, one of the few buildings to maintain its original neon sign. Washington Avenue used to serve as Highway 59, 34, and 10, all of which are now diverted around the core of city business. This created an interesting dynamic with one road serving as a county, city, and state entity.

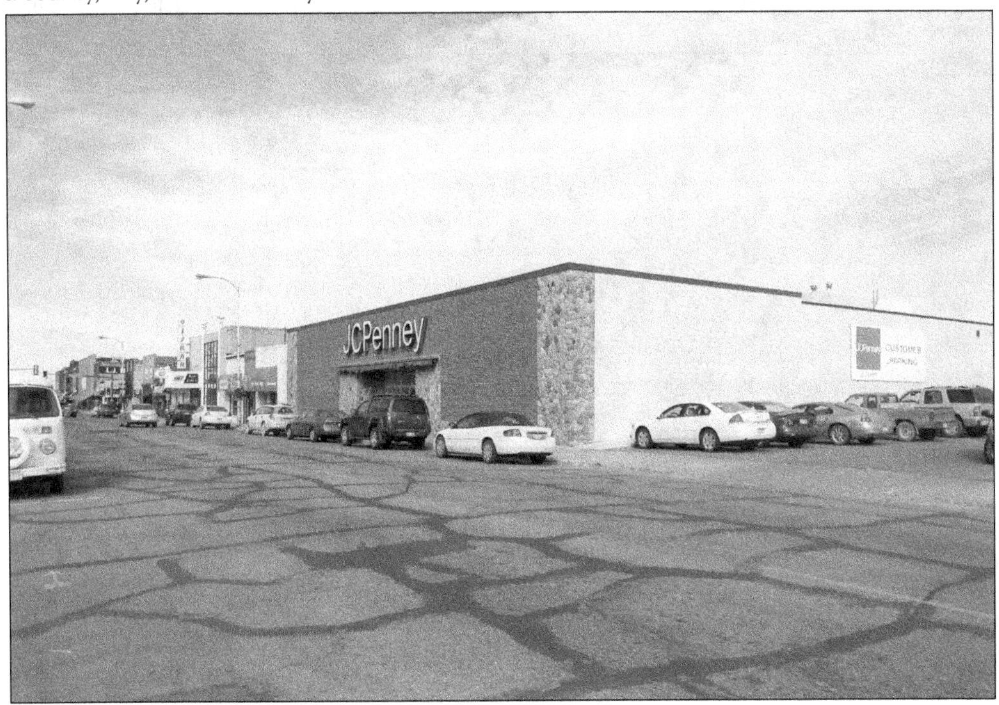

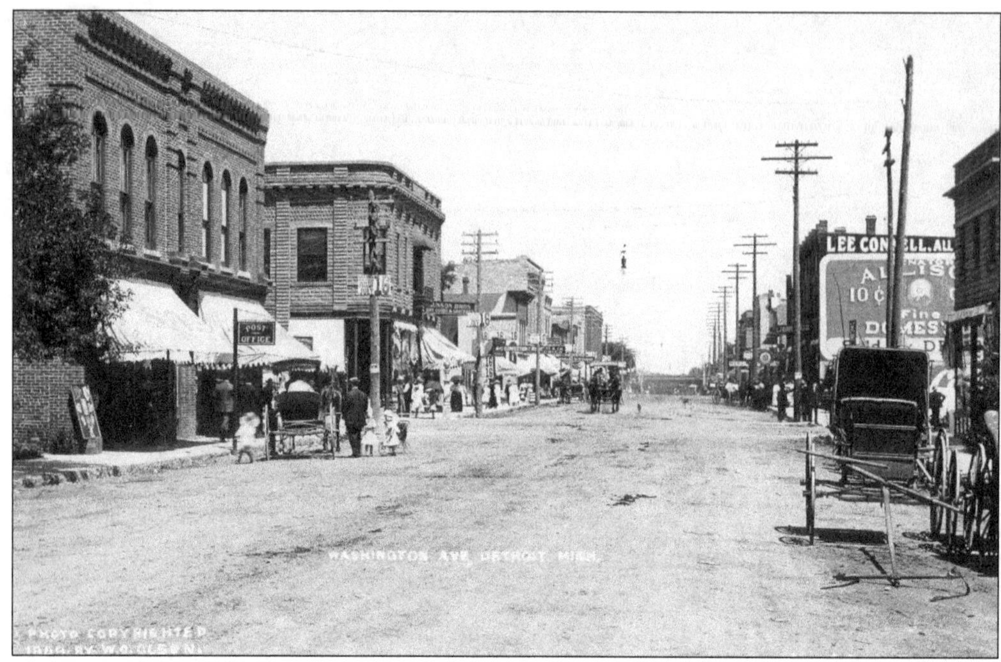

The intersection of Washington Avenue and Holmes Street has served as the crossing point of commerce and civic units in Detroit Lakes for more than 100 years. Seen above, the building that now houses the Main Street Café was once the city and county office building that also included the post office. Civic offices later moved to Lake Avenue, which was the site of the courthouse, town hall, fire department, and post office, pictured here in its fifth location. The Irish Block, named for Jeff Irish, an attorney in the city, featured a curved-corner brick building that later became Schaffer's Ready-to-Wear. This building burned and was replaced by the Washington Square Mall.

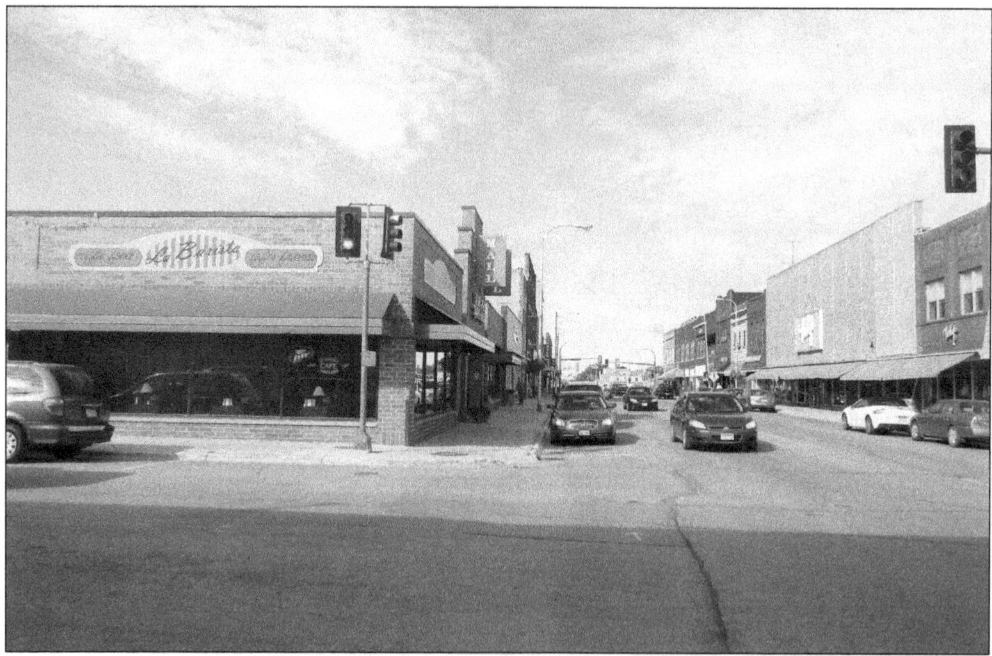

The 800 block of Washington Avenue has, without question, been the heart of the downtown business district throughout the history of Detroit Lakes. Businesses like Schaffer's Ready-to-Wear have become part of the Washington Square Mall. Today, La Barista, a coffee shop owned and operated by Brooke and Courtney Wenzel, occupies this corner. Other former businesses on this block included Diamonds, the McCarthy Hotel, and Mayerson's Clothing. On the east side of the block, the L.J. Norby Company remains, expanding several times over its 105-year history. Originally located in the Teague Block as a Blanding-Norby partnership, the company moved to its present location in 1906 and continues there today.

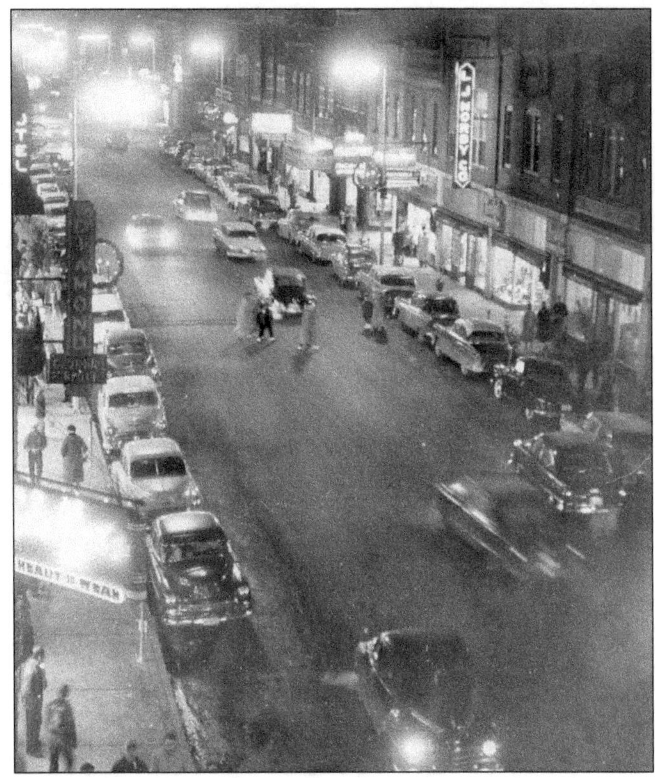

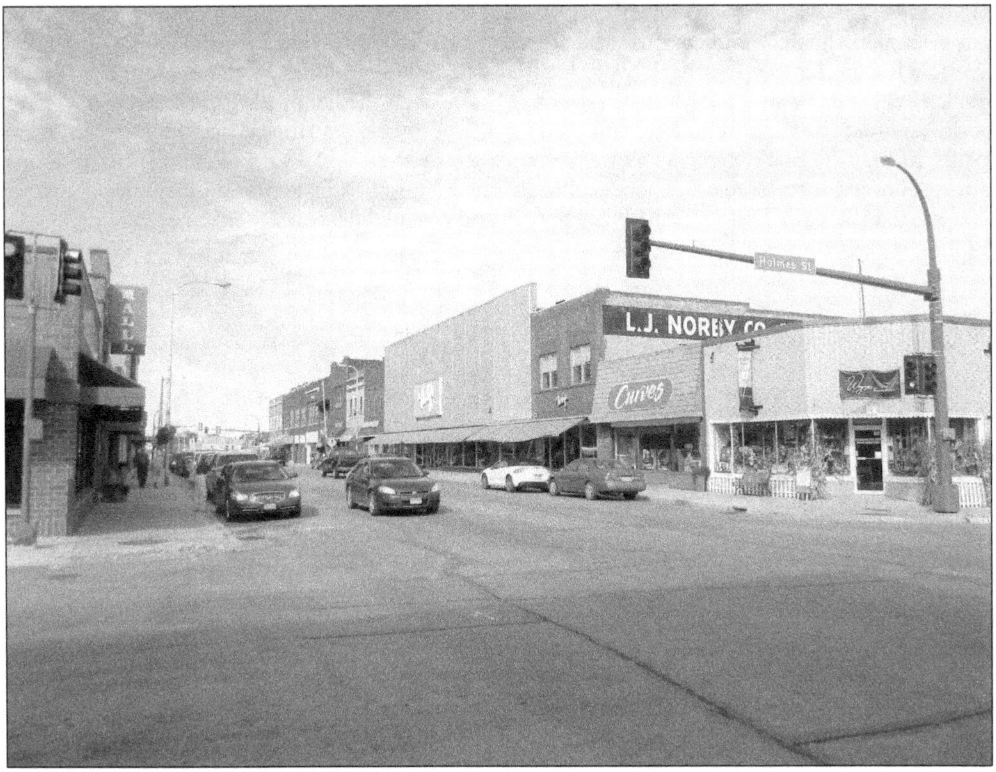

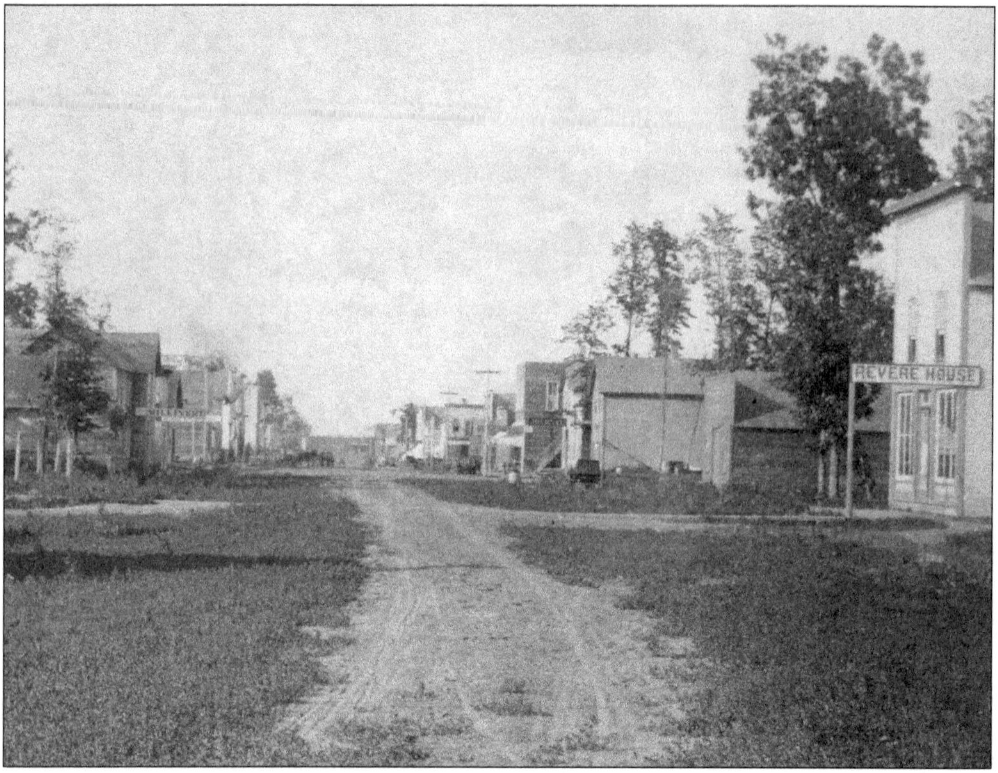

Main Street, now split between north and south Detroit Lakes by Minnesota State Highway 10, was once a bustling commerce district in the city's history. Stores, blacksmith shops, and hotels, like the Revere House seen here, were located within a few blocks of the Soo Line Railroad tracks. As industry shifted, Main Street changed as well. Residential homes sprouted where businesses had stood. Warehouses remained along the tracks, offering storage for freight. In the 1960s, Minnesota State Highway 59 was rerouted to the west of Detroit Lakes and crossed Main Street, allowing it to serve as an access point to the highway and the new business development that started there, including L&M Fleet Supply and Noah's Furniture.

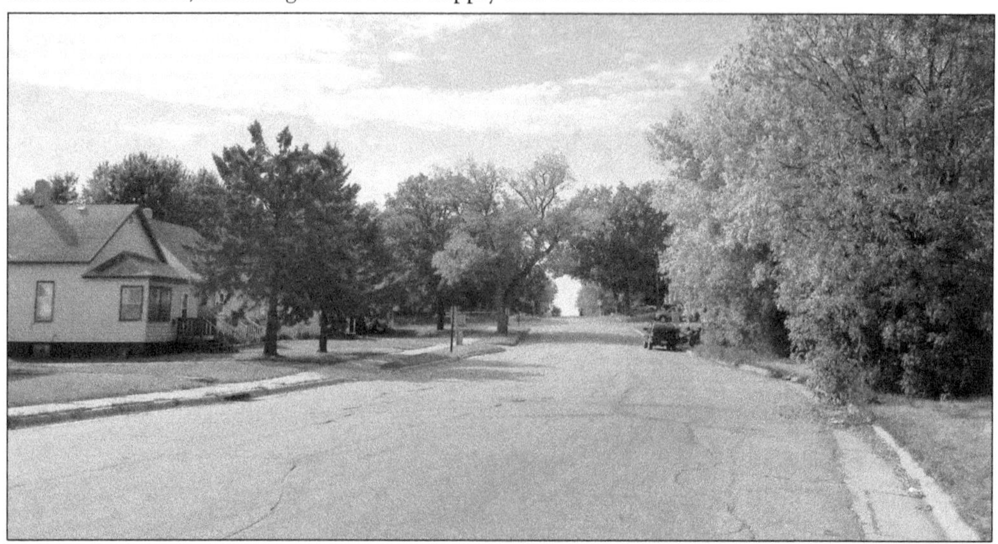

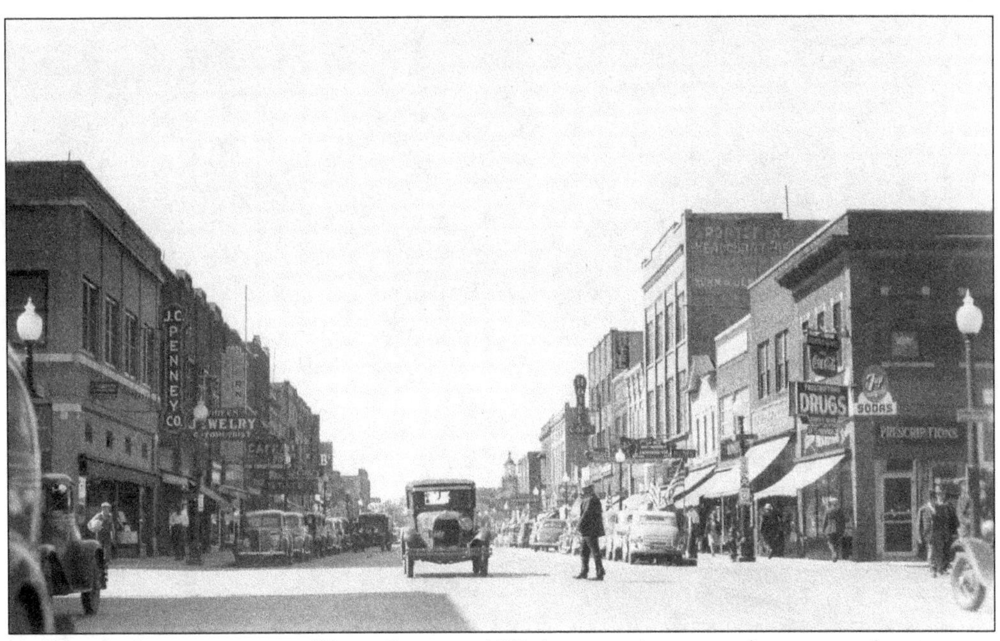

Looking at the intersection of Front Street and Washington Avenue today situates the viewer at the northernmost point of original buildings that still exist before the Northern Pacific Railroad crossing on the east side of the street. This corner, now Beug's Ace Hardware and Vanity, was formerly occupied by J.C. Penney and Nelson Drug. New development brought the destruction of the First Security Bank (Mac's Hardware) building that had stood just to the north, when the Minnesota Highway 10 bypass came through. Today, the area to the east of these buildings is being redeveloped to include Veterans Memorial Park and a strip mall.

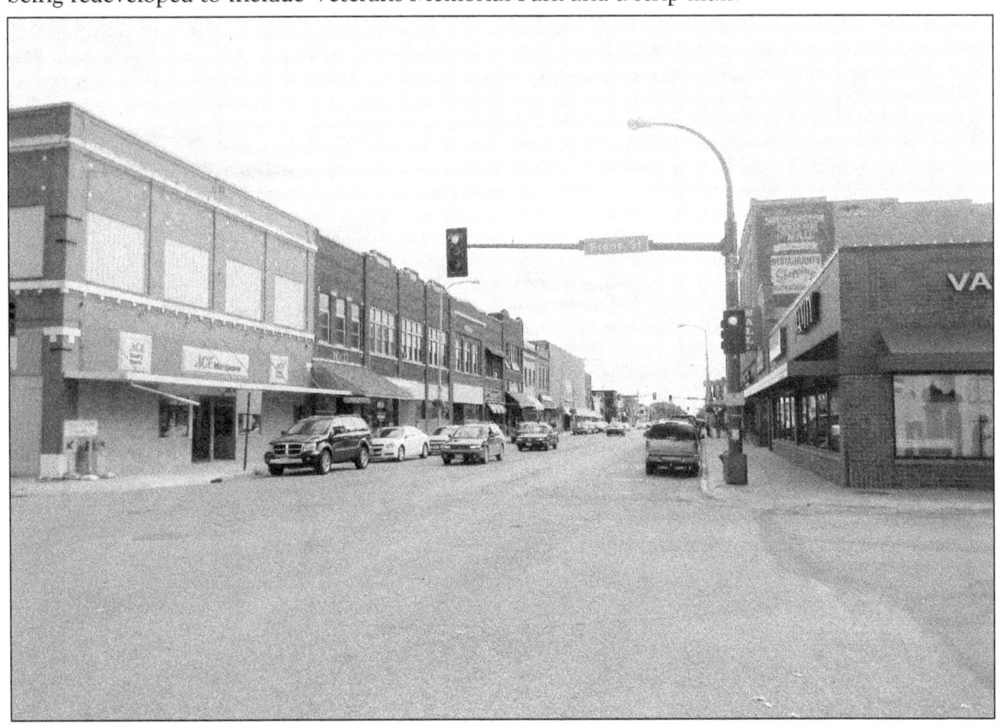

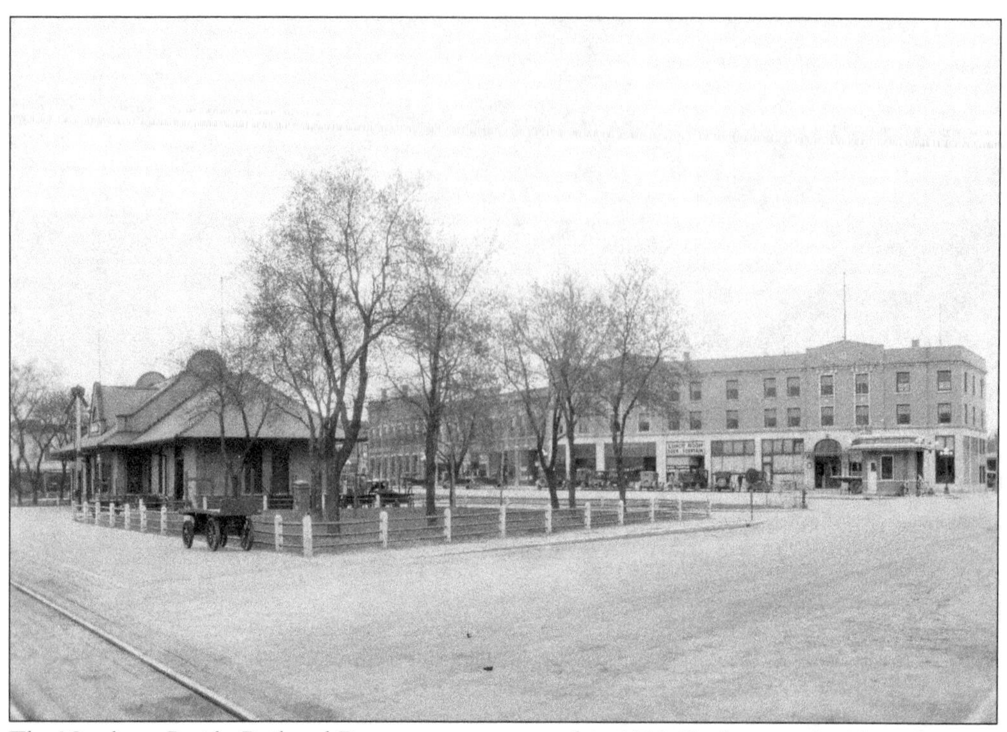

The Northern Pacific Railroad Depot was constructed in 1908. Replacing a building that was originally located north of the tracks, this brick structure offered a tiled waiting area, offices for railroad officials, and indoor washrooms. In 2009 and 2010, the depot was renovated by the White Earth Band of Ojibwe and now serves as a coffee shop and meeting area. It also provides one of only three Amtrak passenger stops in greater Minnesota. Just to the south, the Graystone Hotel building was constructed in 1915 and 1916. It was later attached to the Graystone Annex and then the Holmes and Teague Block to create the angled building we recognize today. Situated on the west end of the Graystone Building, the Saurer Brothers Gas Station, also known as the "World's Smallest," provided quick access to gasoline and basic service for visitors driving through the city. A replica of this station now sits in the Becker County Museum.

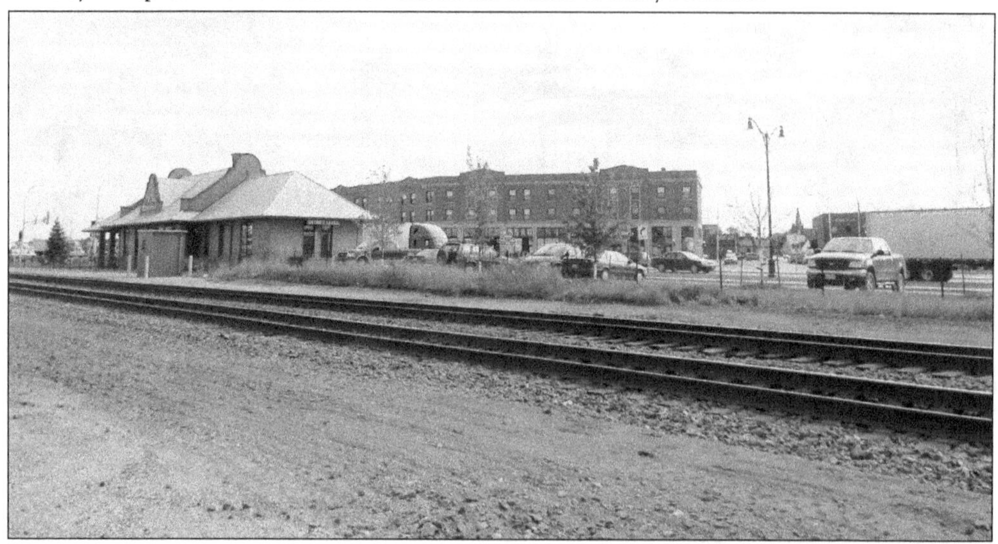

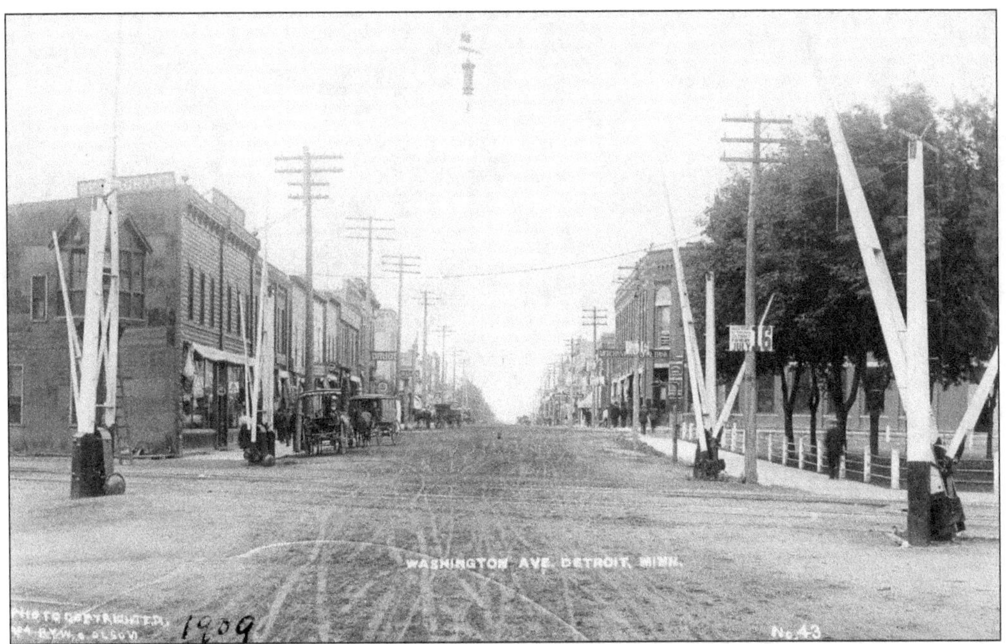

Today, the north side of the Northern Pacific Railroad tracks is a neighborhood in transition. Pioneer Street, which dead-ended just south of the tracks, housed businesses such as the Colonial Hotel and Alvin Wilcox's Land Office. Circuses and parades came down this block, and it was the first that most visitors by train would see of the city. Today, the railroad remains a vital part of the city, going through with deliveries and passengers. Businesses such as TiresPlus and Sinclair's Dinomart keep the neighborhood going. Within the last five years, new brick crosswalks and pedestrian bump-outs have been added, making this busy street easier to cross.

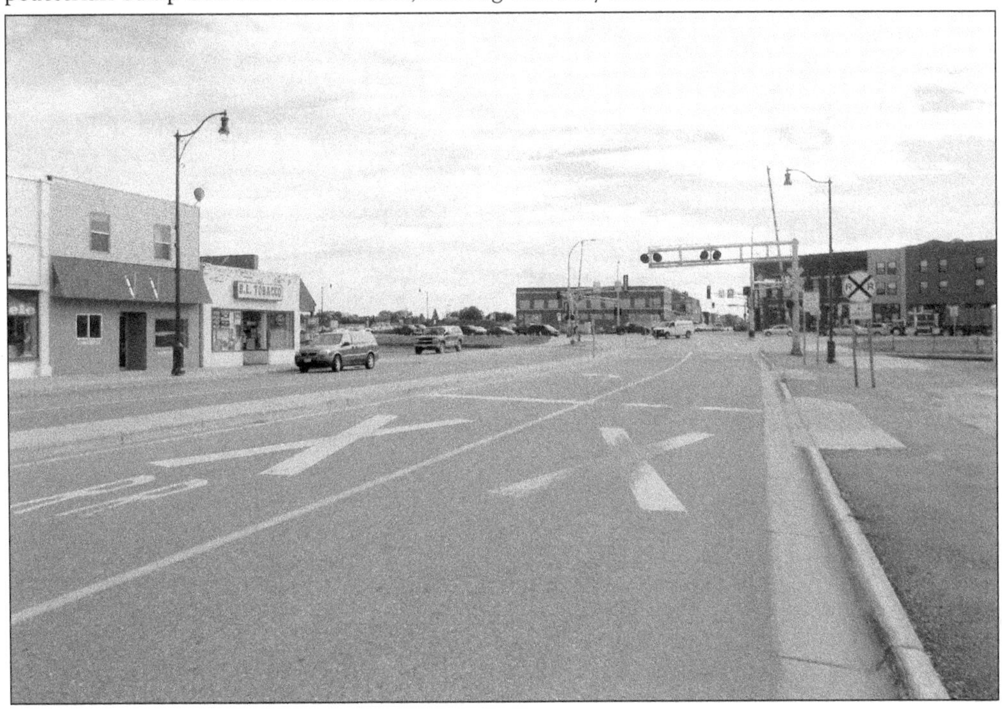

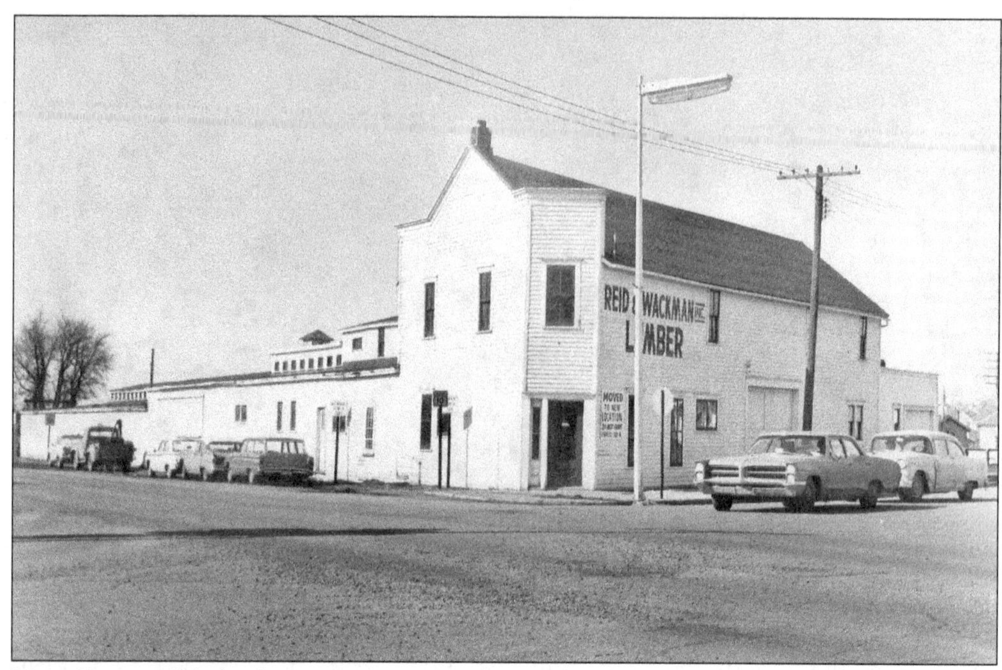

Main Street and Lake Avenue intersect on the north side of Minnesota State Highway 10 at the former site of Reid & Wackman Lumber. A useful site in its day, located directly next to the Northern Pacific Railroad Tracks, this location had many uses before becoming a lumber company. Reid & Wackman was a long presence here, opening in 1886 and closing at this location in 1966. Many other service industries also occupied this neighborhood, including beer warehouses, Hartman Hide and Fur, and numerous freight buildings. Today, the westbound lanes of Highway 10 and parking lot for the depot occupy this spot.

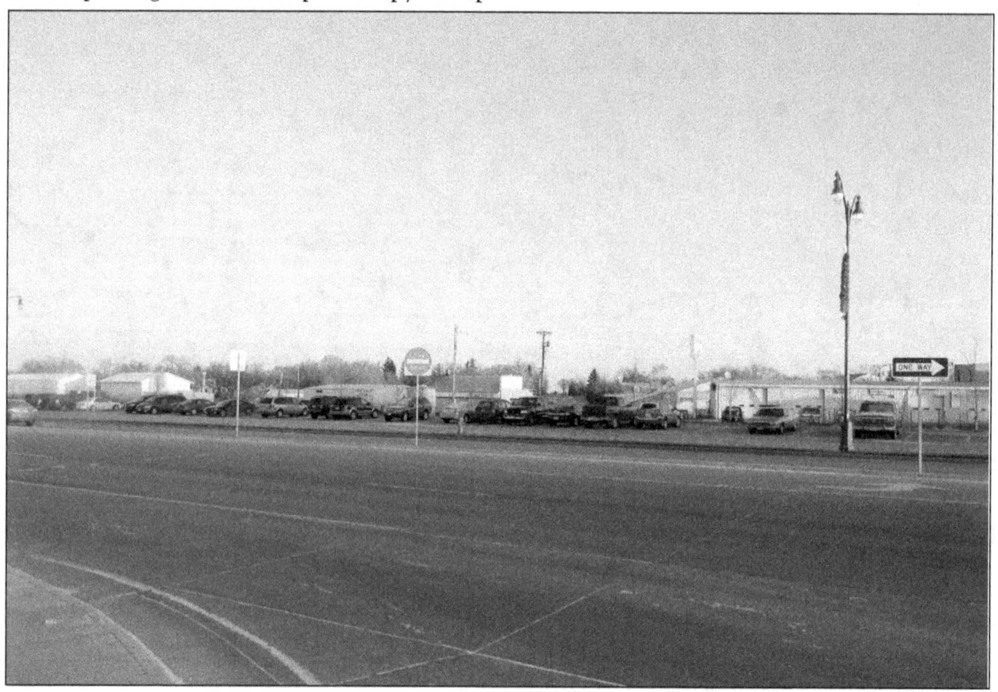

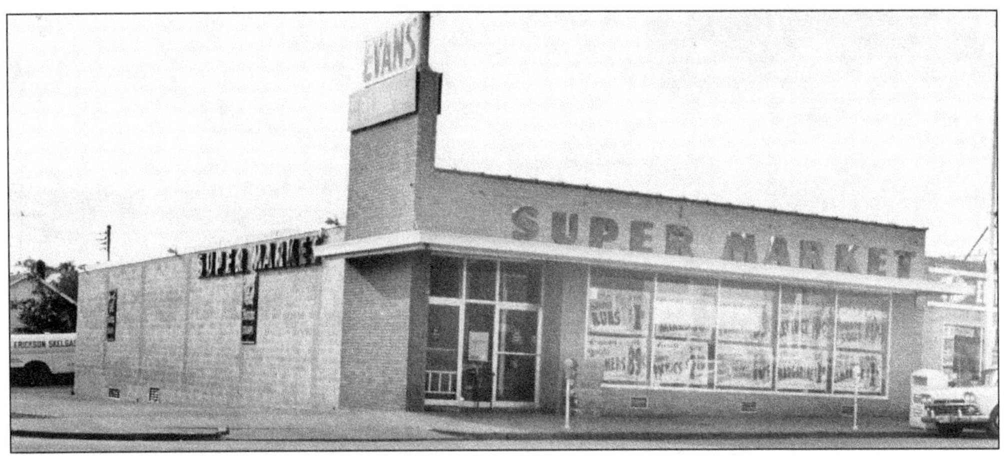

The corner of Washington Avenue and Grant Street is now being revitalized. The Baptist Church, later the first site of Trinity Lutheran, sat in the parking lot of what is now Michael's Furniture and the Social Cup Coffee Shop. The offices of Detroit Lakes Newspapers occupies the building that once housed Evans Super Market, pictured above. The VFW sits on the east side of the intersection, offering a gathering place for veterans. The northern part of the city is now also home to M-State (Minnesota State Technical and Community College), which is part of a five-campus system that brings an influx of students to the community each year. As with any city, Detroit Lakes has gone through many periods of change, emerging as a community with a rich history and bright future.

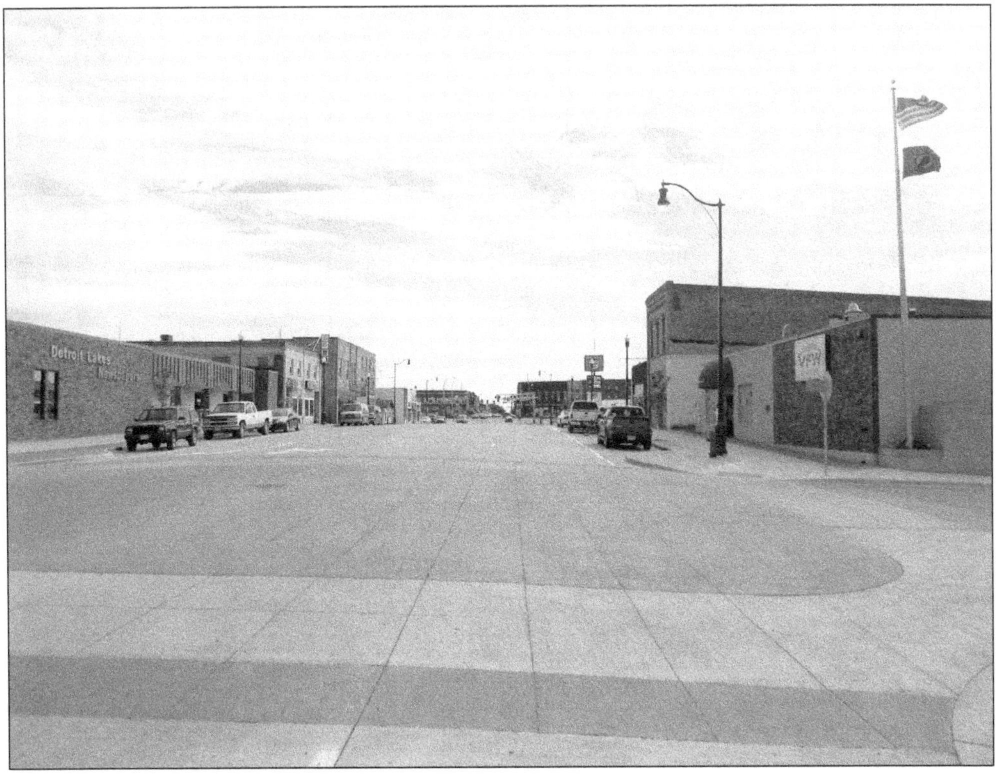

Bibliography

Becker County Historical Society. *The Soldiers of Becker County*. Detroit Lakes, MN, 2011.

City of Detroit Lakes. *100 Years of Progress: Sod to Shoreline*. Detroit Lakes, MN, 1971.

Detroit Lakes Middle School. *Historians 1998*. Independent School District 22: Detroit Lakes, MN, 1998

Lake Park Historical Society. *People's History of Becker County*. Dallas, TX: Taylor Publishing, 1976.

Mayfield, Pippi. *150 Years of Becker County*. Detroit Lakes, MN: Detroit Lakes Newspapers, 2009.

Prentice, Ken and Guy E. Teague. *Horse and Buggy Days at Detroit Lakes*. Detroit Lakes, MN: Lakes Publishing, 1971.

Wilcox, Alvin H. A *Pioneer History of Becker County Minnesota*. St. Paul, MN: Pioneer Press, 1907.

The Becker County Historical Society

The Becker County Historical Society, established in 1882 as the Pioneer Settlers Union, resides in Detroit Lakes, Minnesota, which is the county seat of Becker County. Offering a museum with exhibits, collections totaling more than 10,000 artifacts, a research library with more than 5,000 archival documents, newspapers on microfilm beginning in 1872 to present day, tax records, township records, and countless books, the history of Becker County can be discovered there. The Becker County Historical Society also houses over 18,000 photographs, which help the staff tell the visual history of the county, as they have done in this book. Donations of artifacts, photos, and documents are continuously taken, so please consider preserving a piece of your family's history in our collections. An institution that is dependent on many forms of support for its operations and programming, the Becker County Historical Society appreciates your investment in history by purchasing this book, and hope that you may be inspired to join our society and keep history alive in your county. Information about donations, membership, and volunteer service can be found on our website, www.beckercountyhistory.org, or by visiting the Becker County Museum at 714 Summit Avenue, Detroit Lakes, Minnesota 56502, or call 218-847-2938. For further research and reading, please visit the Becker County Historical Society Research Library at 714 Summit Avenue, Detroit Lakes, Minnesota 56502, or call 218-847-2938.

Consistent with our mission to preserve history on a local level, this book was printed in South Carolina on American-made paper and manufactured entirely in the United States. Products carrying the accredited Forest Stewardship Council (FSC) label are printed on 100 percent FSC-certified paper.

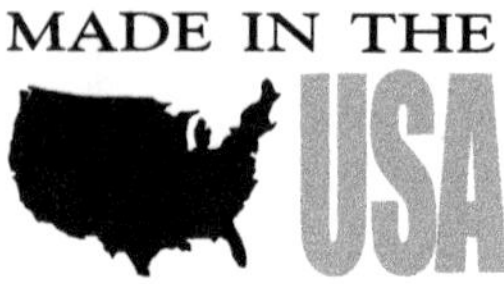

www.ingramcontent.com/pod-product-compliance
Lightning Source LLC
LaVergne TN
LVHW081540100826
845153LV00004B/275

* 9 7 8 1 5 3 1 6 5 5 9 5 2 *